THE ECONOMIC THEORY OF THE MULTINATIONAL ENTERPRISE

This book systematically surveys and extends the economic theory of the multinational enterprise (MNE). The approach taken, based on the internalization rubric and least cost location, is contrasted and compared with other approaches and the results of testing the theory are presented. The alternatives to the multinational are treated in detail. For instance, multiplant firms are contrasted with cartels. Many aspects of MNE behavior are found to be common to all modes of international technology transfer.

The location decisions of MNEs are modelled in detail across countries and through time and the influence of financial and organizational factors is traced. Finally, entrepreneurship, the dynamic element in the management of MNEs, is integrated with the theory and the flows of information and intermediate products within the firm are shown to be of great importance.

Peter J. Buckley is Professor of Managerial Economics at the University of Bradford Management Centre. His publications include books on the theory and practice of foreign direct investment and the multinational enterprise and articles in British, European, American, and Japanese journals.

Mark Casson is Professor of Economics at the University of Reading. His published works span a wide area of economics, including macroeconomics, multinational enterprise, and entrepreneurship.

Also by Peter J. Buckley and Mark Casson
THE FUTURE OF THE MULTINATIONAL ENTERPRISE

Also by Peter J. Buckley
GOING INTERNATIONAL: THE EXPERIENCE OF SMALLER
   COMPANIES OVERSEAS
(*with Gerald D. Newbould and Jane Thurwell*)

EUROPEAN DIRECT INVESTMENT IN THE USA BEFORE
   WORLD WAR I
(*with Brian R. Roberts*)

HANDBOOK OF INTERNATIONAL TRADE
(*edited with Michael Z. Brooke*)

DIRECT INVESTMENT IN THE UNITED KINGDOM BY
   SMALLER EUROPEAN FIRMS
(*with Zdenka Berkova and Gerald D. Newbould*)

THE INDUSTRIAL RELATIONS PRACTICES OF FOREIGN-
   OWNED FIRMS IN BRITISH MANUFACTURING
   INDUSTRY
(*with Peter Enderwick*)

Also by Mark Casson
INTRODUCTION TO MATHEMATICAL ECONOMICS

ALTERNATIVES TO THE MULTINATIONAL ENTERPRISE

YOUTH UNEMPLOYMENT

UNEMPLOYMENT: A DISEQUILIBRIUM APPROACH

THE ENTREPRENEUR: AN ECONOMIC THEORY

THE ECONOMICS OF UNEMPLOYMENT

THE GROWTH OF INTERNATIONAL BUSINESS (*edited*)

THE ECONOMIC THEORY OF THE MULTINATIONAL ENTERPRISE

Selected Papers

PETER J. BUCKLEY
and
MARK CASSON

St. Martin's Press   New York

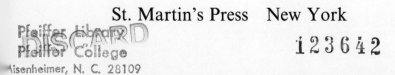

ISBN 0–312–23636–0

Library of Congress Cataloging in Publication Data
Buckley, Peter J., 1949–
The economic theory of the multinational enterprise.
Bibliography: p.
Includes index.
1. International business enterprises—Addresses,
essays, lectures.   I. Casson, Mark, 1945–
II. Title.
HD2755.5.B82   1985   338.8′8   84–18198
ISBN 0–312–23636–0

For Ann

Contents

List of Tables

List of Figures

Preface and Acknowledgements

This book presents a selection of papers on the theory of the multinational enterprise (MNE) that we have written since our first collaboration on *The Future of the Multinational Enterprise* (1976). It contains revised versions of published papers and four hitherto unpublished papers. Two of the unpublished papers have been especially written for this volume.

The book begins with a review of recent literature which covers theoretical work on the MNE published up to the end of 1983. The remainder of the book falls naturally into three parts. Chapters 2–4 are concerned with applications of the concept of internalisation, chapters 5–7 with the location of foreign investment, and chapters 8 and 9 with some of the broader issues raised by the study of the MNE.

Chapter 2 discusses internalisation in the context of an economy in which every market is subject to transaction costs. It focuses upon internalisation motivated by the need for quality control. It analyses forward integration into sales subsidiaries and backward integration into component production, and applies the analysis to MNEs operating in low-technology manufacturing industries and service industries.

Chapter 3 discusses licensing, subcontracting, franchising and other forms of industrial co-operation agreement. It compares and contrasts the various contractual modes of technology transfer which are potential substitutes for the MNE. This chapter develops one of the main themes that permeates our work: that the MNE cannot be properly understood without investigating the alternatives to it. When this is done, it becomes apparent that many aspects of MNE behaviour are common to all the modes of technology transfer. Focusing upon the firm alone can give a very misleading impression of the special characteristics of the MNE.

Chapter 4 examines the relationship between multinational monopolies and international cartels: a subject of considerable importance for the economic history of the inter-war period. The analytical standpoint is that the multiplant firm and the cartel are alternative institutional arrangements for the exploitation of monopoly power. The MNE internalises the pricing and production agreements that are negotiated at arm's length between members of an international cartel. The advantages of internalisation are greatest when the monopoly is based upon marketing and product differentiation skills and lowest when it is based on patented technology. This chapter is specially written for the book and represents a new development of internalisation theory.

Chapters 5–7 examine the location decisions of the MNE. Each of the three chapters involves the formulation and solution of a mathematical model. This reflects our commitment to deriving testable propositions from a reasonably parsimonious set of assumptions about the behaviour of the MNE. It also reflects our view that it is only by following the methodology of mainstream economics that the theory of the MNE will eventually become an integral part of economic theory as a whole.

Chapter 5 presents a dynamic analysis of the decision to produce abroad. It considers the optimal timing of a foreign investment when the size of the foreign market is growing and the set-up costs of foreign investment depend upon the length of time for which the firm has already been exporting.

Chapter 6 introduces financial and organisational factors into the analysis of location. It shows how the financial structure of multinational operations is governed by the different perceptions of risk held by investors in different countries. It examines the complex relationship between the location of international production and the availability of equity and debenture debt in different countries.

Chapter 7 examines the consequences of the growing volume of international trade in intermediate products. It argues that technical advances in product design made by MNEs have been instrumental in promoting trade in components and semi-processed materials. It analyses the connection between intermediate product markets, export-platform investments, the 'new international division of labour' and the growth of intra-industry trade. A computable model illustrates the rationalisation of production within an MNE, with special reference to the impact on location of transport costs, taxes and tariffs.

Chapter 8 synthesises two themes from the earlier chapters: the importance of dynamic factors in the management of international operations, which is stressed in Chapter 5, and the subjectivity of expectations, which is the basis for the theory of international risk developed in Chapter 6. The general theme is the need to introduce the entrepreneur into the theory of the MNE. The entrepreneur specialises in taking business decisions in which subjective perceptions of the environment have a crucial role. Entrepreneurship involves a two-way process by which information is used to take business decisions and the outcomes of business decisions feed back information to the entrepreneur. The theory of the entrepreneur explains, amongst other things, how firms which invest abroad gain access to overseas information and how the use of this information affects their future expansion strategy.

Chapter 9 underlines another of the major themes of the book: the importance of testing the theory of the MNE. A major strength of the theory of the MNE is its practical relevance. It affords a convincing explanation of the growth, the industrial composition and the geographical destination of post-war US and European direct investment overseas. Recent theoretical work, however, too often stresses purely conceptual issues and, as a result, loses immediate relevance. This final chapter considers the problems of testing the theory of the MNE, and identifies the areas where more empirical work needs to be done.

The authors are grateful to a number of editors and publishers for permission to revise and reprint their earlier work. Chapter 1 first appeared in *Aussenwirtschaft*, volume 36; Chapter 2 in Alan M. Rugman (ed.) *New Theories of the Multinational Enterprise* (Beckenham, Kent: Croom Helm); Chapter 3 in *Aussenwirtschaft*, volume 38; Chapter 5 in the *Economic Journal*, volume 91 and Chapter 6 in J. Black and J. H. Dunning (eds) *International Capital Movements* (London: Macmillan). Chapter 7 is based upon University of Reading Discussion Paper in International Investment and Business Studies, no. 70, and was presented at the Annual Conference of the UK Chapter of the Academy of International Business (AIB) at the University of Strathclyde, March 1983. It was prepared under the auspices of the Leverhulme Project on Multinationals and Intermediate Product Trade at the University of Reading. Chapter 8 was originally presented to the Annual Conference of the UK Chapter of the AIB at Manchester University in November 1978.

It is once again the authors' pleasure to acknowledge the help of Jill Turner and Sylvia Ashdown in the preparation of the typescript.

The authors would like to thank Alan Rugman for comments on Chapter 2, Patrick Artisien for his comments on Chapter 3, Hafiz Mirza for help with the Tables in Chapter 9 and Mira Wilkins, John Cantwell, George Norman and Robert Read for comments on Chapter 4.

Special thanks are due to John Dunning for his continued support and encouragement.

Bradford and Reading   P.J.B.
                                                                         M.C.C.

1 A Critical View of Theories of the Multinational Enterprise

PETER J. BUCKLEY

1.1 INTRODUCTION

It is conventional to trace the origins of the modern theory of the multinational firm to the doctoral dissertation by Stephen Hymer, written in 1960 and eventually published in 1979. The strands of the theory, however, go back much further, to Coase (1937), Kaldor (1937) and Robinson (1931, 1934). More immediately, Hymer drew heavily on the work of Bain (1956) and Dunning (1958). Current developments suggest a trend towards a general theory of the firm, encompassing the multinational enterprise as a special case (Buckley, 1983).

This chapter analyses the development of theoretical approaches to the multinational enterprise. The several avenues of theoretical development are classified as (1.2) the Hymer–Kindleberger tradition, (1.3) the place of the multinational enterprise in the product cycle, (1.4) the importance of the concept of internalisation, (1.5) diversification versus internationalisation, (1.6) location theory as applied to the multinational enterprise and (1.7) attempts at achieving a synthesis into a general theory.

The definition of a multinational enterprise

Whole papers have been devoted to the question of defining the multinational enterprise (for example, Aharoni, 1971). Four alternative types of definition would seem to be:

(1) an 'operating' definition, one form of which is the ownership

1

threshold definition – a firm which owns or controls income generating assets in more than one country;

(2) a 'structural' definition where multinationality is judged according to organisation of the company;

(3) a 'performance' criterion, incorporating some relative or absolute measure of international spread (for example, number of foreign subsidiaries, percentage of sales accounted for by foreign sales, etc.);

(4) a 'behavioural' criterion based on the corporation's degree of geocentricity.

Definitions are not right or wrong, just more or less useful. Throughout the book, our definition is the simplest form of a threshold definition – a firm which owns outputs of goods or services originating in more than one country (Casson, 1982). Consequently, we avoid the issue of defining control and do not necessarily imply that the firm is a foreign direct investor. Thus we bring new forms of international involvement within the ambit of the theory (see Chapter 3).

1.2 THE HYMER–KINDLEBERGER TRADITION

The initial core of modern theory of the multinational enterprise was a deceptively simple proposition, that in order to compete with indigenous firms, which possess innate strengths such as knowledge of the local environment, market and business conditions, foreign entrants must have some compensating advantage. At a stroke, this proposition took foreign direct investment away from the theory of capital movements into the theory of industrial organisation. For, in a perfect market, foreign direct investment (FDI) could not exist because local firms would always be able to outcompete foreign entrants.

The initial phase of the Hymer–Kindleberger approach was therefore the search for the compensating 'advantage' which foreign investors possessed. Kindleberger's exposition (1969) examined four main areas of internationally transferable 'advantages'. First, departures from perfect competition in good markets, including product differentiation, marketing skills and administered pricing; second, departures from perfect competition in factor markets, including access to patented or 'proprietary' knowledge, discrimination in access to capital and skill differences embodied in the firm (particularly its management); third, internal and external economies of scale, including those arising from vertical integration; and finally, government intervention, particularly those forms restricting output or entry. Such advantages enable the foreign entrant to overcome its lack of knowledge of local conditions innate in the local firm, which the foreign firm can only acquire at a cost, and also serve to compensate for the foreigner's cost of operating at a distance.

The focus of investigation was thus placed firmly in the field of industrial organisation and was more specifically related to the analysis of imperfect competition. Hymer had relied greatly on Bain's (1956) pioneering work on barriers to entry to an industry and this thread of analysis has been deepened and broadened by Caves (1971, 1974; Caves and Porter, 1977). Caves (1971) suggested that the critical Hymer–Kindleberger advantage was the ability to differentiate a product, thus enabling the firm to service simultaneously several international markets.

Johnson (1968, 1970, 1975) suggested that the significant advantage must have the characteristic of a 'public good', that is, it can be exploited by a subsidiary at a cost which is low in relation to the acquisition costs facing a rival firm. Such an advantage strongly suggests special knowledge or skills.

We must, however, turn to a second critical element in the Hymer––Kindleberger approach. Given the special advantages which enable the firm to invest successfully abroad (that is, the necessary condition) it remains to be proven that direct investment is the preferred means of exploiting the advantage (that is, the sufficient condition). The basis for the decision, according to Hymer and Kindleberger is profitability. In many cases direct investment will be preferred to either exporting or licensing the 'advantage' to a host-country firm. Exporting will in many cases be excluded by tariff and transport cost barriers – also a local producer may be better placed to adapt his product to local conditions and a local presence may have the effect of stimulating demand.

The arguments that firms will often prefer FDI to licensing are more subtle. Hymer (1976) argued that the advantage-possessor cannot appropriate the full return (or rent) from its utilisation because of imperfections in the market for knowledge. Such imperfections arising from 'buyer uncertainty' (the buyer being unable to assess the worth of the knowledge to him until he is in possession of it), lack of an institutionalised market for knowledge and the dependence of the value of knowledge on its secrecy. The seller thus cannot induce competitive bids in order to appropriate the full returns. Further factors which favour FDI over licensing the advantage to host-country firms are the desire for control by the advantage-possessor and the danger that the advantage-seller will create a competitor if the buyer uses the advantage in 'ways which have not been paid for'. Licensing thus may incur heavy firm-to-firm transfer costs, including cost of 'policing' the transferred property rights (Davies, 1977; Buckley and Davies, 1980) – costs which do not arise in the case of transfers from parent to subsidiary.

In summary, therefore, this approach suggests that a multinational entrant must possess an internally transferable 'advantage', the possession of which gives it a quasi-monopolistic opportunity to enter host-country markets. Barriers to trade and barriers which prevent host-country firms from duplicating this advantage mean that direct foreign investment is frequently the preferred form of exploiting the advantage in foreign markets.

It is arguable, however, that the fundamental proposition of the Hymer–Kindleberger approach is not as easily applicable to established multinational firms as it is to firms becoming multinational. How far do the barriers to entry to a foreign market decline as the international spread of the firm widens? Established multinational firms have gained worldwide dominance and have developed techniques to 'learn in advance' local conditions – products, processes, management style, marketing techniques are continually adapted to local markets. The ability of a multinational to forecast and to adapt is one of the major competitive skills. It is now only the entry into unusually isolated markets (such as the People's Republic of China) where heavy 'costs of foreignness' are still encountered. The advantage of locals in other instances can be discounted in advance by an experienced multinational firm.

The whole concept of firm specific advantages must therefore be questioned (Buckley, 1983). The concept is artificially attenuated at the point where the firm first crosses national boundaries, or at least where it has the potential to do so. Firm-specific advantage is a reflection of this cut-off point as a snapshot in time of a dynamic process. The existence of firm-specific advantages depends on a set of assertions on (i) the diffusion of technical and marketing know-how, (ii) the comparative advantage of firms in particular locations, and (iii) the existence of particular types of economies of scale.

The first set of these assertions rests on the size and extent of barriers to the sale of information on the market which are increasingly open to challenge (Carstairs and Welch, 1981). Chapters 2 and 3 of this book as are the assumptions on on the relatively costless nature of internal information transfer (Teece, 1976 and 1983). The second set of assertions is under threat from the rise of multinational enterprises throughout the world (Kojima, 1978; Ozawa, 1979a; Agmon and Kindleberger, 1977; Kumar and Mcleod, 1981; Lecraw, 1977; Franko, 1976). Finally, empirical propositions on economies of scale in Research and Development (R & D) on which firm-specific advantages rest, remain to be proved empirically and there is no guarantee that the R & D undertakers are necessarily the optimum users of the output of R & D units. Separability via the market of R & D and its implementation in production may be a better solution. Additionally, multinational firms often become locked into outmoded technologies and institutional rigidities may prevent the creation and absorption of new developments in established firms. This provides oppportunities for new generation products and processes outside existing multinationals, which gives fluidity to growth paths and often leads to the emergence of new firms.

The notion of firm-specific advantage is thus a short-run one when endowments of proprietary knowledge among firms are fixed. In the long run, the investment policy of the firm is crucial and a dynamic reformulation of industry barriers to entry is necessary to bring about an approach integrating the life cycle of the firm to expansion paths over time (Magee, 1977a; Buckley, 1983).

The MNE as a Currency Area Phenomenon

A variant of the Hymer–Kindleberger approach, particularly associated with Aliber (1970 and 1971) deals with an advantage which is not specific to particular firms but to all firms based in a particular currency area. According to Aliber it is the international financial market in which MNEs have an advantage over host-country firms. Consequently, Aliber argues that FDI can take place *even if* the market for advantages (licensing) is perfect.

The analysis centres on the currency premium. The holder of debt denominated in a particular currency bears the risk that his returns will be reduced if that currency depreciates in value relative to other currencies. If there is no aversion to risk then, in a perfect market, the rate of interest on the debt denominated in a particular currency will exactly reflect the expected rate of depreciation of that currency. But investors are averse to risk and demand a premium for bearing the uncertainty of exchange risk. However, Aliber argues that the market is subject to a *bias* in the application of the currency premium. Investors are myopic – they treat *all* the assets of an MNE as if they were in the same currency area as the parent firm. Consequently, a UK factory is a sterling asset, but when that factory is owned by a US company it is regarded by the market *as if* it were a dollar asset.

The effect of these propositions is that source-country firms are ones which are able to borrow at lower interest rates (those relating to 'hard' currency assets) and are more highly valued by the market because their earnings are all capitalised at the rate relevant to the source-country currency.

Several criticisms of Aliber's theory are in order (Buckley and Casson, 1976; Dunning, 1971). First, it seems unlikely that as a long-term explanation investors' myopia can bear the weight placed on it. Could not speculators turn such a bias to their advantage and thereby eliminate the phenomenon? Surely the international market recognises that MNEs are multiple currency-earners and that such earnings are subject to exchange risk if converted back to source-country currency? Second, the theory fails to explain the industrial distribution of FDI and the phenomenon of simultaneous cross-investment within one industry between currency areas. However, in broad terms, the approach explains well the direction of MNE investment in the post-war world; US expansion followed by extensive German and Japanese outward investment and the invasion of the US by European multinationals during the 1970s and early 1980s.

Oligopolistic Reaction and the Multinational Enterprise

Although closely linked with product cycle models (see next section) the work of Knickerbocker (1973) clearly belongs with the general rubric of industrial organisation. In a carefully designed study using the Harvard Multinational Enterprise Study sample of 187 US corporate giants, Knickerbocker found a close relationship between oligopolistic reaction (demonstrated by the 'bunching' in the time of entry into a particular market by oligopolistic firms) and industry structure. Moreover, the greater the degree of seller concentration, the more closely was entry into a market by the 'leader' matched by 'followers'. Profitability was also related to intensity of oligopolistic reaction. Knickerbocker suggested that brisk 'defensive' investment transplants profitable patterns of oligopolistic behaviour to foreign markets. (See also Flowers, 1976, who applies the approach to direct investment in the USA.)

The Political Economy of the Hymer–Kindleberger Propositions

The political economy implications of the basic Hymer–Kindleberger model were developed by Hymer into a critique of the role of the MNE in the world economy (Hymer, 1970 and 1971; Hymer and Rowthorne, 1970; Rowthorne and Hymer, 1970). The integration of the 'Law of Increasing Firm Size' and 'The Law of Uneven Development' gave Hymer the tools to criticise the MNE as an instrument which channels wealth and power away from 'peripheral' (less developed) nations to 'central' nations (that is, rich source-countries).

Paradoxically, the theory has been extended in an opposite direction by its other begetter, Kindleberger (1969). Kindleberger suggests that although multinational firms may swallow up competitors, they lead the world towards greater economic efficiency by increasing global competitive interaction, breaking up domestic monopolies and surmounting Government-imposed barriers to freer competition. (See Modelski, 1979, for a variety of views on these contrary projections.)

1.3 THE PRODUCT CYCLE MODEL

The product cycle hypothesis (PCH) chiefly associated with Raymond Vernon (1966, 1971, 1977a and 1979) has yielded a large number of insights into the development of the MNE. The models rest on four basic assumptions:

(1) products undergo predictable changes in production and marketing;
(2) restricted information is available on technology;
(3) production processes change over time and economies of scale are prevalent;
(4) Tastes differ according to income and thus products can be standardised at various income levels (Wells, 1972).

The original model (Vernon, 1966) suggested that new products would appear first in the most advanced country (the USA) because demand from (i) discretionary spending on new products arising from high income and (ii) substitution of new capital goods for expensive labour, would be most easily transmitted to local entrepreneurs. Consequently, the *new product stage*, where an unstandardised product with a low price-elasticity of demand is produced on an experimental basis, occurs in the USA. The second stage is the *maturing product*. The product begins to be standardised and the need for flexibility on both supply and demand sides declines. The possibilities of economies of scale lead to expansion in production and this is matched by increasing demand as the product becomes cheaper. The market begins to appear in other advanced countries and is initially satisfied by exports from the USA. Eventually cost factors begin to dictate that these foreign markets should be serviced by local production and the emergence of indigenous producers adds a 'defensive' motive to the advantages of investment by US producers. So other advanced countries are the first recipients of US direct investment. In the third stage, a *standardised product* emerges which sells entirely on the basis of price competitiveness. The imperative now is to produce the product at the lowest possible cost. Consequently, the labour-intensive stages of production are hived off and carried out, via foreign direct investment, in the less-developed countries, where labour is cheapest.

Vernon's initial model thus has the virtues of simplicity and directness. It explains US investment in other advanced countries and the phenomenon of 'offshore production' in cheap labour countries (Moxon, 1974). Despite its virtues of integrating supply and demand factors, it has been outdated by events. Firstly, the US is no longer totally dominant in foreign investment – European and Japanese multinational expansion also needs explanation. Second, MNEs are now capable of developing, maturing and standardising products almost simultaneously, differentiating the product to suit a variety of needs without significant time lags.

It was to counter the first objection that Vernon adapted his model to deal with non-US MNEs (Vernon, 1977) after virtually admitting the redundancy of the 'simple' model (Vernon, 1971). The modified product cycle (Vernon, 1979) brings the hypothesis much closer to the Hymer–Kindleberger model outlined above, resting as it does on oligopoly and market behaviour. The hypothesis is now concerned to emphasise the oligopolistic structure in which most MNEs operate and their attempts to forestall entry into the industry by new firms. The names of the stages tell the story of the competitive devices used to construct and maintain oligopoly – *innovation-based* oligopoly, *mature* oligopoly (price competition and scale economies) and *senescent* oligopoly (cartels, product differentiation and the essential breakdown of entry barriers).

The product cycle model thus yields many interesting insights into the process of global competition. It also led to several valuable empirical studies – notably Hufbauer (1966) and Hirsh (1967). However, its over-deterministic and programmatic nature are features which have to be modified in view of the increasing sophistication of global competitive interaction (Giddy, 1978). In its analysis of the strategy of established multinational firms, the product cycle approach splits three decisions which are interdependent:

(1) investment in product development,
(2) the method of servicing a foreign market and
(3) the firm's competitive stance *vis à vis* foreign firms.

These elements need to be considered simultaneously by MNEs. As the basis for a forward planning model, the PCH has been outdated by the existence of experienced firms facing worldwide competition. Modelling of the process by which a naive entrant firm becomes an established multinational firm represents a gap in the theoretical framework despite several empirical studies (Newbould *et al.*, 1978; Aharoni, 1966; Luostarinen, 1980). Whatever the defects of Vernon's models, their virtues serve to focus attention on a more truly dynamic version of the growth of (multinational) firms.

1.4 INTERNALISATION AND THE THEORY OF THE MNE

Attempts at integration of the various strands of the theory of the multinational firm have centred on the concept of internalisation. It is pointed out in Chapter 8 that two connotations of this concept exist. One aspect is the internalisation of a market where an arm's length contractual relationship is replaced by unified ownership. The other concerns the internalisation of an externality where a market is created where none existed before. Often internalisation of the latter kind is a consequence of the former, but logically the two should be dissociated. The excessive generality ascribed to internalisation has led to it being described as 'a concept in search of a theory' (Buckley, 1983, p. 42) but careful distinctions between types of internalisation and the incidence of costs and benefits on a firm-by-firm basis leads to concrete propositions on the optimal scope of the firm (Casson, 1981; Teece, 1983).

The thrust of the concept of internalisation is that the actions of firms can replace the market or alternatively can augment it. The explanatory power of the concept rests on an analysis of the costs and benefits to the firm of internalising markets, particularly markets in intermediate goods. The predictive power of the concept for the growth and pattern of MNEs is given by a statement of the likelihood of the internalisation of the various markets which the MNE faces. The advantages of internalisation (and therefore of control by the firm versus the market solution) are given by:

(1) The increased ability to control and plan production and in particular to co-ordinate flows of crucial inputs;
(2) exploitation of market power by discriminatory pricing;
(3) avoidance of bilateral market power;
(4) avoidance of uncertainties in the transfer of knowledge between parties which may exist in the alternative (market) solution;
(5) avoidance of potential government intervention by devices such as transfer prices.

Costs arise from communication, co-ordination and control difficulties, and costs of foreignness (Buckley and Casson, 1976). Three cases of empirical importance are (i) the advantages of vertical integration, (ii) the importance of situations where intermediate product flows in research intensive industries and (iii) the internalisation of human skills, particularly in areas with high returns to team co-operation such as marketing and financing.

Magee (1977a, 1977b) bases his explanation on the ease of 'appropriability' of returns from the creation of information, that is, the ability of the private originators of ideas to obtain for themselves the pecuniary value of the ideas to society. This extension of Johnson's (1970) concept and Arrow's (1962) analysis of the public good nature of proprietary information is linked with an industry cycle to derive expectations on the nature of MNE development and their ability effectively to transfer technology (particularly to LDCs) (Magee, 1977a). Parallel contributions have been made by McManus, 1972; Swedenborg, 1979, and Hennart, 1982.

Underlying this internalisation approach is the view that internal solutions will be sought where international market imperfections would impose costs on firms using those markets. Internalisation of markets also imposes severe barriers on new entry. The multinational is thus seen as both responding to market imperfections and creating them. Clearly, strong links with the Hymer–Kindleberger approach and the product cycle hypothesis are apparent. Attention to imperfections on intermediate markets should not obscure the role of imperfections in final goods markets, leading to competitive devices such as product differentiation and administered pricing. Multinationals are not passive reactors to imperfections and internalisation decisions interact. The critical role of information as an intermediate product is an important synthesising element.

The role of multinationals in creating imperfections has not yet been fully incorporated into the theory because more attention has been paid to MNEs' reaction to market imperfections. What is required is a thoroughgoing theory of barriers to entry for industries and markets. Further, the concept of internalisation is a difficult one to measure empirically. The use of internal exports and flows relating to R & D (Buckley and Pearce, 1979 and 1981) do not always discriminate fully between this approach and others. Further empirical work in this field is necessary.

1.5 DIVERSIFICATION AND INTERNATIONALISATION

It is possible to regard the MNE not as an aggressive risk taker, investing heavily in R & D and diffusing the fruits through an international network of subsidiaries and appropriating the returns, but as averse to risk, using multinationality to achieve stability of returns. Moreover, internationalisation may be regarded as an alternative to domestic diversification. Here we bring these two ideas together.

The typical MNE will be diversified in two ways – first, by its product – market position internationally, and second, it will be financially diversified, earning its returns in a variety of currencies. It is argued that the advantages given by international financial diversification have led to superior stock market performance by MNEs over purely domestic firms, even after allowing for size and industry influences (Rugman, 1975, 1976, 1977a, 1977b, 1981). Thus MNEs are regarded as an alternative vehicle for international financial diversification to individual diversification by the purchase of shareholdings. This argument rests on imperfections in the world capital market which prevent individuals from enjoying the benefits of diversification (Stevens, 1974; Prachowny, 1972; Grubel, 1968). Such imperfections must (i) impede individuals from satisfactorily diversifying, and (ii) reduce the optimal diversification of intermediaries so that diversification through controlling interests is more efficient than a large number of smaller shareholdings. Direct investment involves control and without some such supporting argument *control* would involve a suboptimal amount of diversification relative to the amount of each holding.

The arguments adduced for such imperfections are that (i) transactions costs exist in the equity market in the form of costs of acquiring and disseminating the relevant mass of information, and (ii) this results in the application by the market of a premium to the equity valuation of diversified firms. In addition, it can be argued that the divorce of ownership and control reinforces this tendency because managers in an imperfect capital market can pursue policies which enhance their own welfare, within the constraint that returns to shareholders do not fall below those which would make their shareholders receptive to a takeover bid. Managers may be averse to risk (preferring to safeguarding of their jobs to extra returns) and may therefore prefer a widely diversified company with the hoped-for stability which goes with this state. Diversification through foreign investment widens the scope of their discretion. However, this would presumably accord with a strategy of avoidance of high risk R & D, which is not consistent with the evidence (Buckley and Casson, 1976; Hood and Young, 1979).

A further theoretical avenue concerns the choice between domestic (product) diversification and internationalisation. The simplest answer is to regard the MNE as a bundle of sector-specific resources, facing high barriers to entry into other industries but with relatively easy investment access to foreign markets (Kindleberger, 1969; Corden, 1977).

A more rigorous analysis of this choice has been carried out by Wolf (1975) (1977) following work by Horst (1972a,b). Horst showed that it was *total* US sales to the Canadian market (exports plus investment sales) which were explained by the theoretically significant factors (R & D intensity, size). Wolf takes this further by suggesting that domestic diversification and internationalisation should be regarded as alternative expansion routes. Wolf's theoretical underpinning relies on the pioneering work by Penrose (1959), who suggested that underutilised resources within the firm, particularly management (the development of an idea in Robinson, 1934) can be called into service at home or abroad as rent-yielding assets. The opportunity cost of such underutilised resources is close to zero but will have positive marginal revenue when utilised. The difficulty in such an approach is represented in finding appropriate measures or proxies for underutilised resources. Wolf uses average firm size (by industry) to represent economies of scale and he uses the proportion of scientists and engineers in total employment as a proxy for technological expertise.

This avenue of investigation leads us into the area of MNEs as special cases of multiplant firms. The theory of multiplant firms is addressed to the question, 'Why should firms operate several plants of suboptimal size rather than a smaller number of plants which could be above minimum efficient scale?' This question is tackled by Scherer *et al.* (1975) and it is clear that the results are of direct relevance to MNEs. Scherer brings together findings from location theory, optimal lot-size theory, monetary theory and physical distribution theory to derive hypotheses concerning 'optimal unbalanced specialisation paths' for firms. In the international sphere it is clear that many markets are small and do not provide enough scope for even one optimal size plant. In addition, buyers' desire for choice and variety dictates from the demand side that no one firm, let alone plant, shall dominate individual markets. Further, in many industries long-run unit production cost is relatively flat and cost penalties are not imposed severely on less than optimal plant scales. Finally, multiplant operation is often a rational response to problems of manufacturing highly specialised products with volatile demand or other features requiring close managerial supervision or technologies well-suited to low volume production. These findings can be integrated with the above theory and with location theory to yield a fruitful synthesis (1.6 below). The interplay of *plant* level economies and *firm* level economies play a major role in the market servicing (exports versus direct investment) decisions of MNEs (Dunning and Buckley, 1977) and represent central concepts around which to integrate the different theoretical perspectives.

1.6 MULTINATIONAL ENTERPRISES AND LOCATION THEORY

It is fair to suggest that location theory elements in the modern theory of the MNE have been neglected. Yet any viable explanation of the growth, pattern and operations (sourcing policies) of inputs and market servicing policies must include elements of location theory. Under the general rubric already given the MNE can be seen as simply a major vehicle for the transfer of mobile resources (technology, capital, management skills) to areas with immobile (or fixed) complementary inputs (markets, raw materials, labour). Thus Ricardian endowments enter the theory.

The location-specific endowments of particular importance to MNEs are (i) raw materials, leading to vertical FDI, (ii) cheap labour, leading to 'offshore production' facilities (Moxon, 1974) and (iii) protected or fragmented markets leading to FDI as the preferred means of market servicing. Location factors therefore enter the theory not only in their own right, as an influence on the relative costs facing an MNE with a choice of locations, but also may provide the motives for international expansion.

The important connections between location factors and the (internal) organisation of MNEs should however be given due weight. First, the MNE will normally be a multi-stage, multi-function firm and the location of different stages and functions will be subject to different locational influences connected by (international) flows of intermediate products. Second, the internalisation of markets will affect location in two important ways:

(1) The MNE have an incentive to minimise government intervention through transfer pricing, for instance, to reduce the overall tax liability by imputing high mark-ups in the lowest tax countries and possibly by altering its location strategy completely to take in a low-intervention 'tax haven'. (For evidence on transfer pricing see Lall, 1973 and 1978a and for the nature and amount of intra-company trade and its determinants, Buckley and Pearce, 1979 and 1981.)

(2) The increased communication flows in an internal market may bias high communication cost activities towards the 'centre' – usually towards the source country where critical activities are focused on head office. (A forceful extension of this argument is given by Hymer, 1971.)

In his restatement of the product cycle hypothesis, Vernon (1974) gives a great deal of weight to the interplay between the stage of the industry's development and the relevant locational influences upon it. The location of research activities (in the centre) and the changing locational influences on production provide the dynamic for the theory.

Standard location theory can be shown to be of direct relevance to the strategy of MNEs as illustrated by Dunning's paper (1972) on the location of MNEs in an enlarged EEC, which is further developed in Chapter 7, and Horst's work (1972a,b) on the servicing of the Canadian market by US MNEs. The reduction, removal of increase of tariffs between nations will alter MNEs' market servicing decisions and cause a restructuring of the location of MNE activities. This area leads into an interesting discussion centred on the relative 'comparative advantages' of firms and nations (Lundgren, 1977) and thence to relative bargaining capabilities (Vaitsos, 1974; Casson, 1979).

Japanese Direct Investment: A Distinct Approach?

Japanese direct investment is thought by some to require a special approach because of several alleged differences from Western European and US investment (Ozawa, 1979a,b). Amongst these differences are: (i) a later takeoff of Japanese investment, (ii) a clustering in Latin America and Asia of such investments, (iii) the supposed greater labour intensity of Japanese investment, (iv) its openness to joint ventures and (v) the existence of group-controlled investment (Buckley, 1983).

These characteristics have led Japanese analysts to propose alternative explanations specifically related to Japanese conditions. One of the most ingenious is the theoretical framework developed by Kiyoshi Kojima (1973) (1975) (1978) and (1982). Kojima's approach is variously called 'a macroeconomic approach', 'a factor endowments approach' and 'a model of trade-oriented (Japanese-type) foreign investment' to distinguish it from 'anti-trade-oriented (American type) FDI'. Kojima's aim is to integrate trade theory with direct investment theory and to contrast 'Japanese type' investment with 'American type'.

Kojima (1978) begins with the standard two-country, two-factor, two-product Hecksher–Ohlin model of trade. He then introduces Mundell's demonstration that under rigorous Hecksher–Ohlin assumptions 'the substitution for commodity of factor movements will be complete'. The process for achieving this is that capital (homogeneous –money–capital) flows from the capital-rich to the capital-poor country, perhaps in response to the imposition of a prohibitive tariff on capital-intensive exportables, so the recipient country becomes more capital-abundant and reallocates its resources such that production of the capital-intensive good expands and the labour-intensive good declines until equilibrium is reached at a point exactly corresponding to the post-trade situation in the absence of the capital movement. This pattern of output change – that the recipient country's comparatively disadvantaged industry expands and its comparatively advantaged (in terms of its *original* factor endowment) contracts is posited in the Rybczynski theorem. Kojima views American FDI in this light, arguing that the basis for trade is eliminated by outflows of capital from the capital-exporting country's advantaged industry so FDI is a substitute for trade.

In the Japanese case, however, Kojima's argument is that the host-country's production frontier expands in such a direction that the (pre-investment) comparatively advantaged industry expands and the comparatively disadvantaged industry contracts, thus enhancing the basis for trade.

This 'complements' case is achieved by the Rybczynski line sloping in an opposite direction (that is, the line linking the original production point and the post-capital inflow production point moves 'upward'). This effect cannot occur if homogeneous 'money capital', perfectly re-allocable to any industry, is the norm. Therefore Kojima suggests at this point that direct investment capital is a package involving technical knowledge and human skill components (including management skills); it is therefore to some extent industry-specific. This capital moves to the host country because of 'comparative advantages in improving productivity' in the host country and the resultant increase in profitability gives the motivation. Here Kojima introduces a crucial assumption: that productivity in the host country is increased *more* through direct investments in the labour-intensive industry than in the capital-intensive industry 'due to the smaller technological gap and a greater spillover of technology to local firms' (Kojima, 1978, p. 126). The same amount of output is produced with proportionately smaller inputs of labour and capital, that is, Hicks-neutral technological change is deemed to have taken place.

The critical factor in this model is the disproportionate effect on productivity, when sector-specific capital moves into the host's com-paratively advantaged industry. The implicit assumption is that indus-try-specific public goods have been transferred – the proof of this is Kojima's statement (Kojima, 1978, p. 127) that the production frontier in the source country remains unchanged 'since the technology and managerial skills do not decrease even when they are applied abroad and since labour and capital are assumed unchanged' in the source country, for Kojima includes the assumption that FDI involves a negligible transfer of 'money capital'.

The 'comparative advantage in improving productivity' can thus be seen as the result of the combination of internationally mobile inputs transferred by the investing (Japanese) firm, such as managerial and organisational skills, with the vital addition of guaranteed access to (Japanese) markets and distribution networks, together with locatio-nally immobile inputs, notably cheap labour. Kojima suggests that because of the sector-specific nature of these productivity-improving resources, it is easier for firms which possess such attributes to relocate abroad (outside Japan) rather than to diversify into other domestic industries. Consequently, there is no presumption (unlike product cycle type US FDI) that the outward investors are the 'leading' firms. Indeed it is suggested that weaker firms, most exposed to exogenous shifts in comparative advantage, will be most likely to relocate in LDCs.

The crucial element in Kojima's explanation of Japanese foreign direct investment is the improvement in productivity in the host country brought about by the infusion of the 'package of resources' involved in Japanese investment. Of key importance are the market access which the link with a Japanese distribution network brings, and the organisational skills of Japanese management when working with relatively unskilled or semi-skilled labour. The host-country unit, when taken over or set up by Japanese FDI, becomes integrated with a marketing network guaranteeing market access. The addition of a Japanese imprint enhances the quality image of the product. Japanese ownership therefore confers immediate benefit.

The specialist skills infused include the skills developed by Japanese enterprises in response to the particular stimuli which they have faced in Japan; notably a co-operative rather than competitive environment, a docile and relatively cheap workforce and skills in organising high quality, mass production systems. The range of industries over which these skills are crucial is very different from those where US (and European) firms have developed intra-industry specialisms and consequently the industrial structure of Japanese FDI is very different from 'Western' FDI. It has however been differentiated by Kojima more starkly than the version presented here by his concentration on a product cycle interpretation of 'American type' FDI.

Japanese FDI represents a search for location specific inputs (stable environment, low transport costs, but chiefly cheap labour) to complement the skills developed by Japanese enterprise. It corresponds to Western (chiefly US firms') 'offshore production' and exhibits a similar industry structure (Moxon, 1974; Finger, 1975 and 1976).

Japanese outward investment must indeed be explained by reference to locational criteria, notably the relative labour costs in 'nearby' LDCs as compared with Japan. The firm-specific skills – access to a (worldwide) distribution network, organisation ability and managerial skills – of Japanese firms differ significantly from the typical US or European MNEs' strengths and consequently the industrial distribution of Japanese FDI differs from that of other industrialised countries. Differentiation of Japanese FDI has been exaggerated by its comparison with product cycle type US FDI, which is at most only a subset of that country's outward investment – an explanation which has been outdated by events (Giddy, 1978).

1.7 SYNTHESIS – A GENERAL THEORY OF THE MNE

There are now several candidates for a general theory of the multinational enterprise. Amongst these are Dunning's eclectic theory (Dunning, 1977, 1979, 1980 and 1981), which relies on the OLI paradigm: ownership specific advantages, location endowments and internalisation advantages. Several unresolved issues remain in this approach. First, the relationship between these three elements and their development over time is unclear and leaves a classification system which is bereft of a dynamic content. Second, the existence of separate (and separable) ownership advantages is doubtful and logically redundant because internalisation explains why firms exist in the absence of such advantages.

Rugman (1981, 1982) claims that internalisation in itself represents a general theory of the multinational enterprise. This is achieved partly by relegating location factors to a footnote by including 'spatial cost saving' as an internalised firm-specific advantage. Internalisation requires restrictions on the relative sizes of internal and external transaction costs to have any empirical content and without a theory of this incidence, remains tautological.

The 'markets and hierarchies' approach associated with Oliver Williamson (1975, 1981) has also been advanced as a candidate for a general theory of the multinational enterprise (Calvet, 1981). Williamson suggests that his general theory of why firms exist explains the existence of the multinational firm as a special case. Without a theory of the conditions under which one ideal-type form (market or hierarchy) will be replaced by the other, only an arid comparative static framework remains. The transition from market to hierarchy may be explained by the minimisation of transaction costs once these have been carefully specified (Casson, 1981; Buckley, 1983). The concept of bounded rationality in management decision-making utilised by Williamson is useful but sits awkwardly within an essentially neo-classical framework. Further, Rugman's (1981) identification of hierarchy with internal market may be unjustified because internal organisation may more closely resemble a perfect market (with transfer prices approximating to shadow prices of a perfect allocation) than the hierarchical mode.

The theory of the multinational firm therefore requires development in several directions before it can be seen to be adequate. First, the fusion between institutional and neo-classical elements must be made more secure. Second, the general area of the economics of business strategy is in need of greater attention. Third, the role of time must be more carefully defined in the relationship between the growth (and decline) of firms, technologies, products and industries. Finally, the formulation and testing of hypotheses from the theory is an urgent task.

2 Transaction Costs and the Theory of the Multinational Enterprise

MARK CASSON

2.1 INTRODUCTION

The theory of internalisation is now widely accepted as a key element in the theory of the multinational enterprise (MNE) (see Chapter 1). Internalisation is a general theory of why firms exist, and without additional assumptions it is almost tautological. To make the theory operational it is necessary to specify assumptions about transaction costs for particular products and for trade between particular locations. It is typically asserted that:

(1) It is very costly to license unpatentable know-how, so that the market for know-how must be internalised. This leads to the vertical integration of production and R & D, and, because of the 'public good' characteristics of know-how, to the consequent horizontal integration of production in different locations.
(2) It is difficult to specify and enforce long-term futures contracts, so that the market for raw materials used by capital-intensive production processes must be internalised by backward integration.
(3) *Ad valorem* tariffs, international tax differentials and foreign exchange controls create incentives for transfer-pricing, which are most easily exploited through internalisation.

With these additional assumptions about the relative costs of internal and external markets, the theory predicts that MNEs will predominate in R & D-intensive industries – particularly those where patents are difficult to register or enforce – in resource-based industries, and in situations where the international division of labour is inhibited by fiscal intervention which can be avoided by transfer-pricing.

It is apparent, however, that not all industries in which MNEs operate fulfil these conditions. MNEs occur in many low-technology manufacturing industries and are also quite important in the service sector. It is true that US-based MNEs are predominantly R & D-oriented, but this does not apply to the same extent to European MNEs, and certainly not to Japanese MNEs.

The object of this chapter is to extend conventional theory in order to explain the rationale of non-R & D-intensive MNEs. It has been suggested by Giddy and Young (1982) that this can be done simply by broadening the concept of know-how to include a wide range of marketing skills. This chapter suggests that instead the non-R & D-intensive MNE is best explained by extending the scope of internalisation theory to take account of additional sources of market imperfection.

The chapter is arranged in three parts. The first part reformulates internalisation theory in the context of a more general theory of transaction costs. The second part focuses upon a particular component of transaction cost, arising from the need to monitor for product quality, and shows how this may be reduced through internalisation. Using case studies, it is argued that this motive for internalisation explains the presence of MNEs in some non-R & D-intensive industries. The final part considers how far orthodox theory can be regarded as a special case of this more general theory of transaction cost and internalisation.

2.2 THE NATURE OF TRANSACTION COSTS

Orthodox internalisation theory starts from the neoclassical norm of perfectly competitive markets in general equilibrium, and then introduces imperfections which appear as deviations from this norm. These imperfections are obstacles to trade, and are usually assumed to be exogenous to transactors. The imperfections are sometimes identified with transaction costs, but this is not strictly correct. The opportunity cost of obstacles to trade is measured by the gains from trade foregone. Transaction costs are incurred in attempting to overcome these obstacles. Table 2.1 identifies these obstacles and indicates the 'market-making' activities required to overcome them.

The table may be interpreted in two ways. The conventional interpretation is that of an inventory of possible deviations from perfect competition. On this view it is appropriate to analyse each obstacle to

TABLE 2.1   *Classification of market-making activities*

Obstacle to trade	Market-making activity	Major resource input
No contact between buyer and seller	Contact-making *via* search or advertisement	Administrative labour
No knowledge of reciprocal wants	Specification of the trade and communication of details to each party	Administrative labour
No agreement over price	Negotiation	Administrative labour
No confidence that goods correspond to specification	Monitoring: i.e. screening of quality, metering of quantity, timing of instalments, observation of 'contingent' events	Administrative labour
Need to exchange custody of goods	Transport	Energy, applied via manual labour or utilisation of transport equipment
Tariffs, taxes on gains from trade, price regulations, quotas	Payment of taxes and tariffs. Avoidance or evasion of taxes, tariffs, regulations or quotas	Administrative labour
No confidence that restitution will be made for default	Enforcement	Administrative labour, physical force

trade and its corresponding market-making activity as though it were the only deviation present. The objections to this view are twofold. First, it is unrealistic, for in practice many markets exhibit several simultaneous obstacles to trade. Second – and much more fundamental – is that the effectiveness of a market-making activity designed to overcome one obstacle may be strongly influenced by the presence of other obstacles. For example, if contact-making is difficult then markets will be fragmented, transactors will tend to be bilateral monopolists, and so price negotiation may be more difficult too. Again, the accuracy with which the product has to be screened for quality will depend upon the detail with which the product is specified, and this in turn will depend upon the ease with which product specifications can be communicated.

An alternative interpretation is that the table exhibits the logical sequence of steps necessary to take transactors from mutual isolation, through anarchy (or a Hobbesian state of nature, perhaps) by way of strategic haggling towards successful completion of a trade. Logically the first step in a trade is for transactors to make contact, and then to communicate reciprocal wants which are embodied in the contractual specification. It is assumed that they exchange two types of good, one of which may be designated 'the product' and the other 'the payment'. The contractual specification may allow for product supply and/or payment to take place in various instalments at different dates, for the arrangements to be contingent upon particular events on or before these dates and for various penalties or compensations to be paid in the event of default. After negotiating a price the two parties exchange custody of the goods and pay any taxes or tariffs due on the transaction. Each party monitors the exchange: he screens the quality and meters the quantity of the good he offers, and checks the other party's screening and metering of the good which he has received (though in certain cases it may be possible to eliminate this duplication of screening and metering – see Section 2.7). Failure of the quantity of quality to comply with the specification constitutes default. In the final stage the penalties and compensations due in respect of default are enforced.

2.3 SPECIALISATION IN MARKET-MAKING

All market-making activities incur costs, and have (at least to some extent) an uncertain outcome. There is always a risk that the transaction may break down, so that the costs of market-making will have been incurred without anything to show for them.

Suppose to begin with that all transactors are risk-neutral and there is no fiscal intervention (which implies, amongst other things, that taxes and tariffs are zero). In this case economic efficiency requires that expected transaction cost should be minimised for any given set of transactions. Transactions should be effected up to the margin where the increment in expected transaction cost is equal to the value of the incremental gain from trade.

The minimisation of transaction costs normally calls for the specialisation of market-making activities. There are two main reasons for specialisation. The first is to exploit economies of scale arising from increased utilisation of purpose-designed indivisible assets. The classic example of this is the use of a brokerage facility (that is, a purpose-built communication network) to reduce contact-making costs. Second, specialisation permits each resource to be concentrated on the market-making activity in which it has a comparative advantage. For most market-making activities the major resource is administrative labour.

Thus for example specialisation allows people with a comparative advantage in monitoring to specialise in activities such as quality control, while people with a comparative advantage in contact-making can specialise in brokerage.

2.4 SPECIALISATION IN RISK-BEARING

Suppose now that some individuals – possibly all – are risk-averse. The risks associated with each market-making activity are described in Table 2.2. Typically the risks associated with any given transaction are related to the nature of the product and to the personal characteristics of the buyer and seller, as well as to other more general factors. The influence of product characteristics and transactor characteristics on market-making risks is exhibited in Table 2.3.

In the first instance, the risks associated with each transaction, or attempted transaction, will be shared between the buyer and the seller. Prior to contract, the allocation of risk between the two parties will depend upon who takes the initiative in making contact, communicating specifications and opening negotiations. The allocation of the remaining risks will be determined by the provisions of the contract and by the arrangements made for its enforcement.

TABLE 2.2   *Risks associated with market-making activities listed in Table 2.1*

Risk	Loss
Failure to make contact	Sunk costs of search and advertising
Misunderstanding of specification	Sunk costs of setting up the transaction which led to receiving the mis-specified commodity, *plus* the capital loss incurred on resale of the unwanted good, *plus* the transaction costs incurred in the resale
Failure to agree over price	Sunk costs of negotiation
Default on specification caused by dishonesty or incompetence of other party	Costs of remedying the problem *plus* indirect costs of damage or disruption to other activities
Default in transport	
Failure to enforce	Compensation that would have been due *plus* sunk costs of attempted enforcement

TABLE 2.3 Product and transaction characteristics influencing market-making risks

Risks	Product characteristics						Transactor characteristics					Other
	Fewness of potential buyers and/or sellers	Novelty of the product	Complexity of the product's function	Difficulty of inspecting for quality before use	Lag in evaluating performance after use	Difficulty of metering	Market awareness	Knowledge of products	Screening ability	Metering ability	Dishonesty	Legal experience
Failure to make contact	X						X					
Misunderstanding of specification		X	X					X				
Failure to agree over price							X					
Default on specification				X	X	X			X	X	X	
Default in transport												X
Failure to enforce												X

SOURCE Casson (1982) Chapter 9.

In principle most risks are to some extent insurable. This means that ultimately the risks associated with any transaction do not have to be borne solely by the buyer and the seller – they can be shared with other people. It is apparent that in any transaction the buyer's risk and the seller's risk are to some extent inversely correlated. Provided that the contractual form is efficient, in the sense of avoiding unnecessary risk, then the greater is the risk borne by the buyer the less is the risk borne by the seller, and vice versa. Furthermore the risks associated with different transactions will normally be less than perfectly correlated with each other. Both these factors provide individual transactors with an opportunity to reduce their exposure to risk through mutual insurance. Instead of each individual bearing either all the buyer's risk or all the seller's risk in each transaction in which he is involved, each individual can hold a small share of the buyer's and seller's risk associated with all the transactions taking place. By diversifying his portfolio of risk, the 'unsystematic' element of market-making risk is eliminated from his portfolio. If all individuals diversify, then the risk associated with any given level of transaction cost, and any corresponding level of expected gains from trade, is minimised. As a result, economic efficiency is increased (see for example, Fama, 1976).

When individuals differ in their degree of risk-aversion, economic efficiency also requires that the least risk-averse individuals should specialise in risk-bearing, that is, the least risk-averse should insure the 'systematic' risks of the most risk-averse.

Finally, it is necessary to consider the economic implications of the fact that many market-making risks are subjective. They are subjective in the sense that different individuals will form different estimates of the risks associated with the same transaction. *Ex ante*, economic efficiency requires that if two individuals have a similar degree of risk-aversion and one takes a more optimistic view of some risk than does the other, then it should be the more optimistic individual who insures the risk. Thus *ceteris paribus* the insurance of each risk is specialised with the person who takes the most optimistic view of it (Casson, 1982). This point is elaborated further in Chapters 6 and 8.

2.5 THE OPTIMAL DEGREE OF SPECIALISATION

It has been shown that economic efficiency calls for the specialisation of the resources used in market-making activities and also for the specialisation of the bearing of market-making risks. However, specialisation is effected using markets, and the greater the degree of specialisation the more markets are required. It must then be recognised that transaction costs will be incurred not only in the markets where the original obstacles to trade were encountered, but also in the markets both for market-making services, and for the allocation of market-making risk. These markets too will face obstacles to trade, and require their own market-making activities whose costs will offset some of the gains stemming from specialisation. In the context of the economy as a whole, therefore, economic efficiency requires that the specialisation of market-making activities and of the bearing of market-making risks should be extended only up to the point at which the additional transaction costs incurred as a result of greater specialisation are equal to the savings in transaction costs achieved elsewhere as a result of it.

2.6 THE RATIONALE OF THE FIRM

This section summarises the arrangements for the specialisation of market-making, and of its associated risks, that most commonly prevail in the private sector of developed capitalist economies.

(1) The supply of market-making services is generated from plants, most of which take the form of offices, showrooms, trading posts, or some combination of these (for example, a retail shop). These plants combine complementary resources to 'produce' market-making services. The typical plant is constituted as a legal entity, that is, as a firm (or a part of one). The firm hires the market-making resources and owns the market-making services that are produced. The residual income stream from the sale of these services is profit which accrues to the owners of the market-making firm.

(2) Market-making plants sell their services to households and to other plants. To avoid transactors having to make two separate transactions, one for the purchase of market-making services and the other for the purchase or sale of the product itself, the market-making activity is usually integrated with the purchase or sale of the product. So far as households are concerned, for consumer products they buy their market-making services from the firm that sells them the product, and for factor services they buy their market-making services from the firm that buys their factor services (for example, the employer who buys their labour). This means, for

example, that if two households were to trade with each other they would purchase their market-making services from an intermediary. This intermediary would buy the product from the seller and resell the product to the buyer. Ostensibly this doubles the number of transactions, but in fact it actually minimises the number of transactions required to sell to the households the market-making services which are required to accomplish the transaction.

(3) Market-making services are usually sold using a pricing system through which the seller of the services insures the buyer against the risk of failure, by charging for the service only if the transaction is successful. This is most apparent in the relation between firms and households. In consumer-product markets, firms take the initiative in contacting households by advertising and/or by renting retail premises on sites convenient to households. Households are only charged for making contact if the contact leads to a trade, in which case a contribution to the overheads of contact-making is included in the price paid by the household. This arrangement insures the household against contact-making risks by (i) reducing the household's direct expenditure on seeking out the product supplier and (ii) pricing the supplier's contact-making service so that if the contact is unsuccessful no charge is made.

Firms also reduce the risks borne by households in respect of negotiation. They reduce the time the household needs to spend on negotiation by adopting a convention of always quoting their best price first, that is, they quote an initial price on which they subsequently refuse to concede. Once the household recognises this, there is no point in wasting time on negotiation (an exception may be made in the case of very valuable commodities, or where households have a very low opportunity cost of time, in which case haggling may occur). These price quotations are normally freely available and can still be taken up after the household has solicited other quotations for comparison. This protects the household against the risk that protracted negotiations may result in breakdown; the household pays only for the firm's price quotation service if the negotiation is successful, in which case the negotiated price includes a contribution to the firm's overheads.

Similar principles apply when firms purchase factor services from households. Although the firm and the household reverse their role of buyer and seller, it is still by and large the firm that takes the initiative in seeking out the household (for example, by advertising job vacancies) and in quoting prices (for example, in quoting non-negotiable wage rates for the job).

(4) Many firms are constituted as joint-stock companies. This means that no one individual is obliged to bear all the risks incurred by the firm in its market-making activities. Each household can hold equity shares in different firms involved in different transactions and so avoid unsystematic risk through equity diversification. Households who are not risk-averse can avoid holding equity altogether, and so obtain complete insurance against market-making risk.

(5) Each firm specialises in making a particular market, or group of markets. This enables those individuals who take an optimistic view of the risks associated with a particular market to back their judgement by acquiring equity in the relevant firm. Taken together (4) and (5) indicate how the equity market functions to achieve an efficient allocation of market-making risk.

2.7 QUALITY CONTROL AND BACKWARD INTEGRATION

The preceding discussion sets the scene for our main hypothesis, which is concerned with the role of firms in providing quality control. Quality control is a special case of monitoring activity. As Table 2.1 indicates, monitoring activity also encompasses the control of quantity and the timing of supply, but in the present context these may be regarded as of secondary interest.

A household purchasing a product demands insurance against the risk that the product will be substandard. At the very least the household needs to have confidence that its contractual or legal right to replacement of a faulty item can be enforced. Since prevention is better than cure, it is preferable that the quality can be assured before the product is used. In certain cases the buyer may be able to establish the quality by inspecting the good before use. However, such inspection by the buyer may well replicate inspection by the seller prior to the sale. Such replication is wasteful and is only done because of the buyer's lack of confidence in the seller.

If the seller assumes that the buyer will screen for product quality anyway then he may be inclined to abandon screening himself. This will resolve the problem of duplication of screening. However, there are two objections to this strategy. First, the buyer may not be able to establish the quality of the good by inspection, and may not even be able to screen for quality by trial use. If the potential damage caused by utilisation of a substandard good is very great, then it is essential that quality is checked before the buyer takes delivery. This is a special case of our second, and more general, proposition, that the seller of a product has a natural advantage over the buyer in screening for product quality because he is one step closer to the producer, and may indeed be the producer himself. Information about product quality is generated naturally as a joint product of the production process and accrues in the first instance to the person supervising production. The costs of quality control may be reduced significantly by drawing upon this information instead of replicating its discovery at a subsequent stage.

Economic efficiency in quality control therefore normally requires that the producer should assume responsibility for quality control, and that people buying from the producer should have confidence in the producer's quality control (assuming that this confidence is well founded). If the product is an intermediate product, which is going to be transformed or resold again before final use, then it is important that there be a chain of confidence whereby the final buyer has confidence in the seller's quality claims, and the seller has confidence in his own claims because he has confidence in the claims of the intermediate product producer, as well as confidence in his own work that has added value to the intermediate product.

There are three main strategies available for giving buyers confidence in the seller's quality control. The first is simply to build up this confidence through successful experience of repeated trade between the same buyer and seller. If the same seller trades with several buyers then he may be able to build up a reputation among them. This reputation may be disseminated more widely by word-of-mouth recommendations, or may be actively promoted by the seller through advertising. This is really the only feasible method for sellers of final products who wish to build up household confidence in the quality of a consumer good.

The second strategy is for the seller to agree to the buyer supervising the production of his own good. The disadvantage of this is that while it gives the buyer confidence, it may require him to interrupt his other work. In the case of a firm which subcontracts a great deal of work to another firm in which it has relatively little confidence this strategy may be quite reasonable, however, as the volume of trade may justify placing a full-time agent of the buyer (for instance, one of his employees) on the seller's premises.

The third strategy is for the buyer to integrate backward into production, that is, to internalise the product market in order to achieve better quality control. Once internalisation has been achieved the buyer has free access to all the information about quality generated in the course of production, as well as full discretion to take remedial measures without having to negotiate with another party (the seller) first. Equally, a seller who feels it will be a slow or difficult business to build up confidence among buyers may decide to integrate forward into the use of his product.

Internalisation is applicable to the household in only a very limited sense (for instance, 'do-it-yourself' is a simple form of internalisation of the market for manual labour services). Internalisation however is likely to be an important strategy by which the market-making firm can guarantee the quality of the product it offers to consumers. A speculative intermediator who wishes to establish a reputation for the quality of the product in which he deals may wish to integrate backward into production, so that he can have confidence in the validity of the claims he makes for his product in his advertising. If the product he sells is in turn an assembly of different components then he may be involved in backward integration into a number of different production processes. It is this case which is of most direct relevance to the theory of the MNE.

2.8 APPLICATIONS TO THE MNE

For the purpose of this chapter it is useful to work with a very simple definition of the MNE, namely that an MNE is any firm which owns outputs of goods or services originating in more than one country. This definition supposes only a minimal threshold level of multinationality. In particular it includes firms which merely operate foreign sales subsidiaries, since these subsidiaries produce market-making services and so qualify as foreign locations of production, within the terms of the definition. Note also that the MNE does not need to be a foreign direct investor, since all resources (except possibly inventories) in the foreign location can be hired rather than owned outright. This reflects the fact that the definition employs an income, or value-added, concept of production, rather than a capital or asset concept, as do some other definitions.

The simplicity of the foregoing definition emphasises the fact that the MNE is simply a multiplant firm whose operations span national boundaries. The advantages of backward integration from consumer market-making into production mean that any firm which services a host market with imports of a new or sophisticated product is liable to become an MNE. The most elementary example is of a two-country MNE with production located in one country and sales located in the other. There is no need for the firm to have any internationally transferable advantage in market-making. All that is required is that the firm utilises host-country resources which have a comparative advantage in market-making, that international comparative advantage encourages production elsewhere and that there are economies of integrating production and market-making.

There are four main reasons why a market-making MNE may operate in many different countries at once. First, there may be major economies of scale in production which make it efficient to service several entire national markets from the same plant. If the market-makers in each host country were independently to attempt to integrate backward, they would find themselves all trying to share ownership of the same production facility (or alternatively, being obliged to produce in independent plants on a less-than-efficient scale). The solution is for the market-making activities in each of the host countries to be integrated within a single firm which owns the production facility as well.

A second reason is that buyers of the product may be internationally mobile, that is, they may travel frequently between countries. It reduces the buyer's transaction costs if there is a single market-making firm offering its services within easy reach of any location, for the buyer then avoids having to identify separate market-makers in each location. The international mobility of the clientele encourages market-making firms to replicate their activities in many different countries. It should be emphasised that in this case each market-making branch plant can impose severe external costs on the others by failing to provide satisfactory service. Poor service offered by one plant will reduce the consumer's goodwill not only towards that plant but towards all other plants carrying the same name. As a result the maintenance of strict accountability of branch plants is crucial to the success of the firm as a whole.

The third reason is related to the second, but is logically distinct from it. It is that buyers of the product may wish to place orders in one location for supply at another location. In this case part of the market-making service (contact-making, specification and negotiation) is effected in one country and another part (exchange and monitoring) in the other country. In principle, of course, the buyer could communicate direct with the market-making facility nearest to where he wishes to take delivery of the product. However, the cost of international communication may be relatively great to the buyer, particularly if he does it only occasionally and therefore lacks expertise. It may be cheaper, and certainly less risky to the buyer, if international communication is internal to the firm. The buyer will therefore prefer to trade with a firm which offers a facility for placing an order through one branch office to be executed by another. It is obvious that the success of this arrangement depends upon close liaison between the two branch plants involved. The extent to which the operations of the branch plants are integrated is even greater than in the second case, and the need for accountability to avoid potential externalities is correspondingly intensified.

The final reason is that the firm has an internationally transferable absolute advantage in market-making. This brings the analysis to an interface with earlier work on theory of the MNE. The interface is more obvious if the absolute advantage is described as proprietary know-how regarding the differentiation of products (Caves, 1971). The exploitation of an absolute advantage tends to create a set of market-making activities in each country operated on broadly similar lines, but without any of the special features identified in the first three cases. The only link between the market-making branch plants in the different countries is a common dependence on the firm-specific market-making skills. In this case the potential externalities between the branch plants are limited to a tendency to compete against each other in neutral territories. At the same time, the firm as a whole exhibits the familiar characteristics of firms possessing unpatentable proprietary know-how: extreme secrecy regarding operating methods, a tendency to 'lock-in' key employees who have partial access to the know-how, and so on.

In the context of this final case the present analysis has little to add to orthodox theory, except to provide more rigorous foundations for the general concept of market-making skills such as product differentiation. These analytical foundations suggest, however, that the efficiency implications of product differentiation are far more complex than a naive application of partial equilibrium monopolistic competition theory used by previous writers might suggest.

2.9 TOWARDS A MORE GENERAL THEORY OF THE MNE

The foregoing analysis suggests that in the light of the theory of transaction costs, the MNE may be a far more common species of firm than the orthodox theory would suggest. In particular, it highlights a new kind of MNE which specialises in making markets in consumer products. The firm improves the quality of service to the consumer by integrating backward from market-making into production.

Almost all consumer products are likely to have at least some buyers who value quality of service. Perhaps the only exceptions are goods which are consumed only in very low-income countries where consumers are too near subsistence to afford to purchase quality. Consequently there are very few markets where the presence of market-making MNEs can *prima facie* be ruled out. The theory predicts, however, that in whatever markets MNEs occur they will be most strongly represented in those segments of the market where quality is at a premium. Thus in markets where backward-integrated MNEs operate alongside non-integrated indigenous firms the MNEs will be positioned at the high-quality–high-price end of the market, and the indigenous firms at the low-quality–low-price end of the market.

Another major implication of the theory is that the presence of MNEs in low-technology consumer product markets does not need to be interpreted as a manifestation of an absolute advantage in product differentiation. It may be due to this, but it is not necessarily so. It can in fact be argued that recent research on MNEs in non-R & D-intensive industries supports the view that an absolute advantage in product differentiation is not always the crucial factor.

Dunning and McQueen (1982) have examined the involvement of MNEs in the hotel industry (see also McManus, 1972). Although Dunning and McQueen interpret their findings in terms of Dunning's eclectic theory, their data can just as easily be interpreted without this theory. The authors confirm that MNEs are concentrated at the high-quality–high-price end of the hotel market, and not surprisingly cater principally for international travellers and in particular for the businessman. The hotels use an internationally standardised brand name, as one would expect when catering for an internationally mobile clientele. This suggests that the hotel firms represent the MNE of the second kind distinguished in the previous section. Many of the hotel firms offer an international reservation system, which in the past has proved important in attracting first-time visitors to foreign locations, though the authors argue that its importance is diminishing now that repeat-visit business has become relatively larger. Subject to this qualification, it appears that the MNE of the third kind is also significant among hotel firms.

The hotel industry is unskilled-labour-intensive, and one of the crucial elements in maintaining product quality is the efficient management of unskilled labour. Many hotel groups train their own managers, and the authors interpret this, quite reasonably, as a method of imparting firm-specific management skills to their senior employees. It is, however, possible to regard this backward integration into vocational training simply as a method of achieving quality control. Given the key role of the manager, and the potential diseconomies that an isolated failure of management may create, the internalisation of training does not need to be justified by imparting monopolised skills; it may be justified simply in terms of a lack of confidence in managers who have been college-trained or who have just quit jobs with competing firms. Intuitively, it may be suggested that if each MNE in the hotel industry has a monopolistic advantage in some aspect of hotel management then there would be far greater diversity in the hotel services offered by the different groups. The MNEs in the hotel industry do not on the whole appear to be characterised by major product differentiation, but by the supply of a fairly standardised service with rigorous quality control.

Our second example is based upon Read's work on MNEs in tropical agricultural export industries (Read, 1983). Read provides an interesting case study of the banana industry in which, despite the apparent homogeneity of the product, MNE involvement in the export trade is relatively strong. Here again MNEs specialise in the high-quality–high-price trade in a branded product, offering year-round supplies of carefully ripened bananas distributed through selected retail outlets (typically large supermarket chains). The arm's-length export trade which is carried on alongside is predominantly a seasonal trade in unbranded bananas which are sold through small independent retailers. The MNEs invest heavily in quality control using custom-designed reefer ships for transport, and they tag all bananas so that the packing station on the plantation can be readily identified should defects be observed at the point of final sale. The ability of the MNE to control the growing and packing on the plantation gives it the confidence to make the claims for product quality which, through advertising, it hopes that consumers will identify with its brand name.

Because of the economies of scale and agglomeration in plantations (arising from indivisibilities in the infrastructures – for example, road and rail links) several national markets can often be supplied from a single group of neighbouring plantations. In this respect MNEs in the banana industry exemplify the MNE of the first kind distinguished above: production is concentrated in just one or two countries, with numerous sales subsidiaries servicing the various export markets supplied from these locations. It is quite possible that the MNEs also possess certain monopolistic advantages, such as proprietary know-how regarding disease-resistant strains. It is equally apparent, however, that because of the very limited set of locations in which it is feasible to grow bananas, this factor alone cannot explain the multinationality of the operations of banana producers. The key to multinationality lies rather in the integration of market-making and production in order to improve quality of service, and in particular to maintain effective quality control.

2.10 RELATION TO THE THEORY OF BUYER UNCERTAINTY

The previous discussion has emphasised some important differences between the general theory of internalisation based upon transaction costs and those applications of the theory which focus exclusively upon the internalisation of firm-specific advantage. It is worth noting, however, that there is a close analogy between the concept of quality control used above and the concept of buyer uncertainty which occurs in discussions of the licensing decision (see Chapter 3). Essentially the buyer uncertainty which complicates the licensing decision is an extreme case of the buyer uncertainty which complicates the sale of any product. In each case buyer uncertainty arises, not because no one knows the quality of the product, but because those who do cannot communicate the information to those who do not. The seller knows the quality, but cannot communicate it to the buyer. There is an initial asymmetry of information which remains impacted (Arrow, 1975; Williamson, 1975).

In the case of licensing, the information remains impacted for an important strategic reason. Where know-how is concerned, information about the product quality is difficult to separate from the information which constitutes the product itself. The proprietary value of the information can only be protected by enforcing a right of exclusion, and in the absence of patent protection a right of exclusion can be enforced only by secrecy. Maintaining secrecy about the product itself implies that only very limited information about product quality can be divulged. Consequently the seller of know-how cannot allow the buyer to become too well-informed about its quality.

As noted earlier, buyer uncertainty is overcome most efficiently by giving the buyer confidence in the seller's competence and integrity. The buyer's knowledge of the seller's personal characteristics acts as a surrogate for knowledge of product quality. Typically this confidence is built up by the successful repetition of trades. However in the case of know-how, although there is a high value of trade there is a relatively small number of separate transactions and hence a relatively infrequent repetition of trades between the same two parties. This makes it extremely difficult for confidence to be built up and hence for buyer uncertainty to be overcome.

It appears therefore that the concept of quality control used in our extension of internalisation theory is not entirely new to the internalisation literature. However, while it has been implicit in earlier discussions of the licensing decision, its wider implications have not been fully appreciated.

2.11 ALTERNATIVES TO THE MNE

At present there is considerable interest in the issue of contractual alternatives to the MNE. The analysis above has an important bearing on this issue, for it focuses attention on the question of alternatives to internalisation as a method of overcoming buyer uncertainty regarding quality.

An alternative to internalisation mentioned in section 2.7 is that the seller allows the buyer to monitor his production process. When buyer and seller have a long-term contract for supply then this may be an attractive proposition. Indeed it is a method which is quite widely used by sellers of branded products who subcontract production (for example, retail chains selling own-brand products, and manufacturers assembling electronic products from components).

A potential difficulty for the seller is that it may be difficult to separate the functions of monitoring and control. Conflict may arise when the buyer's agent appears to interfere excessively in the management of production. One way of resolving this conflict is for the seller to allow the buyer full discretion in the day-to-day management of production – that is, to enter into a management contract with the buyer at the same time as the contract for supply is made. In this case the parties negotiate a composite long-term contract in which the buyer supplies the management and the seller supplies the production facilities.

Contracts of this kind are fairly common in East–West trade and are a special case of industrial co-operation agreements.

The introduction of a buyer's agent or management team into the seller's premises is a reasonable solution so long as the seller does not have any proprietary know-how to protect. However if the seller possesses such know-how (for instance, an advanced technology) then the introduction of a buyer's agent is likely to result in a premature dissipation of his property rights. For this reason theory predicts that the buyer's direct involvement in production will only occur in firms or industries in which the seller has little proprietary know-how (that is, in industries where there is a fairly standard production technology).

When sellers have proprietary know-how to protect it is extremely difficult to overcome buyer uncertainty except through the creation of mutual confidence. But to build up mutual confidence it is necessary at the very least to get some trade between the two parties initiated, out of which this confidence can grow. It is therefore desirable to have some form of intervention or intermediation in order to 'prime' the trading process. One solution is to introduce an 'honest broker'. The honest broker is usually someone who is legally prohibited from entering into competition with either the buyer or seller – that is, he is barred from production or use of the product. As a result the seller may be willing to accord privileges to the honest broker which he would not be willing to accord to the buyer. Similarly the buyer may be willing to employ the honest broker as an agent, because the broker is unlikely to use the information he acquires from the seller to undermine the buyer's trading position with the seller. The buyer will accept assurances about product quality from the broker because the broker, unlike the seller, has no incentive to mislead.

However, there are very few economic agents who have the reputation necessary to operate as honest brokers. This function is normally institutionalised in major banks, politically stable governments and international agencies. It would appear that in many instances the creation of a viable alternative to the MNE will depend upon such reputable institutions being able to extend their role of honest broker into the underwriting of product quality in a wide range of industries. Whether these institutions – or any other kind of institution that could be devised – can develop the necessary skills to perform this wider role must remain an open question.

3 New Forms of International Industrial Co-operation

PETER J. BUCKLEY

3.1 INTRODUCTION

This chapter is an attempt to bring together the rather disparate literature on a topic which is currently identified as an important area in international trade and development – the growth of 'new forms' of international industrial co-operation. Such new forms are contrasted with traditional technology transfer through the agency of a wholly-owned subsidiary of a multinational enterprise. Consequently, we are able to identify a spectrum of forms of industrial co-operation from joint ventures between multinationals and host-country interests through a variety of contractual agreements such as licensing, franchising and management contracts to time-limited 'contractual joint ventures' and 'fade-out agreements'.

The emphasis of this chapter is on technology transfer between industrialised countries and less-developed countries. Reference is made to the literature on co-operation between Western industrialised countries and centrally planned economies, but this is not treated in depth. The aim is to provide a coherent framework for analysis of new forms of industrial co-operation.

This chapter attempts to provide a typology of the new forms of international industrial co-operation in Section 3.3. Section 3.4 provides an analytical framework for the consideration of such agreements and Section 3.5 examines the issues raised by the new forms including problems of distribution of benefits, the concept of effective transfer and limitations inherent in such institutional forms. The following section examines the context of new forms of international industrial co-operation.

39

3.2 THE CONTEXT

New forms of international industrial co-operation are primarily
vehicles for transfers of technology between the industrial market
economies ('the West') and the less-developed countries ('the South').
(Technology is used throughout this chapter in a very broad sense, to
encompass know-how, skills [both technical and managerial] and
functional competence in, for instance, marketing and utilisation of
labour.) There has, however, been an upsurge of interest in technology
transfer to the Socialist countries ('the East') after liberalisation of co-
operation with the West. West–South and West–East transfers require
new vehicles and we have seen, and are seeing, new modes of transfer
being developed (Dunning, 1982).

Table 3.1 shows the drift away from wholy-owned subsidiaries as
means of technology transfer by multinational firms. This tendency is
very strongly marked in the 'other' ownership group, which includes

TABLE 3.1   *Distribution of ownership patterns of 1276 manufacturing affiliates
of 391 transnational corporations established in developing countries 1951–75*

Home country and type of ownership	Number established as percentage of total				
	Before 1951	*1951–60*	*1961–5*	*1965–70*	*1971–5*
Affiliates of 180 United States based Corporations					
Total	100.0	100.0	100.0	100.0	100.0
Wholly-owned (95% +)	58.4	44.5	37.4	46.2	43.7
Majority-owned (over 50%)	12.2	21.4	19.2	17.8	17.3
Co-owned (50:50)	5.6	7.9	11.4	11.2	10.4
Minority-owned (5–50%)	11.2	18.8	21.7	21.5	28.1
Unknown	12.6	7.4	10.3	3.3	0.4
Affiliates of 135 European (incl. UK) based Corporations					
Total	100.0	100.0	100.0	100.0	n.a.
Wholly-owned	39.1	31.6	20.9	18.9	
Majority-owned	15.4	20.1	15.6	16.4	
Co-owned	5.3	6.6	11.1	6.6	
Minority-owned	9.8	27.9	35.8	42.1	
Unknown	30.5	13.9	16.6	16.0	
Affiliates of 76 other transnational Corporations					
Total	100.0	100.0	100.0	100.0	n.a.
Wholly-owned	27.4	16.7	10.7	6.1	
Majority-owned	8.2	26.2	12.6	8.2	
Co-owned	12.3	7.1	6.3	7.5	
Minority-owned	16.4	42.9	66.7	74.2	
Unknown	35.6	7.1	3.8	3.9	

SOURCE   UN Commission on Transnational Corporations (1978) p. 229, from data supplied by the
Harvard Multinational Project.

Japanese firms and Table 3.2 confirms the strong tendency of Japanese firms to take minority positions in their affiliates. (See also Kojima, 1978; Smith, 1981.)

The variety of modes of technology transfer to the East is attested by Table 3.3, which shows a search for new institutional forms in transferring Western technology to centrally-planned economies. (See also Levcik and Stankovsky, 1979; Zaleski and Wienert, 1980; McMillan, 1981; Scriven, 1980; United Nations Economic and Social Council Economic Commission for Europe, 1978.) 'Non-multinational' firms are also active (Alam and Langrish, 1981).

In this context a study of such forms is of vital importance and it shows the need for a coherent framework for the description and analysis of these new modes of industrial co-operation.

3.3   A TYPOLOGY OF NEW FORMS OF INTERNATIONAL INDUSTRIAL CO-OPERATION

The normal conception of international business activities is a spectrum of 'depth of involvement' of the multinational firm in the host country, running from a wholly-owned subsidiary at one end to very loose time-limited arrangements such as subcontracting at the other

TABLE 3.2   *Japanese investment in Asian developing countries: distribution of ownership patterns, 1977–8*

Host country	Number of firms with Japanese equity participation					
	Total no.	of which: (%)	50 > 98% Japanese-owned no.	50 > 98% Japanese-owned (%)	Wholly Japanese-owned (≥98%) no.	Wholly Japanese-owned (≥98%) (%)
Philippines	97	(100)	6	(6)	2	(2)
Thailand	184	(100)	14	(8)	17	(9)
Malaysia	126	(100)	10	(8)	18	(14)
Republic of Singapore	153	(100)	31	(20)	43	(28)
Hong Kong	224	(100)	42	(19)	113	(50)
Republic of Korea	153	(100)	7	(5)	19	(12)
Total	937	(100)	110	(12)	212	(23)
Total excluding Hong Kong	713	(100)	68	(10)	99	(14)

SOURCE   Reproduced from Oman (1980). Based on data provided in consecutive issues of 'Japan's Overseas Investments', *The Oriental Economist*, December 1978.

TABLE 3.3 *Share of various types of contract in total number of East–West industrial co-operation contracts, by country*
(as percentage)

Type of contract	Bulgaria	Czecho-slovakia	German Democratic Republic	Hungary	Poland	Romania	Union of Soviet Socialist Republics	Sub-total	Yugoslavia	Total
Licensing[a]	17.1	27.3	—	29.5	21.7	19.4	3.2	17.1	9.5	15.6
A.1	17.1	18.2	—	25.3	15.3	15.3	2.6	13.8	7.7	12.6
A.2	—	9.1	—	4.2	6.4	4.1	0.6	3.3	1.8	3.0
Plant delivery[b]	25.7	—	23.5	16.3	24.2	25.5	20.4	20.5	6.5	17.6
B.1	25.7	—	23.5	15.7	24.2	24.5	15.8	18.8	5.9	16.2
B.2	—	—	—	—	—	1.0	3.6	1.2	0.6	1.1
B.3	—	—	—	0.6	—	—	1.0	0.5	—	0.3
Co-production[c]	31.4	22.7	35.3	32.6	32.3	14.2	61.5	38.3	11.9	32.8
C.1	25.7	22.7	17.6	29.0	27.4	11.2	8.7	19.3	9.5	17.3
C.2	5.7	—	5.9	2.4	3.3	1.0	10.2	5.0	1.8	4.2
C.3	—	—	11.8	1.2	1.6	2.0	42.6	14.0	0.6	11.3
Sub-contracting[d]	11.4	9.1	17.7	9.6	6.4	7.1	4.7	7.4	2.4	6.4
D.1	5.7	—	11.8	6.6	2.4	1.0	1.5	3.3	1.8	3.0
D.2	5.7	9.1	5.9	3.0	4.0	6.1	3.2	4.1	0.6	3.4
Joint ventures[e]	3.0	18.2	5.9	10.2	6.4	24.6	7.1	10.5	68.6	22.4
E.1	—	18.2	5.9	4.8	4.8	3.1	5.1	4.9	—	3.9
E.2	3.0	—	—	5.4	1.6	21.5	2.0	5.6	68.6	18.5

Joint tendering[f]	11.4	22.7	5.9	1.2	8.0	9.2	1.6	5.1	1.1	4.4
F.1	11.4	22.7	5.9	1.2	5.6	9.2	1.0	4.5	1.1	3.9
F.2	—	—	—	—	2.4	—	0.6	0.6	—	0.5
Tripartite[g]	—	—	11.7	0.6	1.0	—	1.5	1.1	—	0.8
Total	100.0	100.0	100.0	100.0	100.0	100.0	100.0	100.0	100.0	100.0

Notes

[a] A.1 Supply of licences and/or know-how (sometimes also some special equipment), in exchange – at least partially – for products or components

A.2 Same as A.1, but the supply also includes parts in varying percentage of the final product in exchange for products or components

[b] B.1 Supply of plant or equipment, including the corresponding technology, in exchange for products or components, at least partially

B.2 For the exploitation of natural resources same as B.1, plus studies of the availability and accessibility of the resources and research connected with the application of technology to particular circumstances

B.3 Supply of plant or equipment on a leasing basis in exchange for produce

[c] C.1 Co-operation, including or not including sales, in which each party manufactures parts or components of a final product, the technology being supplied by one or both of the parties

C.2 Co-operation, in which each party specialises in part of the manufacturing programme and then exchanges units in order to complete each other's range of produce

C.3 Co-production and specialisation involving R & D only

[d] D.1 Short-term agreements providing for the delivery of an agreed quantity of finished or semi-finished goods produced through the use of documentation and know-how (and sometimes parts, machinery and equipment) provided by the contractor

D.2 Long-term agreements providing for the delivery on a continuing basis same as above

[e] E.1 Joint ventures involving production, marketing and R & D

[f] F.1 Customer located in a third country

F.2 Customer located in one of the countries

[g] Tripartite co-operation agreements

SOURCE Reproduced from United Nations Commission on Transnational Corporations (1978) based on data supplied by United Nations Economic Commission for Europe.

extreme. (See for example Mason, 1981.) It is useful, however, to isolate several dimensions of involvement before such a concept can be accepted. These dimensions include (i) the locus of control, (ii) transfer of a (limited) set of rights and resources and the mode of transfer, internal to the firm or by the agency of a market transaction, (iii) time limitations, and (iv) space limitations.

The Locus of Control

The issue of control is central to the growth of new forms of international industrial co-operation. Recipient countries, notably the less-developed countries, wish to achieve the transfer of technology and skills without the necessity of accepting foreign control over the use of these resources. Many host countries feel that the exercise of control and potential costs implied in the operation of a wholly-owned subsidiary of a foreign multinational are unacceptable and restrict or prohibit such institutional arrangements by law. (See India, for example, where the normal ceiling is 40 per cent foreign equity, but 74 per cent where advanced technology is involved and up to 100 per cent in wholly export-oriented projects. Foreign investment is viewed as a vehicle for the transfer of technology (India Investment Centre, 1981).)

Consequently, the desire for technology and skills on the part of host countries has to be matched to the profit-seeking desires of source-country firms through new arrangements. The equation of 'control' with 'ownership' is of course only part of the story. However, a frequent attempt to dilute foreign control is the creation of joint ventures whereby host-country interests share the equity (Bivens and Lovell, 1976). Many kinds of arrangements are implied by such a division of equity. For instance a (foreign) investor holding 30 per cent of the voting equity in a company where no other investors holds more than 10 per cent is more likely to be able to exercise control, in spite of his minority holding, than he would be if he held 49 per cent, with the other 51 per cent in one person's or company's hands (Buckley and Roberts, 1982). A further important distinction lies in the nature of the host-country's equity holding. If this is a single shareholder, a prominent host-country company or the host government, then it might be expected that host-country influence will be greater than if the holding is split or if the equity is traded on the host stock-market.

Definitions of joint ventures have been centred on the issues of co-operation and control. Friedmann and Kalmanoff (1981, p. 6) define joint international business ventures as 'a type of association which implies collaboration for more than a very transitory period'. Tomlinson (1970, p. 8) takes this further – a joint venture is 'a commitment for more than a very short duration, of funds, facilities and services, by two or more legally separate interests to an enterprise for their mutual benefit'. Lamers (1976, p. 138) suggests that to this must be added the sharing of control and risk. Sukijasović (1970) states that joint ventures have four properties 'a community of interests involving doing business in common, the sharing of profits, the sharing of business risk and losses and longevity of co-operation'.

The attractions of joint ventures for the multinational firm are time-unlimited access to the market and resources of the host country, possible political preferment and a measure of equity control. The host country, in theory at least, gains access to the full range of the skills and resource package of the foreign firm, whilst not sacrificing full equity control. (See also Paliwoda, 1981; Weralski, 1980).

The limiting forms of joint ventures are minority holdings by foreign corporations where the foreign investor chooses a small equity stake (typically of the order 5–12 per cent, Buckley, 1981) often in order to share research or marketing arrangements. It is to be noted that in companies with diffuse shareholding, 5–12 per cent may give the foreign entrant the largest block of votes.

Resource Transfer

A crucial distinction between types of international industrial co-operation is the nature of the combination of resources and rights which are transferred and the mode by which such transfer is effected.

The wholly-owned subsidiary here provides a polar extreme. A whole 'package' or 'bundle' of resources is transferred, consisting of capital, technology, skills and a wide range of rights usually covering rights to produce, market and develop products and to raise resources backed by the parent (Kindleberger, 1969; Caves, 1971; Dunning, 1981; Balasubramanyam, 1980). The mode of this transfer is internal to the firm rather than through external markets. This internalisation permits effective parental control, allows long-term planning, avoids market uncertainties, allows discriminatory pricing and may reduce external interference, notably by governments (Buckley and Casson, 1976; Buckley, 1983). It is through the use of internal markets in capital, labour, management, technology and intermediate goods, that effective control of foreign subsidiaries is exercised, rather than through equity ownership, although complete equity control means that no external influences are directly concerned in the management of these internal markets.

In cases where dilution of complete control occurs (joint ventures and minority holdings) this complete transfer may be reduced in order to prevent 'leakage' of secrets, competitive devices and new technology to outsiders (Parker, 1978). This cannot, of course, be completely protected in a fully internalised transaction because of quitting among key workers, in 'breakaways' and through industrial espionage, but the more 'outsiders' are involved, the more restricted is likely to be the transfer of resources and rights.

Licensing agreements represent the market alternative to the internalised transfer of resources (including information) and rights (Davies, 1977). Licensing is a generic term which encompasses a wide variety of contractual agreements between a foreign firm and a local firm for effecting transfers of rights and resources. Balasubramanyam (1973) uses the term 'technical collaboration agreements' to cover the sale and purchase of technical information. Typically, licensing will also include certain rights to market the product which embodies the transferred information (a wider term than knowledge) and many ancillary transfers of resources and rights are included.

The transfer process in licensing is complex and time-consuming. Hall and Johnson (1970) say

> Technology can be transferred in two basic forms. One form embraces physical items such as drawings, tools, machinery, process information, specifications and patents. The other form is personal contact. Put simply, knowledge is always embodied in something or somebody, the form being important for determining the transfer process and cost.

The issue of 'effective transfer' through the market route is crucial and will be taken up in Section 3.4.

Telesio (1979) states that 'Licensing of manufacturing technology can be defined as the sale of "intangible property rights, such as patents, secret processes or technical information"'. To this transfer of technology must be added other forms of information transfer, including marketing and managerial aspects. The widest, and most terse, definition of a licence is 'a covenant not to sue' (Prasad, 1981, quoting Finnegan, 1976), although the writer goes on to list the positive aspects of licensing. We discuss later the issues of just what is transferred in different licensing agreements.

One specialised but important type of licence agreement is franchising. Franchising is 'a form of marketing or distribution in which a parent company customarily grants an individual or a relatively small company the right, or privilege, to do business in a prescribed manner over a certain period of time in a specified place' (Vaughn, 1979, pp. 1–2). The franchise contract usually has several elements:

(1) specification of the duration of the commercial relationship,
(2) grant of a set of rights to the 'franchisee' to offer, sell and distribute goods and services manufactured, processed, distributed or organised and directed by the 'franchisor',
(3) the franchisee as an independent business constitutes a component of the franchisor's distribution network,
(4) the franchisee's business is substantially associated with advertising or other commercial symbol designating the franchisor,
(5) the franchisee's operations are substantially reliant on the franchisor for the continued supply of goods and/or services,
(6) the franchisee will be geographically limited (Vaughn, 1979; Izreali, 1972).

A large element of the franchise thus involves the carefully controlled transfer of managerial and marketing skills.

Usually, the franchisee will be an individual or a small independent business. Franchise systems may be of the manufacturer–retailer type (car distributorship, petrol dealerships) manufacturer–wholesaler (soft drinks bottlers) wholesaler–retailer or trademark licensor–retailer types. The most salient franchise relationships occur in 'fast-food' chains and in hotels (see Dunning and McQueen, 1981). A key element of franchising is the ability to segment the market spatially between different franchisees so as to prevent competition between them. Grants of exclusive rights to these territories can then assure full market coverage without internal competition. Services are thus ideal for franchising.

The benefits to the host country from franchising are frequently adduced to be high, because training and development of management skills are frequently integral to the franchising 'package' (Wright, 1981). Management and technical training, assistance in locating, equipping (even decorating) and financial and advertising back-up are valuable imported components added to the franchisee's motivation to 'be his own boss' and to make franchising attractive to small businesses.

For the franchiser, effective market penetration is often combined with minimal capital outlay. However, indigenous alternative products (soft drinks, restaurants, hotels, for instance) are often unable to compete with internationally known alternatives and charges of cultural imperialism are frequently aimed at franchisors.

Management contracts are a growing form of carrying out business abroad.

> The management contract is an arrangement under which a certain degree of responsibility for the operations of one enterprise is vested in another. The latter undertakes the usual management functions, makes available a whole range of skills and resources and trains personnel. The contract covers payment to the company and the handing over of authority to the locals once trained. (Ellison, 1977, p. 25.)

Rarely are management contracts purely concerned with transferring management skills. Most usually, an infusion of technology is involved. (Brooke and Holly, 1981; Ellison, 1977; Gabriel, 1967 and 1972) Importantly though, management contracts are less reliant on transferring information and skills to an already functioning enterprise and they can frequently build a new enterprise from scratch, relying little, if at all, on local experts. Ellison (1977, p. 26) lists the transfer of 'corporate capabilities' as a unique element of such contracts. This is essentially a link with the transferring company, allowing the recipient, through the contract, to rely on the transferor's corporate skills in access to funds, general reputation and worldwide procurement capacity. Essentially, the contract involves access to inherited corporate skills. This implies an ongoing non-market relationship which is difficult to specify fully in a legal contract and which relies greatly on goodwill between the parties. Hence, management contracts can be highly rewarding or difficult to operate, depending on the relationship between the parties, which cannot be written in to the contract.

Turnkey projects are arrangements where the process of constructing, making operative and usually initially running a facility are contracted to outside enterprise (or enterprises) in return for a fee. The facility is then handed over to local interests. Most usually the construction period is followed by a period covered by a management contract (and possibly a licensing arrangement) whereby continuing relationships with the outsiders provide for extended training and 'debugging'. The customers are usually governments who have decreed that a given product or service must be produced locally and under local control (Wright, 1981).

Turnkey contracts which end when the physical plant and equipment has been set up by the supplier in the host country are referred to as 'light' turnkey contracts; those with clauses providing for the extensive training of local personnel are 'heavy' contracts. Contracts referred to as 'product-in-hand' operations mean that the supplier's responsibility is not fulfilled until the installation is completely operational with local personnel. Extension of contracts to 'market-in-hand' calls for the supplier to give assistance in, or in some cases to take responsibility for, the sale of at least part of the operation's output. Under some circumstances, 'buy-back', 'counter-purchase' or 'compensation' agreements call for the supplier to take payment directly in the form of physical output (Salem and Sanson, 1979; Weigand, 1980; Oman, 1980).

Time Limitations

Many market contracts have time limitations directly written into them – licence agreements will run for a specified time period with specified conditions for renewal; management contracts likewise. The essence of turnkey arrangements is the limited time span of foreign control and the detail of the hand-over of control to local interests. However, equity ventures too can be time-limited as in 'fade-out agreements'.

Such fade-out or 'planned divestment' agreements involve the multinational firm in liquidating its investment and selling its stake to locals, usually government (Hirshman, 1972). These fixed term agreements (usually 5–10 years) were first suggested in order to reduce tension in economies where a high degree of foreign penetration is viewed as a political problem. The countries of Latin America are the prime examples. Such arrangements involve a complex move from an internalised transfer of resources to market transfer, for they are usually followed by a licence agreement or a management contract or both. Problems arise over the issues of (i) the price at which the multinational firm is bought out, (ii) specification of the exact nature of the continuing resource transfer, (iii) the timing of the transfer, (iv) the desire of the foreign corporation to reduce its time horizon to the period over which it exercises full control and to 'milk' the project in that period, and (v) ensuring continuing viability.

Space Limitations

It is usual for licence agreements to include limitations on the economic space across which the licence is valid. This is most usual in the export restriction clauses noted in most surveys of licensing (Buckley and Davies, 1980; Casson, 1979). This provides the licensor with a means of segmenting his market effectively, reducing competition amongst multiple licensees and ensuring that his licensees do not become competitors. It also permits price discrimination by the licensor (Casson, 1979).

In internalised transactions, the same objective can be achieved by management fiat, dividing world markets between subsidiaries according to a market-servicing policy based on internal and external pressures (Buckley and Pearce, 1979 and 1981).

Certain forms of international industrial co-operation are designed to be limited in space (most usually also in time). Important amongst these are 'contractual joint ventures'. Wright (1981, p. 500) states that:

> the contractual joint venture is a risk-sharing venture in which no joint enterprise with separate personality is formed. It is a partnership in which two or more companies (or a company and a government agency) share the cost of an investment, the risks and the long-term profits. The contractual joint venture may be formed for a particular project of limited duration, or for a longer-term co-operative effort, and the contractual relationship may terminate once the project is complete.

Consortium ventures by banks to finance large loans and co-publishing agreements are examples. It was noted above that for the individual franchisor, space limitations were essential to segment the market and to prevent competition between franchisees.

A special form of contractual joint venture is 'Tripartite Industrial Co-operation' where at least three firms or organisations domiciled in the East (centrally-planned economy) in the West (industrialised market economy) and in the South (less-developed country) join forces to carry out common activities in the host developing country. Normally these activities would include one or more of: (i) building up of physical infrastructure, (ii) prospecting for, and extracting natural resources, (iii) supply of industrial plant, assembly work and (iv) marketing (joint importing and/or exporting). (Gutman and Arkwright, 1976; Oman, 1980.)

Finally, international subcontracting is a clearly defined market relationship covering an agreement of a foreign firm to purchase from a local firm. Although such arrangements are, in ideal type, purely market-based, linking purchaser to producer, in practice there is often an input from the purchaser to ensure that quality standards meet specification and often to advise on methods of production. Such arrangements are of course limited in space. Such 'production-sharing' agreements usually involve selling in the purchaser's home market. These arrangements are closely related to the tariff regulations in the developed countries and to the proliferation of 'free trade zones' in less-developed countries. (See for example, Watanabe, 1971 and 1972.)

Summary

Table 3.4 provides a typology of modes of international industrial co-operation in five dimensions: equity versus non-equity ventures, time limitations, space limitations, transfer of resources and rights, and

TABLE 3.4   *A typology of international industrial co-operation modes*

Form of co-operation	Equity or non-equity	Time limited or unlimited	Space limited	Transfer of resources and rights	Mode of transfer
1. Wholly-owned foreign subsidiaries	Equity	Unlimited	At discretion of MNE	Whole range?	Internal
2. Joint ventures	Equity	Unlimited	Agreed	Whole range?	Internal
3. Foreign minority holdings	Equity	Unlimited	Limited	Whole range?	Internal
4. 'Fade-out' agreements	Equity	Limited	Nature of agreement	Whole range? for limited period	Internal changing to market
5. Licensing	Non-equity	Limited by contract	May include limitation in contract	Limited range	Market
6. Franchising	Non-equity	Limited by contract	Yes	Limited + support	Market
7. Management contracts	Non-equity	Limited by contract	May be specified	Limited	Market
8. 'Turnkey ventures'	Non-equity	Limited	Not usually	Limited in time	Market
9. 'Contractual joint ventures'	Non-equity	Limited	May be agreed	Specified by contract	Mixed
10. International subcontracting	Non-equity	Limited	Yes	Small	Market

NOTES   See text for full explanation. See also Buckley and Mathew (1980).

mode of transfer (internal versus market). Although some of the entries in the table are contentious, the analysis proves that a simple spectrum running from wholly-owned foreign subsidiary to 'simple contracts' is an inadequate representation of the nuances and complexities of the different arrangements. In addition many of the new forms are linked to each other in particular circumstances, for example, joint ventures and licensing agreements, turnkey operations and management contracts. The following section builds on this to provide an analytical framework for the consideration of these forms of co-operation.

3.4 AN ANALYTICAL FRAMEWORK

All forms of international industrial co-operation involve the transfer of resources and rights either by the agency of the market or within the firm. Typically, the 'new forms' represent an attempt to externalise transactions which had previously been intra-firm. The new forms are best understood as attempts to release the multinational firm's control of resource transfer by replacing such modes by contracts.

The transfer of physical resources between organisations and of intangible information both require a transferable property right. Casson (1979) distinguishes a right of access and a right of exclusion, the former being the right to use an asset, the latter a right to prevent others from using it except at the holder's discretion. In the case of non-diffusable assets the former right necessarily implies the latter, for to give one person access to it automatically denies it to others. Where a diffusable asset is concerned, the capacity to supply users is theoretically infinite and so the right of exclusion must be separately upheld (Casson, 1979, p. 37). Information is a diffusable asset and a legally enforceable right of exclusion over it is known as a patent. A patent can be conferred free of charge or sold to the highest bidder.

Where the transferred asset is easily identified and vested in exclusive and freely transferable property rights, then market transfer, through licensing can be optimal (Buckley and Davies, 1980). This is most easily the case when the asset to be transferred is 'embodied' in a patent, or in a brand name, a machine or a separable process. If this condition is violated, it may be difficult or impossible to make the asset the subject of a transaction. In particular, difficulties may arise in negotiating the limits within which the asset can be used, in economic space and time. In the face of fragmented markets with uncertain and changing boundaries, and given uncertainty about the 'life' of an asset, companies rationally restrict their attention to specific markets and time periods. Consequently, the potential licensor needs to be assured that the terms of the agreement will be adhered to and that the advantage will not be used 'in ways which have not been paid for'. Consequently, the enforcement of a contract gives rise to considerable 'policing costs'. Natural safeguards can be used by the licensor to protect himself. He may restrict supply of a 'secret ingredient' or other essential part to control his licensee's output, or he may rely on technical progress to out-compete his licensee if necessary. If such safeguards are not available, contractual means must be sought with the resultant 'policing costs'.

Rights of ownership are frequently ill-defined and difficult to enforce and to publicise possession is often to invite imitation or replication or to encourage rival claims. In such cases possession is best maintained through secrecy. This gives rise to a severe problem – for to sell the asset requires publicity, with the consequence that ownership may be lost. This problem is avoided by integrating forward into the use of the asset and so internalising the market. The alternative is to offer a contingent contract, including insurance to the buyer that the asset will perform well. This method of avoiding 'buyer uncertainty' (the buyer being unable to assess the worth of the knowledge to him until he is in possession of it) is part of the reason for the search for new forms of co-operation which effectively transfer information without the necessity of foreign control.

Transaction Costs

The minimisation of transaction costs is central to theories of the existence of the multinational firm (Chapters 1 and 2; Casson, 1979; Buckley, 1983). The model in Casson (1981) shows that the tendency to internalise is greater, the higher the volume of trade between plants. But this depends on a large volume of trade being associated with a high frequency of transactions in the external market. The incentive to internalise is reduced if this frequency is diminished by long-term contracts for instance, or by bulk buying. Nevertheless, in many cases the most efficient institution (that is, the institution which minimises transaction costs) for transferring technology internationally will be the multinational enterprise. It has been argued, by Calvet and Naim (1981), that this is frequently true in the less-developed countries where markets are often imperfect in ways which favour a 'hierarchical' solution to the allocation problems, in other words, internalisation of markets within the multinational firm.

There is a shortage of information on the relative size of transaction costs in internal as against external transfer of technology, but some information can be gleaned from extant empirical studies. Teece (1977, p. 247) defines transfer costs as 'the costs of transmitting and absorbing all the relevant un-embodied knowledge'. Teece's survey of twenty-six international projects does not distinguish between internal and external transfer costs but an average figure of 19 per cent of the total project costs was found to represent transfer costs. The range is 2–59 per cent. Interestingly in Teece's twenty-six cases the 'international component' of transfer costs was negative in six cases and zero in four cases. (In other words domestic transfer would have been more expensive than international transfer in six cases.)

Table 3.5 shows a complete breakdown of the costs of foreign

TABLE 3.5   *Relative costs of licensing overseas (Australian licensors)*

Breakdown of total costs of licensing overseas	%
Protection of industrial property	24.8
Establishment of licensing agreement	46.6
Maintenance of licensing agreement	29.0
	100.0
Breakdown of establishment costs	
Search for suitable licensee	22.8
Communication between involved parties	44.7
Adoption and testing of equipment for licensee	9.9
Training personnel for licensee	19.9
Other (additional Marketing Activity and Legal Expenses)	2.5
	100.0
Breakdown of maintenance costs	
Audit of licensee	9.7
Ongoing market research in market of licensee	7.2
Back-up services for licensee	65.0
Defence of industrial property rights in licensee's territory	11.0
Other	7.1
	100.0

SOURCE   Reproduced from Carstairs and Welch (1981).

licensing by Australian licensors. It shows that a quarter of total costs of foreign licensing is represented by the protection of industrial property, nearly half the cost is represented by the costs of establishing a licensing agreement and over a quarter in maintenance costs of the agreement. In the breakdown of establishment and maintenance costs, the most significant items are 'communication between involved parties' (20.8 per cent of *total* costs) and 'back-up services for licensees' (18.9 per cent of *total* costs). Interestingly, search costs for potential licensees account for 10.6 per cent of *total* costs. (Carstairs and Welch, 1981.) It is not possible to suggest the magnitude of such costs for internal transfers, but it is reasonable to assume search costs to be zero and the policing element to be vastly reduced.

A further problem in the external transfer of information is that of time lags. The lag in licensing on joint ventures has been shown to be longer than internal transfers (Mansfield, Romeo and Wagner, 1979).

It is therefore clear that licensing involves continuing expense on the part of the licensor to ensure successful transfer and 'police' his rights. Several studies (for example, Behrman and Wallender, 1976; Baranson, 1978) have emphasised the continuing transfer of skilled personnel in cementing the know-how. In other words, licensing is a relationship rather than an act. Interaction between recipient and seller is both essential to successful transfer and a continuing element of cost.

The importance of the provisions of individual contracts should not be underestimated. The time and effort put into contract design is a testament to the central importance of the legal document.

Absorptive Capacity in the Host Country

It is over-simplistic to place the types of co-operation on a spectrum from wholly-owned foreign subsidiaries to simple contracts in terms of the ease with which the information can be absorbed by the host country (internalised transactions easiest, simple market contracts most difficult). Many multinational firms have found the absorptive capacity of host countries to be a major problem for activities which they substantially control (Baranson, 1967) and there may be an argument in some cases that absorptive capacity may increase when local control is involved.

However it is partly the desire to increase absorptive capacity which leads to simple asset-transfer contracts becoming more complicated because a larger onus is placed on the transferring firm to ensure effective transfer. The lack of expertise on the part of the host country will raise the costs of transfer (borne by the licensee) and increase the benefits of internalisation, if this is allowed by host-country legislation.

The capacity to absorb a borrowed technology depends on (i) indigenous research efforts, (ii) the skills and capabilities of recipient firms and (iii) the transferor firm's commitment (Balasubramanyam, 1973). A distinction needs to be made between the ability to implement technologies which need no alteration and the local firm's ability to restructure, adopt and develop technologies to local conditions. The first needs upgrading of managerial and labour skills at the plant level, the latter requires investment in research and development. Balasubramanyam suggests that (based on Indian experiences) where the transferor has no equity stake in the recipient, the sale of knowledge will often be regarded as marginal and the transferor cannot be expected to evince any interest in restructuring the knowledge (often any improvements will have to be transmitted back to the licensor). Consequently, he concludes that where adapting is the objective, technical collaboration agreements may be fruitful only in the case of large firms in the host country which can provide the resources to undertake the adaptation. See also Tabe (1975). Internally 'conversion personnel' are of great importance as is the availability of high-quality inputs and subcontractors externally (Baranson, 1967).

The Effects of Competition

Much of the analyses of licensing and other new forms of co-operation ignores the competitive process. This is clearly untenable in a world of large firms, proprietary knowledge and imperfect markets (Lall, 1978 and 1981). The search for new forms of co-operation is in part due to a desire on the host-country's part to reduce foreign control but is also made possible by the willingness of multinational firms to compromise on total ownership. This is often the result of competitive pressure.

New forms of co-operation often offer entry into markets which would otherwise be closed to multinational firms. They may be closed to wholly-owned subsidiaries because of government policy (and to exports by tariffs, quotas or other protective devices) but also because of the existing competitive structure. If the market is already oligopolised, entry via setting up a subsidiary may spoil the market for all firms, including the entrant. Some form of co-operation will be preferable. Hence, we observe cross-licensing in concentrated markets (Buckley and Davies, 1980; Parry, 1975).

Host-country firms may resort to entry-forestalling practices, reducing prices or taking political action to protect domestic industry from foreign investors (Kidron, 1965). The result will be to make co-operation more attractive. In terms of follow-the-leader behaviour, noted as typical amongst large firms in several industries (Knickerbocker, 1973) there comes a point, depending on the relation between the host-market size and scale economies, where followers will turn to licensing rather than head-to-head competition. This pattern of behaviour can be exploited by host-country interests and increase their bargaining power. For instance, where the competitive situation dictates a rapid response from 'following' firms, the necessity for a quick entry may be exploited by the host country to dictate the mode of entry. The desire of oligopolistic multinationals not to allow particular host markets to be cornered by one of their number may provide opportunities for host countries to impose conditions on entry.

3.5 ISSUES RAISED BY NEW FORMS OF INTERNATIONAL INDUSTRIAL CO-OPERATION

Effective Transfer

The successful absorption of the foreign technology into the economic structure of the host country is the key to judging the success of any form of international industrial co-operation (Helleiner, 1975). However, as we have seen, international technology transfer can only be achieved at a cost. The minimisation of this cost to the recipient country is a further criterion of success. There may be a trade-off between this objective of minimising transfer costs and host-country political control of projects involving foreign technology. Given this degree of host control, transfer costs must be minimised. A careful 'match' between the foreign firm and local interests is therefore essential and we are seeing a mushrooming of host-country investment authorities whose task it is to liaise with importers of technology and smooth these transfers. Politically, costs may be involved, as investment authorities often wield a great deal of power outside the normal political channels of control.

Bargaining

Any form of international industrial co-operation involves a continuous process of bargaining (Vaitsos, 1974). Casson points out, however, that the nature of buyer's ignorance and its effects on the bargaining process may have been widely misunderstood (Casson, 1979, p. 113). He suggests that it is the buyer's knowledge, not of the product or process itself, but of the alternative sources of supply or the availability of substitutes, which strengthens the buyer's bargaining power. Even when the buyer does not know what the product or process *is*, he may know what it *does* and hence be able to evaluate alternatives. The exception to this rule is where the seller intends to practise deception and the buyer is not suspicious. But once the buyer becomes suspicious, his valuation will decline. Vaitsos, however, acknowledges that lack of knowledge of alternatives is often a problem for less-developed countries and that an 'international search for knowledge and its alternative sources of supply could institutionally prove to be of the highest importance' (Vaitsos, 1977, p. 131). Attempts to improve the host-country's bargaining power are detailed in UNCTC (1979).

Are New Forms Competitive or Complementary to Direct Foreign Investment?

It has become fashionable to argue that the growth of non-direct investment forms of international involvement implies the decline of multinationals and the end of their subsidiaries as primary means of international technology transfer.

Superficially, this seems correct. However, it is pertinent to examine the argument more closely. There remain many areas where the necessity to control information within the corporate family permit little institutional innovation – computers and bio-engineering are perhaps examples. But it may be suggested that the new forms present additional opportunities for multinationals to penetrate markets and countries which would otherwise be closed. New forms of arrangement also benefit multinationals, in reducing risk, improving their sensitivity to local conditions and penetrating awkward market segments (Contractor and Sagafi-Nejad, 1981). A comparison of returns does not always favour the direct investment route (Contractor, 1981b) and a judicious mix of forms of doing business abroad is an increasingly acceptable corporate objective (Wright *et al.*, 1983). Many multinationals are developing 'dispersal skills' even enabling complex higher-order activities such as research and development to be performed abroad (Behrman and Fisher, 1980).

Institution Building: New Inter-company Relationships

Policy towards international technology transfer to the Third World and Eastern bloc has often been negative. Policies on control of technology transfer by UNCTAD and others seems likely to restrict rather than liberate international flows of productive information (Thompson, 1982; Long, 1981). In many cases the 'restrictive practices' adopted by multinationals are second best attempts to extract returns from diffusable knowledge in the absence of perfect information (Casson, 1979). Alternative strategies rest on the ability of firms and host nations to build satisfactory institutional forms partially to reconcile competing interests. Transfer must be profitable for the multinational firm and effective for the host country's objectives. If we accept the premise that technology creators, operationalisers and transferors must be rewarded for their efforts, then the design of institutions which effectively achieve these ends is as important for them as for the recipients of the technology. To this end a more detailed and constructive debate is necessary. (Baranson, 1981; Perlmutter and Sagafi-Nejad, 1981; Singer, 1980.)

3.6 CONCLUSION

Modes of international industrial co-operation are changing under pressure from host countries to achieve greater political and economic control over their development, and from multinational firms to achieve a return on their investment in creating, developing and transferring knowledge. Given that the circumstances of individual firms and nations vary so much, it is not surprising that from this melting-pot emerge new institutional arrangements. Rigidities on legal arrangements, in policies of firms, governments and international institutions, as well as peculiarities in the market for diffusable assets, have meant that the search for acceptable forms has not been easy. In policy-making areas, it is essential to keep in mind the peculiarities of the market for information and its relationship to the markets for final goods. Attempts at making policy which ignore these fundamental relationships are doomed to failure.

4 Multinational Monopolies and International Cartels

MARK CASSON

4.1 INTRODUCTION

Cartels have received little attention in the theoretical literature on the multinational enterprise (MNE). This is surprising because of their important historical role in the evolution of the MNE (Wilkins, 1970, 1974). The relation between MNEs and international cartels is complex. In some industries cartels have been superceded by MNEs, while in others the two coexist. The collective behaviour of the members of a cartel often resembles that of a horizontally integrated MNE. Yet different MNEs are often members of the same cartel, and a multiproduct MNE may belong to several cartels (see Reader, 1970, and Teichova, 1974).

Wilkins (1977, p. 592) has urged that:

> when we talk about the growth of enterprises, we have to concern ourselves with cartelisation. In America, the rise of big business came after the pool and the agreement to restrain trade were ruled illegal ... In dealing with the development of European multinational enterprise, it is useful to see the cartel structure as linked with the development of such enterprises, and also as an alternative possibility. There are cases where multinational behaviour (direct foreign investment) did not occur because agreements between two, or more, independent enterprises precluded it. The strategy of the multinational manager had division-of-territory agreements as alternatives or sometimes complements to direct foreign investment.

The analytical standpoint of this chapter is a very simple one. The

MNE and the international cartel are regarded as alternative institutional arrangements for the exploitation of international monopoly power. International monopoly is achieved by world-wide collusion between production units in an industry. A typology of collusion is presented in Table 4.1. Tacit collusion is exemplified by price-leadership, or by an open-price system in which firms report their prices to each other before they supply quotations to their customers. Explicit collusion involves either voluntary agreement or subjection to a common authority. Voluntary agreement is exemplified by a private cartel; subjection to authority by government output-limitation schemes and by consolidation of ownership in a monopolistic firm.

TABLE 4.1   *Types of collusion*

Degree of understanding	Degree of coercion	Nature of authority	Examples
Tacit			Price leadership
			Informal open-price system
Explicit	Voluntary agreement		Private cartel
	Subject to common authority	Private	Monopolistic firm
		Public	Government output-restriction scheme

Consolidation involves the internalisation of the market in collusive agreements. Collusion between production units is effected by managerial control within a multiplant firm. Consolidation may be achieved either by merger or takeover between established producers or by the expansion of a progressive firm whose competitive advantage forces other producers out of the industry.

The interpretation of multiplant monopoly in terms of the internalisation of oligopolistic collusion stems from Williamson (1975, ch. 12). Williamson shows that colluding oligopolists face the twin problems of 'opportunism' and 'information impactedness'. The monopolist can largely avoid these problems:

Even within the monopoly firm in which semi-autonomous operating divisions have been created, with each operated as a profit centre, interdivisional cheating on agreements will be less than inter-firm cheating because (1) the gains can be less fully appropriated by the defector division, (2) the difficulty of detecting cheating is much less, and (3) the penalties to which internal organisation has access (including dismissing division managers who behave opportunistically) are more efficacious. (Williamson, 1975, p. 246.)

Williamson's analysis focuses almost exclusively on the benefits of monopolistic organisation, however, and has little to say about its costs. While he discusses in detail the internal organisation of the monopolistic firm, he says little about the administration of cartels. It is hoped that the present chapter will correct this imbalance in previous analysis.

Section 4.2 charts the historical growth of the international cartel and the MNE. Section 4.3 reviews basic concepts and definitions, and discusses earlier analysis of the subject. Sections 4.4–4.13 present a systematic step-wise development of the theory. The analysis is confined narrowly to the subject of cartels and little is said about the related issues of restrictive licensing agreements and commodity-price stabilisation schemes. Section 4.14 summarises the main hypotheses and demonstrates the richness of their predictions. Section 4.15 considers implications for policy and for future research.

4.2 AN HISTORICAL PERSPECTIVE

In European history attempts at international monopoly can be traced back to the thirteenth century. At this time there emerged monopolies in both production and trade. The best known trading monopoly is the Hanseatic League (Dollinger, 1970). A lesser known monopoly was created in the mining and marketing of alum. Alum was used as a mordant to prepare textiles for dyeing: it was an indispensable input to the major manufacturing industry of medieval Europe (Stone, 1956). In the thirteenth century the world alum market was controlled by a Genoese speculative syndicate, but towards the end of the fifteenth century control passed to an international cartel organised by Pope Paul II and the King of Naples. This cartel is especially interesting because of its great sophistication. In 1470 the Pope and the King agreed a common price policy.

Profit-sharing and sales quotas were established, exchange of statistical information arranged, and a common policy was adopted to fight outsiders. There were to be agents acting as 'joint sales comptoir' (that is, a sales syndicate). Credit and other conditions of sales were regulated uniformly and heavy penalties were stipulated in case of violation of the agreement. The social position of the contracting parties did not prevent a certain cartel distrust, mitigated somewhat by the provision that each party was to possess keys to the store-houses of the other in order to supervise possible circumventions. The mines were to be exploited by private companies, but the sovereign owners were highly interested in the prosperity of those companies. Whereas the cartel agreement conspicuously resembled a 'modern' international cartel agreement, there was one provision which belonged to the arsenal of ancient times. In order to fight Turkish 'outsider' competition the Pope obligated himself to enjoin, at least once a year, all Christianity from buying and selling alum of Turkish origin. Turkish alum was outlawed and could be seized by anybody. The whole profit yielded to the Pope by the monopoly was to be used to finance wars against infidel Turks and Protestant Hussites (Hexner, 1945, pp. 26–7, footnote 15; for details of later alum monopolies see Sutherland, 1936, and Stocking and Watkins, 1948, p. 25).

It is difficult to trace a direct link between the medieval cartel and its modern counterpart, however. It is customary to ascribe the origin of the modern cartel to the development of German mercantilist policy after the establishment of the Zollverein in 1834. At first, the formation of cartels proceeded fairly slowly, but by the turn of the century it had accelerated considerably: it has been estimated that there were 385 domestic cartels in Germany by 1904 and between 550 and 600 of them by 1911. At least forty products entering into international trade were subject to cartel agreements before 1896, with German interests involved in most, if not all, of them. Cartels were also prominent in Belgium, and in the emerging heavy industries of France.

In the United States, cartels played an important role in the transition from isolated local monopolies to nationwide multiplant monopolies that followed the development of the rail network after the Civil War (Chandler, 1977). Some of the most enterprising business leaders regarded the cartel merely as an expedient to maintain prices during temporary spells of overcapacity. They believed that long-run economies could only be achieved through full horizontal and vertical integration. This multiplant monopolies such as the Standard Oil Trust did not merely enforce inter-plant collusion, but also disseminated technical and managerial skills to the plants under their control. These skills included the exploitation of mass production technologies and the marketing of consumer products to a population of considerable cultural and ethnic diversity.

The Sherman Act of 1890 was directed against these monopolies, but it was not until 1911 that it really began to bite. It was about this time that the open price agreement became a popular instrument of tacit collusion (O'Brien and Swann, 1968, p. 22). Open pricing administered by trade associations was very popular in the US in the 1920s, and was given a further boost by the National Recovery Act (NRA) of 1933.

The Webb–Pomerene law of 1918 legalised export associations in the US, and the vesting of German business assets in the hands of Alien Property Custodians during World War One encouraged the development of arm's length international agreements.

American and British firms acquiring the properties frequently lacked the technological experience and foreign outlets of the German parent firms; they entered into business agreements with them and thereby substituted an American–German or a British–German cartel relationship for a German parent–subsidiary relationship (Mason, 1946, p. 11).

The promotion of industrial combinations in both Germany and the US was associated with a high domestic tariff (Pierce, 1907). In the UK, protection was much lower, and consolidation did not get under way until the late 1920s and early 1930s. At this time there was a general movement among Western industrialised countries towards the centralised control of production, underpinned by protection of the domestic market. Regulatory boards for agricultural commodities were established in the US, the Bank of England promoted the rationalisation of production along the German model in the UK, the Nazis restructured the cartels in Germany and the Fascists established state control of production in Italy. Business leaders such as Sir Alfred Mond of Imperial Chemical Industries popularised the view that the multiplant monopoly was a higher form of cartel. He believed that the formation of domestic monopolies was a necessary and desirable step towards the regulation of world production by a cartel agreement between national firms. During the 1930s in Europe, *laissez-faire* capitalism was written off in political terms: centralised control was widely believed to hold the key to the restoration of economic stability, and the only questions were how tight the control should be, and whether it should remain in private hands or be vested in the state. In the US, the reports of the TNEC expressed dissent from this view. Nevertheless, Stocking and Watkins (1948, p. 93) using a broad definition of a cartel, estimated that in 1939 cartels regulated 86.9 per cent of all mineral products sold in the US, 47.3 per cent of all agricultural products and 42.7 per cent of all manufactured products. Cartel control of production was even further advanced in Germany and Japan.

Since World War Two there has been a major political reaction against the concept of a corporate state run in the interests of producers. Business leaders now espouse an individualistic philosophy. Nevertheless, corporatist attitudes remain. For example, modern corporations continue to enjoy close ties with government in the provision of defence equipment and other products. Cartels have also a role in raw materials markets and in international transport (shipping, airlines). Inter-governmental cartels continue to control the export trade in some agricultural products. But the role of cartels in manufacturing industry has diminished. The predominant feature of the post-war era has been the rise of MNEs in manufacturing industries – particularly those industries characterised by product differentiation and technological progressiveness. Unlike the first generation of US-based MNEs born in the 1880s, which were created largely by mergers between cartel members, the post-war generation of US-based MNEs has been created largely by the expansion of progressive firms through green-field investments overseas. This expansion has driven out less progressive uninational firms. This difference in patterns of growth is very important, though it should not be overstated. Green-field investments were a significant instrument of international expansion even amongst first generation MNEs, and very recently, mergers and acquisitions have acquired renewed importance as part of a movement towards greater industrial diversification among large firms.

From a broad long-run perspective, the post-war MNE may be regarded simply as the latest and most sophisticated manifestation of a tendency towards the international concentration of capital. This view emerges most clearly from the work of Lenin (1970). It is not only this long-run trend that is interesting, however – if it exists – but also the reasons why this trend manifests itself in different ways at different times and in different industries. The analytical sections of this chapter show that modern theory can go a long way towards explaining the factors which govern the choice of the institutional arrangements for international monopoly at particular times and in particular industries. The theory can explain not only the long-run trend, but also the comparative growth of international cartels and MNEs at the various stages of their development.

4.3 CONCEPTS AND DEFINITIONS

A cartel may be defined as an institution for implementing an agreement for the maintenance of the prices or the limitation of the outputs of independent producers. The outputs of the producers are assumed to be substitutes for one another; in the special case of a homogeneous product they are perfect substitutes.

Because demand for a commodity is normally a decreasing function of price, the maintenance of its price implies the limitation of its output and vice versa. The cartel may have other objects too, but the control of price or output must be one of them. Notice that the cartel is defined, not as an agreement itself, but as an institution whose rules and procedures are devoted to monitoring and enforcing a collusive agreement – and perhaps for renegotiating it too, should circumstances require this. An international cartel is a cartel concerned with restricting the outputs of independently owned plants in more than one country.

This definition is more general than Hexner's (1945, p. 24) which requires membership of the cartel to be voluntary – ruling out many government-inspired restriction schemes – and to be transitory rather than permanent. It is more restrictive than Stocking and Watkins' definition (1948, p. 3), which includes any licensing agreement which imposes restrictions on the licensee.

Cartel literature is mainly concerned with the general issue of competition versus monopoly (Macgregor, 1906; Macrosty, 1907; Levy, 1911; Liefmann, 1932; Plummer, 1934). The choice between alternative modes of monopoly organisation has received relatively little attention. In particular, there has been little analysis of the choice, at the far end of the collusive spectrum, between a sophisticated cartel and a fully integrated firm.

The most penetrating and succinct discussion of this issue is given by Robinson (1941). He distinguishes three categories of collusive organisation: *short-term forms*, consisting of informal undertakings, price-fixing and quota agreements, pooling associations and associations for allocating contracts; *transitional forms*, consisting of sales syndicates, cartels with a dominant member, and financial communities of interests; and *long-term* forms, consisting of trusts, holding companies and integrated multiplant firms.

Robinson argues that the transitional form will be preferred to the short-term form when the prospective life of the monopoly is a long one. Long life is to be expected in circumstances in which there is 'less divergence of interest between high- and low-cost producers, or between producers of slightly differing products, or between producers for slightly different markets' (Robinson, 1941, p. 98). The transitional form is preferred when the incentive to cut prices is greatest and when it is necessary to control non-price competition.

The long-term form is preferred to the transitional form when:

> an important motive for combination is the possibility of securing technical economies which can be achieved only by a wholesale reorganisation of all the various undertakings included. A preference for the holding company or for the merger may be explained by a variety of considerations. The holding company may perform any, or all, of three quite distinct functions. It may be a device for the central office management of a number of separate plants, it may be a central marketing organisation controlling and selling the output of separate plants; or it may be a financial device to facilitate the extension of limited liability to units smaller than the whole combined undertaking. The first two functions can, however, be performed if necessary by special offices or departments within a merger, and the third consideration must be partially relevant in order that a holding company may be preferred. [. . .] The holding company has a further advantage in those industries in which goodwill applies rather to the care and methods of manufacture, as it does, for instance, with motor cars, or gramophones, than to the selection of raw materials, as it does, for example, with cigarettes or cement.

The holding company as a device of central management is most likely to be discovered in industries in which the optimum management unit is larger than that of technical production, or in which, since transport costs are high, production must take place in a number of plants near the market, even though they be of less than optimum size. As a device for central marketing it is most likely to be found in any industry where the optimum scale of marketing is markedly larger than that of manufacture. As a device for the subdivision of limited liability it is most likely to be employed where the anticipated fortunes of different parts of the combined undertaking are most widely different. This will be the case where a combination is lateral as well as horizontal, extending not only into similar, but also into dissimilar branches of activity. It will be the case where a horizontal combination contains technical units of markedly different natural efficiency, such as is common in mining. It will be the case where technique is in transition and each unit is something of an experiment, or where fashion can affect earnings in a way not easily retrievable. This may serve to explain the common practice of many shipping companies in making small numbers of ships into separate companies. It will be the case also where different units sell in different geographical markets, so that one may encounter difficulties without all others suffering equally.

The complete merger, on the other hand, is most likely where combination has been strictly horizontal, where the market for all the separate plants is uniform and identical, where the ultimate aim of technical policy is concentration into one single plant (Robinson, 1941, pp. 99–102).

It is possible to disagree in detail with some of the arguments advanced by Robinson. Nevertheless, it is clear that Robinson's analysis anticipates much recent work based upon the 'markets and hierarchies' approach (Williamson, 1975) and is made all the more profound by his view of the integrated firm as a limiting form of cartel. The following sections synthesise the work of Robinson and Williamson using recent developments in oligopoly theory.

4.4 ADMINISTRATIVE PROBLEMS OF COLLUSIVE OLIGOPOLY

Cartels are most easily analysed within the framework of the theory of collusive oligopoly. In this theory, individual firms maximise profits. Collusion occurs when firms recognise their interdependence and attempt to maximise industry profits. Each firm's long-run interests is best served by maximising industry profits and then bargaining for as large a share of these profits as possible (Chamberlain, 1933; Fellner, 1949).

A simple model of collusion may be developed under the following restrictive assumptions. These assumptions are relaxed in later sections: they are relaxed one at a time and in reverse order.

(a) Buyers of output and sellers of inputs are atomistic
(b) There is no government interference in economic activity as a whole, and in particular no legal constraint on collusive arrangements
(c) The long-run structure of industry demand and industry costs is fixed
(d) The number of production units is fixed
(e) Short-run industry demand is stable
(f) The number of product varieties is fixed and so are the product characteristics
(g) Each firm has full information about the price charged by its rivals
(h) There are no transport costs or tariffs
(i) Production takes place under increasing marginal costs

It is convenient to begin by considering two production units generating differentiated outputs, and then to outline how the results extend to homogeneous outputs and to more than two production units. Unless otherwise stated, each plant generates just one type of output.

Let x_i be the output of the ith plant, p_i its price, and c_i the total production cost of the plant ($i=1,2$). For each product there is a well-behaved demand curve

$$x_i = x_i(p_i, p_j) \qquad\qquad (j \neq i, i, j = 1,2) \qquad (4.1)$$

where demand is a decreasing function of the own-price, p_i, and an increasing function of the cross-price, p_j. Under suitable additional conditions (Friedman, 1983, p. 63) the demand equations (4.1) can be inverted to give the price equations:

$$p_i = p_i(x_i, x_j) \qquad\qquad (j \neq i, i, j = 1,2) \qquad (4.2)$$

where price is a decreasing function of both the own-output and the cross-output. When the products are homogeneous the pair of prices collapses to a single price, and the own-output and cross-output variables interact additively:

$$p_i = p = p(x) \qquad\qquad (i = 1,2) \qquad (4.3)$$

where

$$x = \sum_{i=1}^{2} x_i \qquad (4.4)$$

The benefits of collusion may be measured by comparing the industry profits earned under collusion with those earned under rivalry. The profits earned under rivalry depend upon how the two firms behave, and this in turn depends upon how each firm expects its rival to respond when it changes its own price or its output. The coefficient of conjectural variation measures the proportion of any change that the rival is expected to match. Cournot (1838) suggested that each firm anticipates zero conjectural variation in output, while Bertrand (1883) argued that zero conjectural variation in price is a more realistic assumption. Stackelberg (1952) argued that one firm – the 'leader' – would anticipate a Cournot-type response by its rival – the 'follower'.

Cournot rivalry can be applied to both homogeneous and heterogeneous products, while Bertrand rivalry yields a determinate outcome only for heterogeneous products. For analytical purposes the Cournot assumption is most useful even though it is less realistic (see Section 4.7).

Under Cournot rivalry the ith firm maximises profit:

$$\pi_i = p_i(x_i, x_j)x_i - c_i(x_i) \tag{4.5}$$

taking its rival's output x_j as fixed. Equating marginal revenue to marginal cost

$$p_i + (\partial p_i / \partial x_i)x_i = dc_i / dx_i \tag{4.6}$$

determines the reaction function

$$x_i = x_i(x_j) \tag{4.7}$$

which expresses the firm's output as a function of its rival's output. Under the assumed conditions, the intersection of the two reaction curves (one for each firm) determines a unique and stable Cournot equilibrium.

It is readily established that the Cournot equilibrium does not achieve a maximum of industry profit. To maximise

$$\pi = \sum_{i=1}^{2} \pi_i \tag{4.8}$$

it is necessary to equate *industry* marginal revenue to *industry* marginal cost for each of the two outputs:

$$p_i + (\partial p_i / \partial x_i)x_i + (\partial p_j / \partial x_i)x_j = dc_i / dx_i \quad (i = 1,2; \ i \neq j) \tag{4.9}$$

Solving the pair of questions (4.9) determines the industry-profit-maximising outputs x_i, x_j.

Comparing the left-hand sides of equations (4.6) and (4.9) shows that the marginal revenue of the individual firm is higher than the marginal revenue of the industry as a whole. The left-hand side of equation (4.9) contains an additional term $(\partial p_j/\partial x_i)x_j$, which is negative whenever the rival firm's output is positive. When a firm increases its output, the price of its product falls, and to maintain its output constant the rival firm must reduce its price and so sustain a loss of revenue. The individual firm does not, therefore, bear the full consequence of its output decision, since the consequent loss of revenue on intramarginal output spills over onto the rival firm. Successful collusion must take account of this interdependency by discouraging each firm from expanding its output.

In the special case of a homogeneous product the interdependency between the firms can be resolved in a very simple way. Substituting (4.3) into (4.8) allows industry profit to be expressed in the form

$$\pi = p(x)x - \sum_{i=1}^{2} c_i(x_i) \tag{4.10}$$

Maximising (4.10) subject to the constraint (4.4) gives the first order conditions

$$dc_i/dx_i = \lambda \qquad\qquad (i=1,2) \tag{4.11}$$

$$p + (\partial p/\partial x)x = \lambda \tag{4.12}$$

where λ is a Lagrange multiplier. The value of λ may be interpreted as the shadow price of output. Equation (4.11) shows that both firms produce up to the point where marginal cost is equal to the shadow price of output. Equation (4.12) shows that the discrepancy between the industry price and the shadow price exactly matches the loss of industry revenue on intramarginal output when either firm expands production at the margin. Industry profit is maximised when each firm behaves as though it faced an infinitely elastic demand for output at the equilibrium shadow price.

The simplest way to implement this solution is for the firms to establish a sales syndicate – that is, a jointly-owned sales subsidiary – to which they supply all their output at a uniform price. The managers of the syndicate set this price in the light of demand conditions so that it reflects the industry marginal revenue. The use of the shadow price completely solves the problem of allocating industry output between the two firms. The managers of the syndicate do not need to know the cost conditions in the individual plants. So long as they adjust the shadow price to achieve a balance of supply and demand, total industry costs will be minimised for any level of industry output.

In the Lagrangian formulation, the industry output, x, and its shadow value, λ, are 'dual' to each other. This indicates that an alternative arrangement would be for the two firms to establish a production board which would fix, not a shadow price, but a total output quota. Each unit of quota would be transferable and could therefore be traded between the firms. If the quota units were auctioned in Walrasian fashion then each firm would value a quota unit at the excess of the industry price over its marginal cost of production. This would establish an implicit price of output. Since the quotas would command a uniform price, the implicit price of output would be the same for both firms. It would, in fact, be equal to the shadow price that would prevail under the syndicate arrangement. Thus industry output, and its allocation between the two firms, would be exactly the same as before.

The managers of the sales syndicate or the production board would behave as though they were maximising profit. Their respective profits would be earned from the resale of output and from the sale of production quotas. Their behaviour would be analogous to that of a market-making entrepreneur (Casson, 1982, pp. 140–4). There is a qualification, however: while the managers would be expected to exercise to the full their monopoly power against the final buyers, they would not be expected to exercise any of their monopsony power against the producers.

The main problem with these two arrangements arises because at some stage the profits of the sales syndicate or the production board have to be distributed to the producers. When using these arrangements, efficiency normally requires that the problem of allocating profits must be divorced completely from the problem of maximising the profits to be earned, but in practice this can rarely be done (see Section 4.5).

It would be possible to eliminate the profits of the production board by making the output quotas non-transferable, so that they could not command a price. This modification, however, encounters a difficulty which the other arrangements avoided. It becomes necessary for the production board to solve the industry maximum problem directly, and so the board requires full knowledge of the cost structures of the firms. The two arrangements discussed do not require the colluding firms to pool their cost information, whereas a system of non-transferable quotas does. If the quotas are fixed without the pooling of cost information then there is no guarantee that the allocation of output between the firms will minimise total industry cost.

When the products of the two firms are heterogeneous, the interde pendencies are more difficult to resolve. To extend the previous arrangements to cope with this case, it would be necessary for the sales syndicate to set shadow prices for both commodities, and to attune both the average of the absolute prices and their relativity to the demand conditions specified in equation (4.1). Likewise, the production board would have to set quotas for both the products. In determining the quotas, the board would need to take account of the same set of factors as did the sales syndicate. The benefits to the firms of devolving price and output decisions are much less clear than before because of the greater complexity of the decisions involved.

The extension of the analysis to more than two firms is straightforward. The principles are unchanged. The main effect is to heighten the disparity between the cases of homogeneous and heterogeneous products. Adding more producers of a homogeneous product increases the administrative burden for the managers of sales syndicates and production boards, but does not increase the complexity of their decision: there remains just a single shadow price or output quota to be set. By contrast, when each additional producer generates a different variety of product, the number of prices or quotas to be set increases in direct proportion to the number of producers, and the number of demand interactions that need to be considered in setting them increases asymptotically as the square of the number of producers. Collusive arrangements thus become very complex as the variety of products increases.

4.5 ECONOMIES OF SCALE AND THE RATIONALISATION OF PRODUCTION

This section considers the consequences of relaxing assumption (j) by allowing for constant or decreasing marginal costs of production. Assumption (j) is important for two reasons. First, it guarantees that there exists a unique and stable Cournot equilibrium when the producers do not collude. Second, and more important, it affects the desirability of allocating industry profits between firms through bargaining over production quotas. It is the latter point that is considered here.

It is only in the special case where marginal costs are constant and are the same for both firms that it is efficient to determine the allocation of industry profits through quota bargaining. In this special case, a reallocation of industry output between the plants leaves total industry costs unchanged. Since the inter-plant allocation of industry output is irrelevant for efficiency, it can be used without loss as a mechanism for allocating industry profits as well.

When these cost conditions are not satisfied, however, bargaining over quotas becomes an inefficient method of allocating profits. This is because a quota allocation which reflects the relative bargaining strengths of the parties is unlikely to reflect also their relative production costs. The minimisation of industry costs requires, roughly speaking, that the lowest-cost producers should produce the largest outputs. The lowest-cost producers will tend to have the greatest bargaining strength because of their ability to drive out the highest-cost producers through price warfare. Inefficiency may occur, however, if the relative bargaining strength does not exactly correspond to the relative cost advantage of the most efficient firms.

When marginal costs vary with output, efficiency requires that quota allocations must be supplemented by side payments which are unrelated to output (Bain, 1948). This is particularly important when all the firms produce under decreasing marginal costs. Industry efficiency then requires that, in the absence of tariffs and transport costs, all production should be concentrated on a single plant. If quotas alone were used to allocate profits then the owners of the plants which closed down as a result of the rationalisation of production would receive no compensation at all. Assuming that these producers have some bargaining strength – however little – they cannot be persuaded to close down unless they receive a positive payment. This payment is necessarily additional to the non-payment they would receive under a pure quota arrangement.

The rationalisation of production under decreasing marginal costs encounters other problems besides the unsuitability of quota bargaining. One of these is the need to prevent re-entry into the industry by plants which have been closed down. Members of the cartel may sell off their plants to non-members wishing to enter the industry. To secure their position the members who continue to produce must insist that plants going out of production are dismantled and sold off for scrap. This eliminates the possibility that a potential entrant could acquire his capacity at a 'knock-down price'; it forces the potential entrant to finance investment in new capacity.

It is clear that the problems of cartel administration are much greater when production does not take place under constant marginal costs. Cost minimisation requires side-payment contracts which may be difficult to enforce. The multiplant monopoly avoids this problem because side-payments between plants are internalised within the firm

This is especially relevant when there has been excessive entry into an industry in which there are decreasing marginal costs. Elimination of excess capacity through a merger which forms a multinational monopoly may be a more secure arrangement than rationalisation through a cartel.

4.6 IMPACT OF TRANSPORT COSTS AND TARIFFS

This section considers the consequences of relaxing assumption (h) by allowing for transport costs and tariffs. Suppose that demand is concentrated at the two plant locations; the maximisation of industry profits under these conditions has been analysed by Horst (1971).

Transport costs and tariffs affect behaviour in two main ways. First, they make it possible for the producers to discriminate between the prices charged to buyers at different locations. When price discrimination is possible, an efficient sales syndicate will normally charge different prices for the same product in different countries, the mark-up in each country reflecting the elasticity of demand. The discrepancy between the prices cannot, however, exceed the combined cost of transport and tariff payments, because of the threat of arbitrage through resale. Resale can be controlled by designing variants of the product which can only be used in a specific country (right-hand drive and left-hand drive motor cars, for example).

Second, transport costs and tariff payments complicate the administrative arrangements for allocating outputs between plants. An efficient sales syndicate will no longer purchase the same product at the same price from both plants. It will discriminate in favour of the plant located where demand is highest relative to supply. It was noted in Section 4.4 that the sales syndicate has monopsony power over the producers, but that it is not supposed to use this power. When efficiency dictates that the sales syndicate charges discriminatory prices, however, it may be difficult for the producer against whom there is discrimination to be sure that the discrimination is not merely the result of the selective exercise of monopsony power.

One solution is for the firms to establish two sales subsidiaries – one for each market – to compete for supplies at each location. However, when tariff and transport costs are high, competition from the sales subsidiary at the distant location will provide only a weak constraint on the exercise of monopsony power. Under these conditions, it may be simpler to allow each firm a monopoly of sales at its own location. The firms are then free to bargain with each other if they wish to 'top up' their domestic supplies. This suggests that when transport costs and tariffs are high, cartel arrangements will be based upon an international division of the market between the colluding firms (this point is developed further in the next section).

In practice, products produced for export are often qualitatively different from those produced for domestic consumption. There are several reasons why this may be so: social conventions, legal requirements, health and safety standards may differ between countries, complementary factors required for the utilisation of the product may differ in abundance, the differential impact of transport costs may encourage the export of only high-quality–high-value items, and so on. Under these circumstances, oligopolistic rivalry may be confined largely to export products, and so only product varieties that enter into international trade will be subject to collusion.

The advantage of the multinational monopoly over the international cartel is likely to be greatest when transport costs and tariff payments are fairly modest: not so low that the sales syndicate charges uniform prices when buying from producers and selling to consumers, and not so high that the allocation problem can be solved simply by segmenting the market.

The advantage of the MNE is greatest of all when it is tariffs rather than transport costs which are the main obstacle to trade. When tarrifs are levied on an *ad valorem* basis, payments can be minimised by understating the value of imports through transfer pricing. With a cartel arrangement, the profits of transfer pricing accrue in the first instance to the sales syndicate, and the direct receipts of the producers are actually reduced. This arrangement therefore requires the producers to place very considerable trust in the management of the syndicate. It is also more difficult to keep transfer pricing confidential when it is administered by a cartel than when it is internalised within a firm. Thus when transport costs are fairly low and tariffs are relatively high, the MNE has a significant advantage over the international cartel in generating gains from transfer pricing.

4.7 SECRET PRICE-CUTTING

Secret price-cutting is one of those subjects on which economic theory is curiously silent. Much of conventional theory assumes perfect knowledge of prices. Thus in the Cournot model, for example, each firm can adjust its price instantaneously to what its rival is charging, so that sales are never lost because of undercutting. In the long-run competitive model, undercutting would never be profitable anyway, because the normal price only just covers each firm's average costs.

In oligopoly, however, price normally exceeds average cost, so that undercutting may well be profitable. Oligopolists face a 'Prisoner's Dilemma' regarding price-cutting (Osborne, 1976): it is in the interests of each individual firm to cut the price secretly, but against their collective interest for any one of them to do so.

Suppose now that assumption (g) is relaxed by introducing costs of acquiring information about rivals' operations (an analogous situation involving an information lag is considered by Cubbin, 1983). The dual relation between price and output revealed by equations (4.1) and (4.2) indicates that secret price-cutting can be controlled by monitoring *either* price *or* output. If prices are more easily monitored than outputs then it is more efficient for colluding firms to fix prices and to punish secret discounting, while if outputs are more easily monitored than prices then it is better to fix output quotas and to punish those who exceed them.

Individual firms can quite easily perform some of the monitoring activity themselves. For example, if a firm experiences a sudden contraction of sales, it is likely that a rival firm is secretly undercutting its price (Stigler, 1964). This is very probably the cause, for example, when casual buyers suddenly stop buying and only regular buyers remain. It is not so easy, however, to determine precisely which rival firm is cutting its price. This may require detailed research into changes in market shares – the firm which has gained the largest increase in market share being the principal suspect.

Information about price-cutters is of potential interest to all the members of an industry, and it is therefore natural that they should co-operate by forming a club to carry out the monitoring activity. Where the products are homogeneous the problem of price-cutting is particularly acute, and at the same time the remedy is especially simple: to agree a uniform price and to establish a secretariat to co-ordinate the detection and punishment of those who undersell. This arrangement, however, may encourage indirect price-cutting through bribes or lavish entertainment provided to agents or employees of the buyer. A more effective solution is to channel all sales through a syndicate; the problem is then reduced to monitoring sales through unauthorised outlets, such as special sales of goods 'direct from the factory'. To identify illicit sales, the syndicate may affix its own labels to the products it handles; this makes it possible to assess the magnitude of unauthorised sales, even though pinpointing the actual supplier may be more difficult.

An alternative to the sales syndicate is the allocation of particular customers to particular producers. This arrangement is especially suitable if the products are heterogeneous, and firms specialise in particular varieties of the product. The arrangement also has the peculiar characteristic that it may be easier to enforce internationally than it is domestically, for the cartel secretariat may be able to use customs statistics to check on illicit international flows of the product. Because of the large distances involved, centralised selling may incur high transport and communication costs and so theory predicts that geographical division of the market will be particularly favoured by international cartels and that centralised selling will have mainly domestic applications.

Once a price-cutter has been identified, he must be punished as a deterrent to others. In this respect, the theory of cartels becomes a special case of the economics of crime (Gravelle and Rees, 1981, p. 333). The form of punishment available depends crucially upon whether the cartel agreement is enforceable by an outside power. In some countries collusive agreements are enforceable in law, but this is the exception rather than the rule. In some cases an outside enforcer can be hired by the cartel: members could, for example, contract with a 'Mafia' to punish offenders on their behalf. Perhaps the most straightforward arrangement is for the cartel members to deposit funds with a reputable stake-holder who acts as arbitrator in price-cutting disputes. In the absence of a stake-holder, the most the cartel may be able to do is to spoil the market for the offending party. If the products are homogeneous, for example, then all the other firms could increase their output by the same proportion as the increase in the price-cutter's output: it has been claimed that this strategy has certain disirable properties in comparison with other ways of spoiling the market (Osborne, 1976). If the products are heterogeneous, the firms who produce the closest substitutes may agree to increase their outputs proportionately more than the others, though they may need to be compensated for this through side-payments.

The obvious disadvantage of this last procedure is that it almost inevitably spoils the market for the other members as well. The MNE has the advantage over the international cartel that it can solve this and other problems 'at a stroke'. When all plants are brought under common ownership, the incentive to undercut prices is eliminated. The information channels created within the organisation allow the culprits to be easily identified should price-cutting occur. The enforcement problem is solved, since managers who undercut other plants can simply be fired. It is, of course, possible that undercutting may still occur because of X-inefficiency within the organisation (Leibenstein, 1976). If managers are rewarded by growth of sales rather than profitability, for example, then undercutting may develop as an instrument of rivalry between the managements of subsidiaries.

Theory suggests that the advantage to the MNE is greatest when monitoring is most costly: for example, when it is difficult to channel all sales through a central agency and to prevent direct selling from the factory. It is also greatest when cartel agreements are most difficult to enforce: in other words, the more hostile the legal environment is to the cartel, the greater are the advantages, *ceteris paribus*, to the MNE.

4.8 PRODUCT DIFFERENTIATION AND THE AVOIDANCE OF UNANTICIPATED QUALITY CHANGES

It has hitherto been assumed that when products are heterogeneous, the characteristics of each product are fixed. This section relaxes assumption (f) by recognising that, in the long run, product characteristics are variable. Each product can be 'positioned' in the market by choosing the appropriate value for some characteristic. In fact, products may be regarded as having 'bundles' of characteristics (Lancaster, 1979), so that the positioning of the product involves the selection of a point in a multi-dimensional space.

The positioning of rival products is a key aspect of oligopolistic interdependence. The choice of product design and quality, and the timing and location of supply may be just as important as the setting of price. The tactical problems involved in price-setting and in the control of secret price-cutting have their analogues in the choice of product characteristics and in the control of secret or unanticipated adjustments in the characteristics of rival products.

Product characteristics are, on balance, easier to observe than prices. Changes in characteristics, however, typically involve longer 'lead times' than changes in prices because of the need to re-tool production, etc. This means that once a rival's change has been observed, it may take considerable time to respond. If firms keep their plans confidential therefore, a change in product characteristics may confer a major temporary advantage on the firm that implements it.

Unanticipated changes in product characteristics may substitute for secret price-cutting as a strategic weapon within an oligopoly. In markets where opportunities for product differentiation abound, price-fixing agreements may merely stimulate non-price competition. This can be wasteful in generating excessive expenditures on R & D and advertising, and in inhibiting economies of scale in production through the proliferation of varieties.

If the colluding firms decide to rationalise the varieties they produce, then they must standardise the product range, grade the different qualities, agree timetables and base-points for supply, and so on. They must also decide how production of the different varieties is to be allocated between them. If each firm produces just a single variety – as heretofore assumed – then its total revenue will be very sensitive to the price of that variety relative to the others. To insure itself against the risk that its own variety will be overpriced relative to other varieties, the firm may attempt to produce the whole range of varieties itself. If there are economies of scope at the plant level – so that the output of one variety is a close technical substitute for the output of another – then there may be no efficiency loss. If, on the other hand, there are diseconomies of scope, then industry production costs will be raised as a result of each firm replicating the product range. The ability of the MNE to eliminate this replication through administrative fiat gives it a major advantage over the international cartel. The advantage is greatest in industries where product differentiation is easy but there are substantial diseconomies of scope at the plant level. The MNE can concentrate the production of different items in the range on different plants much more easily than can the members of an international cartel.

4.9 UNPREDICTABLE DEMAND AND PRICE STABILISATION

This section considers the consequences of relaxing assumption (e) by allowing industry demand to be volatile and unpredictable. The discussion focuses upon short-run volatility of demand, but analogous results may be derived by considering long-run volatility as well.

When there are stochastic shifts in the demand curve, the adjustment costs incurred by producers depend upon the sensitivity of marginal cost to the output level in the region of normal capacity. If the marginal cost schedule is very steep in this region then under competitive conditions an increase in demand would lead to a sharp rise in price and very little expansion of output; conversely a fall in demand would lead to a sharp fall in price with very little reduction in output. The marginal-cost curve is most likely to be steep when capacity tolerances in durable equipment are low, when there are economies of continuous flow production and when the output is perishable, so that buffer stock inventories are difficult to maintain. The volatility of the price will be further enhanced if the product-demand curve is price-inelastic.

The combination of a volatile and inelastic demand with steeply increasing marginal cost makes the profitability of production highly variable. The allocative benefits of price adjustment are very small. The main effect of price adjustment is to redistribute income between the buyers and the sellers. The benefits of price adjustment are therefore quite small compared with the cost they exact in greater income uncertainty. Buyers and sellers have a mutual interest in price stabilisation, though while buyers desire a maximum price the sellers will want to set a minimum one.

Although the stablisation of price provides an opportunity for sellers to raise the average price level, it is possible that as a result of the price-fixing agreement the average price level may actually fall. In the absence of barriers to entry, sellers must resign themselves in the long run to earning, on average, no more than normal profits. Portfolio equilibrium between industries implies that in high-risk industries average profitability will be higher than in low-risk industries. This means that the reduction of risk through a price-fixing agreement will increase the threat of entry and force existing firms to reduce their profits by reducing the average price.

When the product is storable, price fluctuations can be damped by the operation of buffer stocks. It is, however, a moot point whether the operation of buffer stocks should be the subject of a collusive agreement, and to what extent it is advantageous to hold the stocks in a central store, or to intervene collectively in a forward market – if one exists. A full discussion of these issues is beyond the scope of this chapter.

It is likely that the advantages of a price-fixing agreement will first become apparent to sellers when they are confronted with a fall in demand, and a consequent 'excess capacity' problem. The immediate effect of a price-fixing agreement may be merely to restore short-run price to its long-run normal level. Entry is unlikely to be stimulated by this effect alone, since all that has happened is that the 'incentive to exit' has been removed. It is only when the long-run significance of the ability to keep price at, or above, this new level is appreciated that entry is likely to be stimulated, and the minimum price must be allowed to fall.

It is important to appreciate that industries with steeply rising *short-run* marginal costs are not necessarily industries with increasing *long-run* marginal costs. Indeed the reverse is probably true: sharply increasing short-run marginal costs are associated with decreasing long-run marginal costs. This is because capital-intensive industries using highly specific durable equipment are likely to have very precise capacity limits and hence steeply rising short-run marginal costs. At the same time the design features embodied in the equipment are liable to generate long-run economies of scale. Boilers, warehouses and goods vehicles, for example, yield outputs of services in proportion to their cubic capacity but have construction costs and running costs that are related, to some extent at least, to their surface area; thus average costs diminish as the design is altered to increase the rated capacity.

Capital-intensity also provides a long-run dimension to the discussion of the volatility of demand. Uncertainty about demand is an endemic problem in capital-intensive industries because investments in durable goods must be made using estimates of demand in the distant future. This long-run problem is superimposed upon the short-run problem of the impact of volatile demand on rigid capacity constraints. When economies of scale are present too, the investment decisions of oligopolistic firms will be strongly interdependent since each firm will be contemplating a 'lumpy' investment which will represent a significant addition to industry capacity. Successful investment planning may therefore call for collusion at the industry level. The tactical problems of negotiating and enforcing investment agreements are very complex. In certain cases, access to an advanced proprietary technology may allow one firm to dictate terms to the others through licensing agreements. Where there is no natural leader in the industry, however, it may be possible to achieve effective collusion in investment planning only through full financial consolidation of the oligopolistic firms.

It has already been shown in Section 4.5 that the MNE is likely to be more effective than the international cartel in rationalising production when there are economies of scale. It has also been shown in Section 4.7 that the MNE has a strong advantage over the international cartel in the enforcement of price agreements. Synthesising these lines of argument suggests that the advantages of the MNE over the international cartel are greatest in capital-intensive industries servicing a volatile and inelastic demand through the utilisation of rigidly-determined capacity which exhibits increasing returns to scale.

4.10 THE NUMBER OF PLANTS

This section relaxes assumption (d) by allowing the number of plants in the industry to vary. In the long-run, the number of plants is determined by the relation between the minimum efficient scale (m.e.s.) and the size of the market. In process industries the m.e.s. is determined mainly by technology and is independent of location. In extractive industries, m.e.s. varies according to the size of the resource deposits, since it is normally efficient to have just one plant to mine each deposit. If deposits are geographically concentrated, then the number of plants in the industry will normally be small.

The number of plants affects the cost of organising a cartel in several ways. First, it affects the costs of negotiating the terms on which the cartel is formed. In this respect, two counteracting effects may be discerned. The more producers there are, the lower is their individual bargaining power, since the smaller is the output of any one producer relative to the other producers as a group. This makes it less likely that any producer will hold out against the others for better terms. On the other hand, the more producers there are, the more likely there is to be a divergence of opinion amongst them about the size of the potential gains from the cartel and the best means of appropriating them (Fog, 1956). Negotiations are likely to be protracted until these expectations have converged.

Sherman (1972) points out that in a market of given size, an increase in the number of producers affects both the rewards of compliance and the effectiveness of monitoring. As the number of producers increases, the potential gains from secret price-cutting and unanticipated quality changes also increase, since each producer has a smaller initial share of the market. The problem of detecting the identity of the secret price-cutter increases too, because there is a larger number of suspects to be investigated.

The potential gains from replacing a cartel by an MNE increase with the number of plants because the MNE can avoid secret price-cutting and unanticipated quality change. The MNE, however, involves far more detailed management than does the international cartel, so that diseconomies of bureaucracy are likely to set in sooner. It seems probable, therefore, that the cost of organisation increase rapidly beyond a certain point both for the cartel and for the MNE.

This suggests that an efficient collusive strategy may involve the partial agglomeration of plants into a few integrated firms, with cartel arrangements being implemented between the firms. This avoids the very high costs of either bringing all the plants into a single cartel or merging them all into a single firm. In this case, the view that cartels and MNEs are pure alternatives is no longer tenable: they become, in fact, complementary methods of exploiting monopoly power at the industry level.

4.11 INNOVATION AND BARRIERS TO ENTRY

This section relaxes assumption (c) by allowing for innovation to occur. Innovation may involve the development of a new product or new technology, the discovery of new inputs or new low-cost locations of production, and so on. Because innovation disturbs the structure of production, it increases the costs of collusion, whether collusion is effected through a cartel or an MNE.

The extent to which innovation undermines collusion depends upon whether the innovation originates inside or outside the industry. Innovations that originate with established firms are likely to be easier to accommodate than innovations that originate with new entrants to the industry. There are two reasons for this. The first is that when innovations originate with established firms, the parties to any new collusive agreement will be the same as the parties to the original agreement. The second is that established firms are more likely to make only minor innovations and new entrants are more likely to make major ones. This is because where marginal advances are concerned, such as the refinement of a conventional technology, the operating experience accumulated by established firms gives them an advantage over outsiders. Where radical innovations are concerned, however, the experience of established firms may be of little value, and their traditions and customs may prove a positive hindrance to change. For example, if a new technology reverses the relative status of different professional groups within the management team then the dominant group may oppose its introduction. Those who wish to innovate may have to leave to start their own firms or join rival firms who wish to diversify into the industry. Alternatively, the gap may be filled by people who initially have no connection at all with the industry.

Because innovation complicates the administration of collusion, cartel agreements may have written into them clauses designed to discourage, or even outlaw, new technologies and products. For similar reasons, the managers of multinational monopolies may adopt a very conservative attitude toward change. In addition, cartel members may agree to collude in erecting barriers against outside innovators who wish to enter the industry. They may, for example, threaten a co-operative effort to spoil the entrant's local market. Threats of this kind capitalise on the established firms' reputation in financial markets. They force the entrant to adopt lower gearing and to carry greater liquidity than would otherwise be necessary (Shubik, 1959); the estab-lished firms are less affected because it is easier for them to borrow funds to finance the losses incurred during economic warfare in the industry.

This strategy must be qualified, however, when the entrant is a firm diversifying out of another industry. Not only is such an entrant likely to have ready access to external finance but he may also have access to internal sources of finance through cross-subsidisation from other activities. The most effective threat against such an entrant is likely to be a threat that the established firms will diversify into his industries if he diversifies into theirs (Utton, 1979).

The existence of a cartel may affect the method of entry chosen by an outside firm. The simplest method of entry into a collusive industry is by the takeover of an established firm. This minimises administrative disruption since the entrant is effectively 'buying out' the production quota allocated to the firm that has been taken over. Takeover is particularly suitable if the entrant has unpatented know-how which it would otherwise be difficult to transfer to other firms. If the know-how is patentable then a licensing agreement may provide a suitable alternative arrangement (see Chapter 3).

The main alternative to takeover is that the entrant invests in new plant and gradually expands by driving some of the established firms out of business. This method of entry is most likely when new know-how has to be embodied in new capital equipment or when new working practices are needed and workers in established plants are too conservative to adjust to them.

Entry by new investment is potentially quite disruptive. It is by no means certain that the entrant would wish to join the existing cartel even if he were invited to do so. However, the logic of the situation – a few firms operating behind an entry barrier – may eventually encourage the entrant to join in. The main issue will be the *terms* on which the entrant joins. Since the entrant is likely to be one of the 'fittest' firms in the industry, and the firms it has driven out are likely to have been amongst the weakest, the entrant may not be content with the terms enjoyed by the firms it replaces. This may lead to a period of intense, rivalry before the cartel agreement is renegotiated.

4.12 THE IMPACT OF GOVERNMENT POLICY

This section relaxes assumption (b) by allowing for government intervention in economic activity. Four types of intervention are considered. The first is intervention designed to protect strategic industries by ensuring that in time of war essential resources remain under domestic control. This policy rules out dominant foreign ownership of manufacturing industries such as armaments and aircraft engineering, and service industries such as shipping.

The second type of intervention is opportunistic expropriation of foreign-owned assets. The main considerations here are (i) political – were the assets acquired by war and conquest, or other 'unethical' means? (ii) custodial – how easy is it to appropriate the assets? and (iii) economic – how probable is retaliation? On all these counts, the easiest targets for expropriation are mineral deposits. Foreign ownership of minerals is often the legacy of imperial freebooting, and may therefore be objectionable on political grounds; the deposits tend to be concentrated and immobile, and so are easy to appropriate and defend; and as the output is relatively homogeneous it is easy to market and immune to boycott by established customers. Minerals often have relatively inelastic demands and so afford large rewards to monopolisation. The threat of expropriation discourages monopolisation through an MNE, except where there are very substantial economies of vertical integration between mining and processing. On the whole, the mineral industries are therefore particularly suitable for the operations of international cartels.

The third type of intervention is government prohibition of collusion. This normally rules out explicit collusion through either a formal cartel or an integrated firm. It may unintentionally stimulate tacit collusion though, since the implementation of a policy to promote competition is often tempered by a respect for business secrecy. Prohibitions on collusion therefore promote tacit collusion at the expense of both international cartels and the MNE. There is one notable exception to this rule: in inter-war Germany, collusion was favoured but secrecy discouraged, so that formal bureaucratic arrangements became very popular. Under these exceptional circumstances, government intervention favoured the growth of international cartels and MNEs.

The fourth type of intervention is government regulation of output in the interests of greater efficiency in distribution and greater security of incomes for producers. This type of intervention encourages cartelisation under the auspices of governments and international agencies, and correspondingly discourages collusion effected through MNEs.

It is apparent that some types of government intervention discourage collusion, while others actively promote it. In some cases tacit collusion is favoured at the expense of explicit collusion, while in others the reverse applies. By and large though, when explicit collusion is favoured, government intervention discourages the formation of MNEs and encourages international cartels instead.

4.13 BILATERAL OLIGOPOLY AND OLIGOPSONY

This section relaxes assumption (a) that the buyers of the outputs and the sellers of the inputs are atomistic. It has been shown in Section 4.10 that increasing the number of traders increases the costs of collusion, whatever form the collusion takes. When buyers are atomistic, it is therefore natural to suppose that they will not collude with each other. Where a few sellers confront atomistic buyers it will be only the sellers that collude. When there are only a few buyers too, collusion between buyers becomes much easier, and if the sellers are already known to be colluding, the buyers will be encouraged to collude for purely defensive reasons. This leads to the emergence of bilateral bargaining between two collusive institutions. The bargaining may involve either two MNEs, two cartels, or an MNE and a cartel, depending upon the relative costs of alternative collusive arrangements on the two sides of the market.

The number of buyers also affects the viability of a seller negotiating a special discount with a particular buyer. Because of the fixed costs of haggling, negotiating special discounts is unlikely to be economic when there are many buyers (Stigler, 1964). When a few buyers purchase a large amount each, however, negotiations over price may become economic. The determination of price through individual bargaining is equivalent to the seller discriminating between buyers on the basis of information the buyer discloses during the bargaining process.

If the discount terms are made public then if they are favourable to the buyer they are liable to be cited by other buyers with whom the seller is negotiating; there is therefore a good reason for the seller to insist that the negotiation process remains confidential. This in turn poses problems for collusion between sellers, since if the outcome of negotiations is to be kept secret then checking on secret price-cutting becomes difficult too. It is necessary to arrange that the price is disclosed to the sellers, but not to the other buyers as well.

The organisation of a secret discount between a particular buyer and seller is equivalent to a realignment of collusion, in which the seller colludes with a buyer rather than with other sellers. The collusive arrangement may develop into a long-term one. It may be an informal arrangement, based upon 'goodwill' built up by repeated trades between the same parties. On the other hand, it may be a formal relation involving a long-term contract. The limiting case of this formal arrangement is where the seller integrates forward into the buyer's activity, through merger or other means.

Finally, it must be recognised that oligopoly in an output market implies a degree of oligopsony in input markets, wherever the supply of an input to the industry is less than perfectly elastic. It follows that collusion between oligopolists may lead not only to the exercise of monopoly power in the output market but also to the exercise of monopsony power in input markets. Similar reasoning suggests that collusion between oligopsonists may stimulate either collusion between suppliers in the input markets or backward integration by the oligopsonists into the supply of inputs. Unionisation of the labour force exemplifies the former effect: backward integration by manufacturers into raw materials supply exemplifies the latter effect.

A full analysis of these possibilities is beyond the scope of this chapter. The discussion is sufficient to demonstrate, nevertheless, that when collusion is analysed as a general concept, it embraces goodwill agreements as well as cartel agreements and includes vertical as well as horizontal integration. It also embraces factor markets as well as product markets. When examined in this light, it can be seen that collusion is a perfectly natural activity. From an analytical point of view, the appropriate question is not 'Why do people collude?' but 'Why do people collude only with certain other people and not with others?'

The answer, in essence, is two-fold. First, the administrative problems of collusion become acute as the number of parties involved increases. These problems can be minimised by forming a hierarchy of collusion in which individual parties join groups and the groups then join higher-level groups, and so on. This hierarchical structure only reduces the magnitude of the large numbers problem, however; it does not resolve it.

The second part of the answer is that collusion is particularly difficult to organise between certain pairs of firms or individuals because of a lack of trust between them, stemming from social, cultural and legal barriers.

Collusive arrangements, it therefore appears, are not exceptional arrangements doomed to failure in the long run, as the conventional wisdom of liberal economic thought suggests. Collusive agreements are perfectly normal and may persist in the long run, particularly where small numbers of parties are involved and there are close social ties between them.

4.14 THE MAJOR HYPOTHESES

This section summarises the results derived in Sections 4.4–4.13. Six main issues are identified:

(1) Under what conditions is collusion most likely to occur?
(2) What are the conditions that favour a cartel rather than a multi-plant firm?
(3) When a cartel is the preferred arrangement, how will the organisation of the cartel reflect the characteristics of the industry concerned?
(4) When a multiplant firm is the preferred arrangement, is it most likely to be formed by merger, by takeover, or by the internal expansion of a particular firm?
(5) What is the effect of the international dimension? Will international cartels be favoured even though domestic cartels are not, and will MNEs be favoured even though domestic multiplant firms are not?
(6) In the light of (1)–(5) to what extent are MNEs and international cartels substitutes, and to what extent are they complements?

The first issue has been extensively discussed in the cartel literature and the present chapter confirms many of the earlier results. Collusion between sellers is most likely when demand for the product is inelastic, buyers are atomistic, and sellers are few. Sellers will be few when the m.e.s. of plant is high relative to the size of the market. This is the case in manufacturing industries characterised by economies of scale and in mining industries where deposits are geographically concentrated. It is also likely where the market for the product is small. Collusion is least likely in industries where products are varied, technology and management is progressive and entry from outside is likely. All these factors increase the costs of negotiating, monitoring and policing a collusive agreement. Anti-trust policy also discourages collusion.

Tentative support for these results is provided by Asch and Seneca (1975), who examined a sample of 101 large US manufacturers for the period 1958–67; their sample consisted of fifty-one firms found by US courts to have colluded, and a control group of fifty randomly selected non-collusive firms. Asch and Seneca examined industrial structure and firm characteristics as determinants of the propensity to collude. They found significant effects caused by industrial concentration, advertising intensity (a possible surrogate for product heterogeneity) barriers to entry, growth of the market, size of firm and firm profitability. The interdependencies between these variables were complex, however, and interpretation of the results was further complicated by an inability to distinguish between collusive firms and firms that were prone to prosecution by the authorities. On the whole, though, the results confirm that the variables identified by the theory do indeed influence collusive behaviour.

The analysis in Section 4.9 shows how collusion can reduce risks in industries characterised by volatile demand, rigid capacity limits and long-run economies of scale. These characteristics apply most particularly to transport industries, and especially to long-distance freight shipping. In practice, the rail, air and shipping industries are almost universally regulated by either statutory bodies or a private 'conference system'. Furthermore, these institutions have shown a remarkable ability to persist over time. The persistence of collusion in the transport sector may be regarded as one of the more striking confirmations of the theory.

The remaining issues are most easily discussed with reference to Table 4.2. The conditions which favour collusion by cartel rather than by multiplant firm include product homogeneity, the absence of economies of scale, low capital-intensity, static technology, a general absence of innovation and a high risk of expropriation of foreign assets. Conversely, the conditions which favour the multiplant firm are product heterogeneity, economies of scale, high capital-intensity, dynamic technology, general innovativeness and a low risk of expropriation of foreign assets.

Support for these hypotheses may be found in the empirical literature on the MNE (see Chapter 1 of this book, and Caves, 1982) Numerous studies confirm that within manufacturing industry, multi national organisation is most prevalent in industries with high advertis

TABLE 4.2 *The role of industry characteristics in the organisation of collusion*

Industry characteristics	Favoured arrangement
Number of product varieties	
low	Production quotas or sales syndicate
high	
with economies of scope	Standardisation of product range, with quota or syndicate system for the entire range
with diseconomies of scope	Tied customers, or full integration
Production technology	
decreasing returns to scale	Sales syndicate
constant returns to scale	Production quotas
increasing returns to scale	Full integration
Obstacles to trade	
low	Production quotas or sales syndicate
high	
caused by high transport costs	Local sales monopolies (closed markets)
caused by high tariff payments	Full integration (with transfer pricing)
Stability of demand	
stable	—
volatile	
with rigid capacity limits	Minimum price-fixing
with rigid capacity limits, high capital-intensity and economies of scale	Full integration
Innovativeness	
static	Cartel arrangement
dynamic	
based on patents	Licensing arrangement
based on secrets	
disembodied	Full integration by takeover
embodied in plant or culture	Full integration by internal expansion
Strategic importance of product	
low	Full integration
high	Cartel arrangement
Expropriability risk for physical assets	
low	Full integration
high	Cartel arrangement
Government industrial policy	
sympathetic to secrecy but opposed to collusion	Covert price-fixing with covert production quotas
opposed to secrecy but sympathetic to collusion	Formal cartel arrangement or full integration
in favour of raising incomes of independent producers	Government marketing board

ing expenditure, economies of scale, high capital-intensity, and high levels of R & D expenditure. If advertising expenditure is regarded as a surrogate for product heterogeneity and brand innovation, and R & D expenditure as a surrogate for technological progressiveness, then these results are in full accord with the theory.

Of all these factors, the innovativeness of the industry is probably the most important. It is this aspect of MNE behaviour which has attracted most attention in the post-war period. Conversely, it was lack of innovativeness that attracted the attention of the critics of cartels in the inter-war period.

> Believers in a dynamic competitive economy cannot fail to see in the entire cartel philosophy a denial of the ideals of growth and expansion. Cartelists are obsessed by stability: they are concerned with 'partitioning a livelihood', ignoring the possibility of expanding old markets and developing new through a vigorous policy of innovation, price reduction and competitive elimination of high-cost elements. Even when the restrictive effects of cartels are not directly discernible, the economic philosophy of cartelists is opposed to the trade expansion upon which they base their case for the legal authorization of cartels. (Whittlesey, 1946, p. 65.)

The third issue concerns the choice between alternative cartel arrangements. The number of different types of cartel arrangement is limited, in principle, only by the imaginative powers of those who devise collusive arrangements. Many different types of cartel have been devised in the past, and unsuccessful experiments are often repeated because the lessons of history have not been learnt. Thus newly-formed cartels often raise prices without discouraging output, so that they quickly disintegrate under the pressure to cut price in order to reduce unsold stocks. Only a few types of cartel appear to have long-run staying power, and these are the types predicted by the theory. They represent the administratively simplest methods of co-ordinating collusive behaviour under the most commonly occurring conditions. They include the sales syndicate, the production quota board, and the agreement which divides the market into monopolistic areas.

The theory indicates that the sales syndicate is the natural form of cartel when transport costs are low, there are few varieties of product and there are many producers of each variety. The sales syndicate is also appropriate when production takes place under increasing marginal costs.

The production quota board, like the sales syndicate, performs best when there are few varieties of product. However, it is entirely successful only when all producers have the same level of constant marginal cost.

Obstacles to trade, such as transport costs and tariffs, favour a geographical division of the market. On the other hand, the existence of many product varieties with diseconomies of scope in production favours a division of the market by buyers.

There exist both simpler and more sophisticated types of cartel, but these are efficient only in very special circumstances. A simple price-fixing agreement, for example, may solve the problem of price instability caused by volatile demand and rigid capacity constraints, but as soon as the arrangement is used to increase long-run profitability it is liable to break down.

Sophisticated cartel arrangements may be used to control the proliferation of product varieties and to rationalise production under increasing returns to scale. However, sophisticated incentives are normally administered most effectively within a multiplant firm and it is only when other factors deter multiplant operation that such cartel arrangements are likely to prevail. They are most likely to occur in strategically important industries where there is product differentiation and economies of scale, and the risk of expropriation of foreign assets is high.

The fourth issue is concerned with the formation of the multiplant firm. Merger is the most likely method when no firm has a technical or marketing advantage over the others and when the managers of the firms share a common perception of the gains from collusion. Takeover is most likely when one of the firms has skills it wishes to transfer to the others and there are obstacles to licensing these skills. It is also likely when the managements of other firms resist a merger because they are opposed to change, favour independence, or over-value their firm. In this case the firm that favours collusion may go 'over the heads' of a recalcitrant management and approach the shareholders directly.

The formation of a multiplant firm through merger or takeover does not involve any increase in industry capacity. Internal growth of a leading firm, by contrast, is liable to increase industry capacity in the short-run, until the less efficient producers have been driven out of the industry. Internal growth is therefore most likely when one of the firms enjoys an advantage which has to be embodied in new plant and equipment or new working practices. The new capacity is qualitatively different from the old; there is, therefore, little point in the expanding firm taking over other existing firms.

It was noted in Section 4.2 that the first wave of consolidations in the US, which followed the end of the civil war, involved several important mergers between members of cartels. A later wave of consolidation around the turn of the century involved many takeovers instigated by a few key individuals; these individuals were company-promoters who enjoyed the confidence of the New York capital market. Mergers and takeovers accounted for many of the inter-war consolidations in Europe. After World War Two however, the internal expansion of firms in new high-technology industries became a major factor in the growth of the multiplant firm. This historical transition from merger and takeover to internal growth may be interpreted as reflecting the increasing importance of firm-specific skills in the growth of the large firm – in particular skills which are difficult to license and which have to be embodied in new plant and new working practices. One example of such skills is the ability to design differentiated products with mass market appeal (Caves, 1971). Product differentiation combines marketing know-how with the technology of the automatic production line and sophisticated quality control. The increasing importance of skills in product differentiation may be one reason for the shift towards internal expansion in the process of formation of the multiplant firm.

The fifth issue concerns the international dimension. International collusion involves greater obstacles to trade and higher costs of communication than does domestic collusion and the risks of expropriation are greater, too. Because obstacles to trade are greater, the advantages of basing a cartel upon a sales syndicate are reduced, while the advantages of a simple geographical division of the market are increased. This suggests that international cartels will typically have different arrangements from domestic cartels: geographical division will predominate internationally, and the sales syndicate domestically. Production quota boards may occur in either case.

The increased costs of communication and the greater risk of expropriation suggest that multiplant operation is less efficient internationally than it is domestically. As a result, global collusion may be effected in two stages, with an international cartel linking domestic multiplant firms. This arrangement is also efficient from the point of view of the 'number problem' discussed in Section 4.10, since it involves a hierarchy of small-number groups instead of a single very large group.

This pattern of domestic and international collusion was very apparent in the inter-war period, when many international cartels partitioned global markets between domestic multiplant firms. What has to be explained is why this pattern became obscured in the post-war period. The answer seems to lie in five main factors: first, the emergence of new skills which were best exploited by the fully integrated firm, as described above; second, the reduction in the costs of managing at a distance made possible by cheaper telecommunications and air flights; third, lower transport costs (because of containerisation, etc.) and lower tariff levels, which facilitated the international division of labour and made the geographical partitioning of markets obsolete; fourth, improvements in accounting practices which made it possible to avoid taxation through transfer-pricing on international transactions; and finally, the consolidation of US hegemony, which brought greater political stability to Western Europe and reduced the risks of the expropriation of foreign assets.

Because of these five factors, the costs of international multiplant operation fell relatively to the costs of domestic multiplant operation, so that in some cases there was little difference between them. It seems to have been as a result of this that in many industries the international cartel was replaced by the MNE as the predominant form of international collusion. The form of domestic collusion that emerged in the US before the turn of the century, and moved its centre of gravity to Europe in the inter-war period, became the pattern for international collusion after World War Two.

Turning to the final issue, it is clear that when organising collusion in any given product market, and over any given geographical area, the MNE and the international cartel are substitutes for one another. It must be recognised, however, that the domestic multiplant monopoly and the international cartel are also complementary, in so far as they combine to generate a two-stage hierarchy of global collusion. This point may be generalised. It is possible that several multinational monopolies, each with a sphere of influence on some particular continent, could organise global collusion through an intercontinental cartel. In this case, the MNEs and the cartel would be complementary in respect of global collusion and would be substitutes only at the intra-continental level. It is apparent, therefore, that substitutability and complementarity between MNEs and international cartels is more complex than a naive interpretation of the theory would suggest.

4.14 CONCLUSIONS

The hypotheses presented in the previous section are supported by a limited amount of anecdotal evidence. Many of them have never been subjected to a formal test, however. There is a world of difference between a casual search for confirmatory examples and a systematic attempt to falsify a hypothesis. Much more empirical work therefore needs to be done on this subject.

The shortage of data is no worse than in other branches of industrial economics. There are several books which survey cartel arrangements in the inter-war period fairly thoroughly (for example, Stocking and Watkins, 1946). Information from these sources could be used, for example, to test the hypotheses about the conditions under which various types of cartel arrangement will prevail.

A study of this kind would have important implications for future policy. The current outlook for the world economy suggests that many hitherto innovative industries are becoming static or even beginning to decline. It is possible that barriers to trade will increase as countries attempt to protect domestic employment against the competitive consequences of international recession. Any return to static protectionist conditions, such as those of the 1930s, is liable to favour the growth of international cartels. The cartels will not, as before be composed chiefly of domestic firms, but of the major MNEs instead. The cartels will seek to restore profitability by raising prices; and to secure higher prices they will restrict output and reduce competition through the partitioning of international markets.

Another factor promoting the growth of international cartels is economic nationalism in developing countries. Raw materials, it has already been noted, are relatively easy to expropriate, and are precisely the kind of commodity where monopoly rents are high and collusion easy to administer. Mineral-rich developing countries have enormous incentives to collude: the major barriers seem to be cultural and political rather than economic. Any tendency towards political unification in the developing world is liable to lead to the emergence of intergovernmental cartels in extractive industries. Cartel experiments have recently been made in bananas, bauxite, cocoa, coffee and copper, to name just a few industries. The most successful experiment has been the OPEC cartel. The theory has no difficulty in explaining the persistence of this cartel. The real question is why many countries have been so slow to follow the OPEC example.

In the field of international monopoly, the pendulum has hitherto swung away from the international cartel and towards the MNE. It may now be starting to swing the other way. It is unlikely to swing the whole way back, since managing at a distance is now so much easier for the MNE than it was before. But if an increasing number of industries cease to be technologically progressive, and a 'new protectionism' emerges, then international cartels may become prominent once again. The theory already exists to predict the form that these cartels will take, but it is important to test the theory using available historical data; then, if events turn out as anticipated above, a reliable analysis will be available as a guide to policy.

5 The Optimal Timing of a Foreign Direct Investment

PETER J. BUCKLEY AND MARK CASSON

5.1 INTRODUCTION

Analyses of the optimal timing of foreign direct investment (FDI) decisions have been curiously lacking in the general literature on multinational enterprises (see Chapter 1). Although comparative static analyses exist, comparing exporting to the host country with market servicing from a production unit sited in the host country (Horst, 1971; Hirsh, 1976) the only attempt to predict the timing of the switch from exporting to foreign-based production is that of Aliber (1970) (although Vernon, 1966, gives a cost-based rationale for the switch). This chapter attempts to fill this gap in the theory of FDI. Section 5.2 outlines and criticises previous attempts to deal with the problem, Sections 5.3–5.5 present a simple model, which ignores set-up costs, and Sections 5.6 and 5.7 give a more detailed analysis including such costs. Further extensions of the theory are considered in Section 5.8 and the conclusions are summarised in Section 5.9. The problem emerges as being more complex than had previously been appreciated.

5.2 RECEIVED ANALYSIS OF THE OPTIMAL TIMING OF A FDI

Analyses which are concerned with the dynamics of the foreign expansion of the firm should be able to specify those factors which govern the timing of the initial FDI. Aliber's model covers exporting, licensing a host-country firm and FDI.

Aliber assumes that the source-country firm has a monopolistic advantage or 'patent' which it can choose to employ either in the host or source country, and either internally or externally, the latter by sale of a licence to a host-country producer. The patent is a capital asset, the income from which is measured by the decline in the cost of production from the reduction in the amounts of various factors required to produce a given output. The value of the patent is the capitalised value of this cost reduction. In a world of unified currency areas but separate customs areas, Aliber argues, the FDI decision is merely one of the economics of location, although tariffs should be included as a type of transport cost. Initially, when location costs indicate foreign-based production, licensing would be the preferred alternative, for although Aliber includes 'cost of doing business abroad' as an extra cost for a foreign investor, he assumes that the licensor would be able to extract the full rent from the licensee (cf. Casson, 1979). However, at a larger market size 'costs of doing business abroad' decline and FDI is preferred. Aliber rather fudges this issue by claiming that at a 'certain point' in the growth of the host-country market 'the inference is that the host-country firm is no longer willing to pay the scarcity rent demanded by the source-country firm' (Aliber, 1970, p. 24) that is, the capitalised value of the patent to the source-country firm is greater than its value to the host-country firm. It is to be noted that Aliber here introduces elements of the monopolistic advantages (Hymer–Kindleberger) approach, for in a footnote (Aliber, 1970, pp. 24–5) he assumes that the source-country firm can appropriate greater rent from the patent when utilised internally than it can from selling the patent on the external market *after a certain market size* (see Hymer, 1976; Kindleberger, 1969; Buckley and Casson, 1976).

We now turn to a multiple currency world. Aliber suggests that interest rates on similar assets denominated in different currencies may differ, because of the premium demanded by currency holders for bearing the uncertainty that exchange rates may be changed. Financial markets therefore apply a different capitalisation rate to the same income stream according to its currency of denomination. A source country is one with a strong currency: a source-country firm applies a higher capitalisation rate to the same income stream than does a host-country firm. Consequently, FDI becomes the preferred form of market servicing at a lower market size than in a unified currency area. The choice between licensing and FDI is determined by the balance of the 'costs of doing business abroad' (which favour licensing) and national differences in capitalisation rates.

In Aliber's scheme, the market servicing decision is dependent on (i) the relative costs of production in source and host countries, (ii) transport costs and tariffs, (iii) the 'costs of doing business abroad' – an extra cost which is relevant only to the FDI mode of market servicing, (iv) different rates of capitalisation of income streams, depending on the currency of denomination and (v) market size and market growth in the host country, which provides the main dynamic element in the theory.

5.3 A SIMPLE MODEL OF THE MARKET SERVICING DECISION

We begin by distinguishing three types of cost associated with a particular mode of market servicing (Alchian, 1959):

(a) A non-recoverable set-up cost, which is a once-for-all cost incurred as soon as the mode is adopted

(b) A recurrent fixed cost (that is, independent of the rate of output) which results from indivisibilities in the factor inputs hired in connection with the market-servicing activity (for example, the salary of the local manager);

(c) Recurrent variable cost (that is, the usual output-related costs of labour, materials, etc.).

The simplicity of the first model depends on ignoring category (a) costs which are reintroduced in Section 5.6. We assume throughout that there is no change in host-country tax policy nor in transport costs.

Let there be n modes of market servicing indexed $i = 1, 2, \ldots, n$. When costs (b) and (c) above are the only ones under consideration, we plot in Figure 5.1 the average cost curve for each mode and determine the least-cost Viner envelope (Viner, 1931). The envelope, shown as a heavy line in the figure, tells us the average cost (AC) at each output when only the efficient mode relevant to that output is used.

For outputs less than q_1, mode 1 is efficient, for $q_1 \leqslant q \leqslant q_2$, mode 2 is efficient and for $q \geqslant q_2$ mode 3 is efficient. For any given output, a profit-maximising firm will select the efficient mode.

We now introduce further assumptions to make the analysis dynamic:

(1) In the foreign (or 'host') market, the firm is faced with a limit-pricing situation, such that for a wide range of different cost conditions the profit-maximising strategy is to supply exactly the

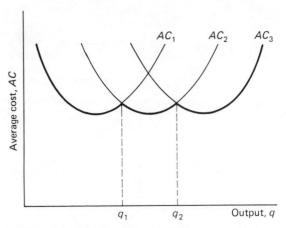

FIGURE 5.1   *Average cost by mode of market servicing*

amount demanded at the limit price. As shown in Figure 5.2, because of the discontinuity in the marginal revenue (MR) curve of the firm, the profit maximising output is q^* for any marginal cost (MC) in the range between p^* and p^{**}.

(2) The 'size' of the market, q, is the quantity demanded at the limit price, and exhibits autonomous growth over time. The pattern of growth is logistic, with size approaching a constant ('saturation') level after a certain time.

(3) The different modes of market-servicing are regarded as alternatives, so that only one mode at a time is used.

(4) For any given mode average variable cost is constant (and so equal to marginal cost, which is also constant). Superficially, this assumption rules out economies of scale in production. But if we are prepared to identify different modes according to the size or type of plant to be used, then economies of scale can be included by giving the mode 'production with large plant' higher fixed costs and lower variable costs than the mode 'production with small plant'.

(5) If all the modes are ranked in ascending order of fixed costs (type (b) above) they will be in descending order of variable costs (type (c)). This assumption is weaker than it seems. It is bound to be true if we consider only modes which could possibly be efficient, for clearly if one mode has a higher fixed cost *and* a higher variable cost than another, it would not be worth considering at any scale of output. If all such inferior modes are eliminated then condition (5) always holds.

102   *The Economic Theory of the Multinational Enterprise*

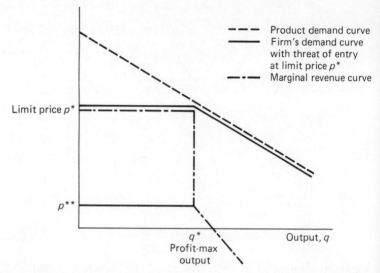

FIGURE 5.2   *Profit-maximising strategy in the foreign market with limit pricing*

Assumptions (1) and (2) enable us to map from the static cost function $c(q)$ to the 'dynamic' cost function $c(t)$, where $t \geq 0$ is the time that has elapsed since the market was entered. Assumption (3) tells us that only the cost functions for each mode need to be considered – 'linear combinations' of them can be ignored because it is possible to use only one mode at a time. Assumptions (4) and (5) tell us that the total cost function for the ith mode is

$$c_i = a_i + b_i q \tag{5.1}$$

with fixed cost $a_i > a_{i-1}$ and marginal cost $b_i < b_{i-1}$ ($i = 1, 2, \ldots, n$), where $b_1 \leq p^*$ and $b_n \geq p^{**}$.

Plotting the total cost functions $c(q)$ (quadrant 3, Figure 5.3) and determining the 'envelope' shown by the heavy line gives the outputs at which switches of mode should occur. Transferring from market growth (quadrant 2) to the time dimension indicates the *times* at which the switches will occur (quadrant 1). If the market size is limited then some switches may *never* occur, as shown by the absence of a switch to mode 3 in quadrant 1.

Assumptions (4) and (5) imply that 'reswitching' can occur only if the market, having expanded, were then to begin to contract.

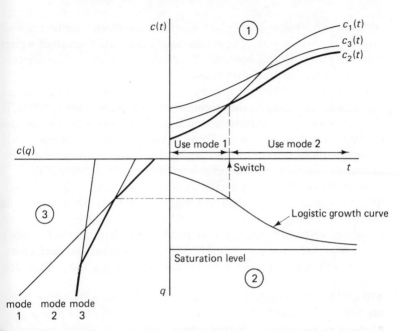

FIGURE 5.3   *A dynamic analysis of foreign market servicing with switches of mode*

5.4 AN APPLICATION OF THE SIMPLE MODEL

Consider three possible modes of market servicing: exporting, licensing and FDI.

When exporting, the firm's fixed production cost is negligible so long as the exports are produced by increasing the utilisation of existing plant in the source country. On the other hand some fixed costs will be incurred in establishing a distribution network in the host country. Variable costs are almost certain to be high under exporting, since they include not only variable production costs but international transport costs and tariff payments as well.

To analyse licensing, we assume that the firm's monopolistic advantage is auctioned competitively to indigenous producers. Assuming that the two highest bidders have identical cost structures, the highest bid will value the licence at the excess of the potential revenue over the minimum indigenous cost (Casson, 1979).

However the licensor must also take account of the transactions costs borne by him, in particular the costs of monitoring the licence and insuring against default. These transaction costs are fixed costs which must be added to the licensee's fixed costs to arrive at an implicit measure of the licensor's fixed cost.

The firm most likely to become a licensee is one which possesses assets complementary to the monopolistic advantage – for instance, it already possesses a distribution and retail network suitable for the product offered under licence. Thus the typical licensee will exploit his licence partly by hiring new fixed assets (for production) and partly by increasing the utilisation of existing fixed assets (in distribution).

When the fixed costs of policing the licence are added to the licensee's fixed production costs, then the total fixed costs associated with licensing are likely to exceed the fixed costs of exporting (which are associated with the exporter's investment in distribution). On the other hand, because licensing avoids international transport and tariff costs, the variable costs are likely to be correspondingly lower than for exporting.

With FDI, fixed costs are likely to be higher than for licensing, since the investor normally has to hire new production equipment and establish an independent distribution system as well. Similar reasoning suggests that the variable costs of FDI are likely to be lower than for licensing.

Our analysis therefore suggests that exporting, licensing and FDI are in ascending order of fixed costs and descending order of variable costs. This is, of course, not an invariable rule. It is most likely to apply when the firm is investing abroad for the first time. Other possibilities are considered in Section 5.8.

Suppose that each mode of servicing is efficient over some range of output. In a market subject to autonomous growth the theory then predicts that the firm will begin by exporting, switch to licensing as market size increases, and then finally switch to FDI. By following such a policy the firm is in effect ensuring that existing fixed assets, wherever located, are utilised fully before new fixed assets are installed (cf Robinson, 1931; Penrose, 1959).

Suppose now that one or other of the modes is inefficient. For example, licensing may have a significantly higher fixed cost than exporting, and a significantly higher variable cost than FDI (see Figure 5.4). In this case, as the market grows, it may be efficient to switch directly from exporting to FDI and forego the use of licensing altogether. Another reason why the licensing stage may be omitted is discussed later.

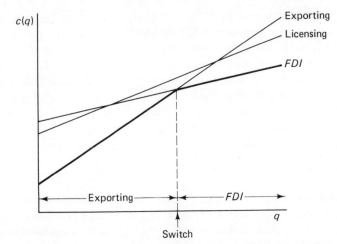

FIGURE 5.4 *The choice between exporting, licensing and foreign direct investment*

It is quite possible that the market will become saturated before all of the modes have been used. If the potential size of the market is small then the firm may export indefinitely. If the potential market is of only moderate size, the firm may switch from exporting to licensing, but not from licensing to FDI.

Alternatively, if the market is large to begin with, the firm may omit the exporting stage and begin with licensing; if the market is very large it may even commence servicing with FDI.

Thus even in this simple model, with its very restrictive assumptions, there are many possible ways in which market-servicing strategy can evolve, depending upon the cost structures of alternative modes, and the pattern of market growth. The only firm prediction that can be made is that in an expanding market where two or more different modes of servicing are used, FDI will never precede licensing, licensing will never precede exporting, and FDI will never precede exporting.

5.5 EXTENSIONS OF THE SIMPLE MODEL

Possible extensions of the model are to include discounting over time, and dynamic cost reductions arising from familiarisation with the market.

Suppose that there is an efficient integrated capital market embracing both source and host economies in which the instantaneous cost of capital is $r(t) \geqslant 0$ at time t (writing r as a function of t enables us to consider non-trivial yield curves – see Samuelson, 1937). Let $p_i(t)$ be a multiplicative factor indicating how costs of the ith mode reduce with the length of time the firm has been servicing the host market ($p_i(0) = 1$, $dp_i/dt \leqslant 0$). We may then define the adjusted cost $c^*_i(t)$ of servicing the market by mode i at time t to be the discounted value of cost, adjusted for familiarisation, that is:

$$c^*_i(t) = p_i(t)c_i(t)\exp[-\int_0^t r(T)dT] \tag{5.2}$$

It is readily established that a wealth-maximising firm will select the mode with the lowest adjusted cost at any given time. It follows that the analysis of switching based on adjusted cost functions parallels exactly the analysis of Section 5.3. The only difference is that the time-dependence of cost is more complex; the typical form of an adjusted cost function is illustrated by the graph BCF in Figure 5.5.

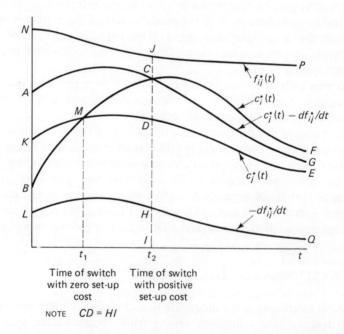

FIGURE 5.5   *Switches of mode of market servicing, with positive set-up costs*

The introduction of discounting does not affect switching behaviour so long as all modes have the same cost of capital. In this case the timing of switching is invariant with respect to the yield curve, because all the cost functions are modified in exactly the same way and so the marginal conditions for a switch are unchanged. The timing of switching is exactly the same as that predicted by the analysis of unadjusted cost functions. A similar result applies if all modes experience the same cost reductions through familiarisation.

The analysis given depends crucially on two assumptions. The first is that familiarisation applies to the market in general, and not to each specific mode. If costs reduce according to the time that the market has been serviced by a particular mode then φ_i becomes a function of t_i, the time elapsing since the ith mode was adopted. In this case the economics of switching becomes extremely complex. In practice, however, this case does not give too much cause for concern because the empirical evidence suggests that it is familiarisation with the market, rather than the mode of servicing it, which is of prime importance in reducing 'the costs of doing business abroad' (see Newbould *et al.*, 1978; Johanson and Vahlne, 1977; Robock, Simmonds and Zwick, 1977, who refer to the process as 'creeping incrementalism').

The second crucial assumption is that there are no set-up costs. If this assumption is relaxed then the yield curve can exert a significant influence on the choice of mode, and on the times at which switches are made. This case is examined in the following section.

5.6 OPTIMAL MARKET-SERVICING WITH SET-UP COSTS

Suppose that switching at time t from mode i to a mode $j > i$ with lower recurrent variable costs incurs a non-recoverable set-up cost $f_{ij}(t)$. The existence of set-up costs influences switching in two ways; it almost invariably induces postponement of a switch, and it may also result in a switch that would have been made never being made at all – in other words it may result in a switch being postponed indefinitely.

When set-up costs are present, a switch between modes represents an investment made by the firm. The 'initial outlay' is the set-up cost, while the subsequent 'net cash flow' is represented by the stream of savings due to the adoption of a mode with lower recurrent costs.

Investment decisions are often analysed as though they involved a once-for-all decision whether or not to invest. It is well known that with an efficient capital market the appropriate criterion for this decision is to invest if the net present value (*NPV*) is positive (Levy and Sarnat, 1978). But this represents an essentially static analysis of a fundamentally dynamic problem. In many contexts, including the present one, the issue is not so much whether the investment should be undertaken at all, but rather *when* it should be undertaken. It may be profitable to undertake it today, but even more profitable to undertake it tomorrow. In this case the appropriate criterion is to time the investment to maximise its *NPV*. Only in very special cases is this equivalent to undertaking the investment as soon as the *NPV* becomes positive.

It is readily established that the *NPV* at time zero of a switch undertaken at time $t \geqslant 0$ is

$$NPV(t) = C^*_i(t) - C^*_j(t) - f^*_{ij}(t) \tag{5.3}$$

where

$$C^*_i(t) = \int_t^\infty c^*_i(T)dT, \tag{5.4a}$$

$$C^*_j(t) = \int_t^\infty c^*_j(T)dT, \tag{5.4b}$$

$$f^*_{ij}(t) = \exp[-\int_0^t r(T)dT]f_{ij}(t) \tag{5.4c}$$

Among the necessary conditions for a maximum of *NPV*, there are two of particular relevance in the present context.

The first is the marginal condition

$$c^*_i(t) - c^*_j(t) = -df^*_{ij}/dt \tag{5.5}$$

Eliminating the factor $\exp[\int_0^t r(T)dt]$ which is common to both sides of (5.5) gives

$$\varphi_i(t)c_i(t) - \varphi_j(t)c_j(t) = r(t)f_{ij}(t) - df_{ij}/dt \tag{5.6}$$

The marginal condition (5.6) states that the additional recurrent cost incurred by failing to switch to the new mode of servicing equals the saving due to a marginal postponement of the set-up costs; this saving has two components: the avoidance of interest charges on the capital outlay and the capital gain due to the net reduction over time in the outlay required.

The application of this marginal condition to the timing of a switch is illustrated graphically in Figure 5.5. The net saving in recurrent cost at any time is measured by the difference between the heights of the graphs *BCF* and *KDE*. The saving of interest and capital costs by postponing the switch is measured by the height of the graph *LHQ*. The optimal time of the switch is t_2; it is at this point that the saving of recurrent costs, measured by the distance *CD*, is equal to the saving of interest and capital costs, measured by *HI*. Geometrically, the easiest way to determine t_2 is to add the graph *LHQ* to the graph *KDE* and determine the point of intersection *C* of the resultant graph *ACG* with the graph *BCF*; the ordinate of *C* is t_2.

In the absence of set-up costs the optimal timing of the switch would have been t_1, corresponding to the intersection *M* of the graph *KDE* and the graph *BCF*. It can be seen that the effect of set-up costs is to postpone the switch from t_1 to t_2. That set-up costs always postpone the switch can be proved from the second order conditions for a maximum of *NPV*.

Another necessary condition for a maximum of *NPV* is that an indefinite postponement of the switch is uneconomic. Any switch which is postponed indefinitely has $NPV = 0$. Thus any switch which is undertaken should also satisfy the static criterion that at the optimal time of switch the NPV is positive, that is:

$$C^*_i(t) - C^*_j(t) > f^*_{ij}(t) \tag{5.7}$$

This condition is also illustrated in Figure 5.5. The present value of the total saving in recurrent costs after the switch (the left-hand side of the inequality (5.7)) is measured by the area CDEF. The present value of the set-up costs (the right hand side of the inequality (5.7)) is measured by the height of the graph *NJP*, which is *IJ* at time t_2. The condition indicates that the switch is undertaken if the area *CDEF* exceeds the height *IJ*.

Both the static and dynamic conditions must normally be satisfied for the timing of the switch to be efficient. If the firm uses only the static condition then there will be a tendency for it to switch *as soon as* the *NPV* of the switch becomes positive. In this case it will normally invest too early. For at the optimal time of the switch the *NPV* may be quite high. As the time of the switch is brought forward the *NPV* will be reduced, but only gradually. Thus even some time before the optimum is reached the *NPV* may still be positive. Thus firms which switch using only the static criterion are liable to invest well before the optimal time.

This analysis is confined to a single switch between two specific modes. It becomes much more complex when a sequence of switches between different modes is contemplated. The problem is that the choice of the initial mode is not independent of subsequent modes to which it is planned to switch, nor of the time when it is planned to make these switches. The solution of such problems calls for techniques of dynamic programming, which are beyond the scope of this chapter.

5.7 AN APPLICATION: THE SET-UP COSTS OF TRANSFERRING TECHNOLOGY

In this section we apply the preceding analysis to the timing of the switch between exporting and FDI. Following Hirsh (1976) and others, we identify the set-up cost of FDI as the cost of transferring technology to the foreign subsidiary. The product cycle theory (Vernon, 1966) suggests that this cost will be related to the degree of standardisation of the product: the greater the standardisation, the lower the cost. The degree of standardisation reflects the stage the product has reached in its technical development; Hufbauer (1970) has suggested that a surrogate for this is the age of the product (see also Teece, 1977). We therefore postulate a time-dependent set-up cost which represents the dependence of the cost of technology transfer on the age of the product.

If we now invoke the marginal condition (5.6), it can be seen that there are two reasons why FDI will be deferred until after its recurrent costs are lower than those of exporting. The first is that deferring FDI delays the payment of interest on the capital tied up in the technology transfer. The second, and much more interesting, reason is that deferring FDI reduces the cost of technology transfer, by allowing the product to be transferred when it has become more standardised. Intuitively it seems that rapid standardisation ought to bring forward the date of technology transfer, but so long as the potential for further standardisation remains, transfer is liable to be postponed. This is the difference between the static and dynamic criteria outlined in the previous section.

5.8 EXTENSIONS

Three extensions of the theory are considered briefly below. They are concerned with the following possibilities:

(a) that the limit price may decline over the life-cycle of the product because of increasing competitive threats;
(b) that the firm may already have gained some familiarity with the market by producing a substitute product,
(c) that the firm has already invested abroad and so has a production and distribution infrastructure ready to receive the product.

So far it has been implicitly assumed that the limit price is constant over the life-cycle of the product. In practice, however, the limit price is liable to decrease as information about the monopolistic advantage diffuses and potential imitators appear. Eventually the advantage may be lost altogether: limit price falls to minimum average cost and the firm's market share becomes indeterminate.

Before this point is reached, however, the falling limit price shows up in the investment decision only through its tendency to increase the rate of growth of the market. Let demand for the product be denoted $q(p,t)$, where p is the price, that is, the limit price, and t represents the time-dependence of the demand curve. Taking the total derivative of q shows that the rate of growth of demand is:

$$dq/dt = \partial q/\partial t + (\partial q/\partial p)(dp/dt), \qquad (5.8)$$

where the first term on the right hand side is the growth of the market caused by the outward shift in the demand curve, and the second term is the growth because of a movement along the demand curve caused by a fall in the limit price. In so far as the increasing threat of imitation is perceived by the firm, and reflected in its pricing policy, there will be a tendency for demand to grow faster than it otherwise would. This will encourage the firm to accelerate the switch to licensing, and also to accelerate the switch from licensing to FDI.

Hitherto it has also been assumed that the firm is a single-product firm. In this case it is reasonable to suppose that prior to the creation of the monopolistic advantage the firm has no familiarity with the market. However if the firm has previously been manufacturing a close substitute for the product – perhaps a lower-quality version of it – then a reasonable degree of familiarity may have already been obtained. This may be easily incorporated into the analysis by setting $\varphi(0) < 1$. Under the assumption that familiarisation is independent of the mode of servicing this in itself has no effect on the firm's investment decision. However the fact that φ is low initially means that the scope for further familiarisation may well be small.

Finally, it is interesting to compare the decision of a firm investing abroad for the first time with the decision of a firm that has already invested abroad. If the firm is already operating in the host country, then it may well be able to produce the new product abroad by increasing the utilisation of existing assets (just as it does when exporting). In this case there is no longer any reason to suppose that the fixed costs of FDI will exceed those of exporting. However, variable costs will still be higher for the exporter than for the foreign investor: first, because the exporter incurs tariffs and transport costs, and second, because most monopolistic advantages are developed in high-income countries where labour costs are higher; since labour costs are a major component of variable costs, variable costs in the typical source-country will exceed those in the typical host-country. With FDI having no higher fixed costs, and lower variable costs than exporting, the firm is likely to invest abroad immediately, and so the exporting phase will be eliminated altogether.

This prediction is borne out well by the history of the product cycle in the post-war period. In the early years when many firms were investing abroad for the first time, exporting almost invariable preceded FDI. But as firms became increasingly multinational there was a tendency for the product cycle to shorten, and eventually for the exporting phase to be eliminated altogether. Obviously there are many factors that could explain this trend. The theory above suggests that a particular pattern will be associated with this trend, namely, that the exporting phase is shortest for products whose producers have already invested in the host-country.

5.9 CONCLUSION

This chapter has analysed the foreign market-servicing decision of firms in terms of the costs of servicing the foreign market, demand conditions in that market and host-market growth. We are able to specify the optimal timing of a switch in modes of market-servicing by reference to the above variables. Decisions on market-servicing are more complex than is sometimes assumed, particularly where time-dependent set-up costs are involved. However the model developed is of sufficient generality for it to be applied to many different special cases. It therefore affords an opportunity for unifying the treatment of different aspects of the market-servicing decision.

6 The Theory of Foreign Direct Investment

MARK CASSON

6.1 INTRODUCTION

The concept of foreign direct investment (FDI) is a rather ambiguous one. To begin with, is the foreign investor the individual whose postponement of consumption enables the investment to be financed? Or is the investor the firm whose shares are owned by the individual concerned, and which owns the real assets on his behalf? If the investor is the firm then by what rules of nationality is it established that the firm is a foreign one – in particular, is there a meaningful economic criterion for the nationality of a multinational enterprise (MNE)?

Second, is investment to be defined in terms of real or financial variables? For the individual investor a financial criterion is normally used, and for the firm a real one. But of what does real foreign investment consist? Can it be identified with imports of producer goods into the host-country, or does it also include imports of, say, management services which increase host-country human capital and transfers of proprietary technology as well? Do we need a different theory for each type of investment, or is it only the aggregate investment that is important?

Finally, what precisely is the significance of the 'directness' of investment? Direct investment is usually assumed to be important because the investor acquires outright control of the asset. However, control over assets can be obtained not only by owning them but also by hiring them – indeed an investor who owns an asset but hires it out continuously will never have day-to-day control over it. A firm may be a major producer without owning any assets (except perhaps work in progress) simply by renting land and hiring labour and producer durables. In this case the decision to 'invest' may involve a marginal decision whether to rent land or to purchase it outright. If it decides to rent, the firm is a foreign producer, but only if it decides to buy is it a foreign direct investor.

The various ambiguities are reflected in the theoretical literature. Orthodox trade theory approaches FDI through the MacDougall model (MacDougall, 1960; Kemp, 1962) the theory of finance approaches it through the Grubel theory of international portfolio diversification (Grubel, 1968; Friend and Losq, 1979; Rugman, 1979) while students of the MNE approach it through both the theory of industrial structure (Lall and Streeten, 1977), and the Coasian theory of the firm (Buckley and Casson, 1976; McManus, 1972; Magee, 1977a; Swedenborg, 1979). Each of these theories exhibits a different facet of FDI. Some emphasise the firm more than do others; some emphasise the financial aspects and others the real aspects; and some emphasise the issue of control, while others relegate it to a minor role.

It is argued later that the theory of FDI is a 'logical intersection' of three distinct theories – the theory of international capital markets, the theory of the international firm, and the theory of international trade. The theory of international capital markets focuses on the international allocation of 'waiting' and 'risk-bearing' between individuals, that is, on the ultimate sourcing of investment. The theory of the international firm is concerned with the optimum size and structure of firms in the international economy. It regards the firm as a unit of ownership and control, designed to minimise transaction costs in international markets. Trade theory focuses on the interplay of production technology and consumer tastes in determining the optimal location of each type of asset used in production. When integrated, these theories provide a comprehensive analysis of the issues which appear in discussions of FDI.

Recent developments in the theory of FDI have centred on the theory of international capital markets and the theory of the international firm. These theories are reviewed in the next two sections of the chapter. The theories are presented using highly simplified models of general equilibrium in the world economy. The justification for this is that the logical fundamentals of each theory are most apparent in a general equilibrium formulation, and the relations between the theories are exhibited most clearly when each is reduced to its essentials by radical simplification.

The remainder of the chapter considers how the two theories may be integrated with each other, and with trade theory, to explain FDI. It is shown how different authors have combined different aspects of these

theories; as a result, the relations between alternative theories of FDI
are seen in a clearer light.

6.2 FUNCTIONAL SEPARATION IN INTERNATIONAL CAPITAL MARKETS

The theory developed in this section distinguishes three economic
functions involved in the creation and exploitation of foreign assets:
funding, ownership and utilisation. Funding an asset involves postponing consumption in order that the asset can be produced. Ownership
and utilisation both involve risk-bearing. The owner holds legal title to
the asset and bears risks of a speculative nature, arising from permanent changes in the economic environment which alter the future value
of the asset. The utiliser hires the asset from the owner and bears risks
which are essentially short-term, arising from transitory changes which
affect the value productivity of the asset while it is on hire to him.

Each of these functions is discharged by individuals. In principle
each function is separable and individuals should specialise in the
function in which they have a comparative advantage. Functional
separation is effected by financial markets in which equities and
debentures are traded.

The theory also distinguishes between international capital movements which are pure consumption loans and those which involve
adjustments of the physical capital stock in the two countries. Even if
endowments of physical capital in each country are fixed (as in the case
of land and natural resources) it is still possible for one country to
finance another through a purchase of debentures. It is necessary only
that debenture claims are internationally enforceable, and that there is
at least one tradable good through which real interest payments can be
effected.

The case where the physical capital stock is adjustable embraces two
possible situations. The first is where the capital stock, though immobile, is producible and either circulates or depreciates, so that both
positive and negative net investment are possible in each country. In
this case net investment in one country may be financed by net dis-
investment in another country, without any movement of physical
capital. Replacement investment is cut back in the source-country to
provide increased consumer goods for export, and these goods are used
in the host-country to maintain consumption standards while indigenous resources are switched into capital goods production. The net

effect is a transfer of physical capital between the two countries, but through an export of consumer goods rather than capital goods.

In the second case the physical capital is mobile and capital stock adjustment is effected in the two countries by the export of physical capital from one to the other.

The theory is loosely based on Fama's model (Fama, 1976), which integrates inter-temporal consumption choice with portfolio choice between risky assets. The model is adapted here to analyse international equilibrium in a two-country world (though the restriction to two countries is inessential). The seminal work is Solnik (1974); for a review of later models of this kind see Lessard (1979).

It is assumed that there is just one kind of physical asset, which is infinitely durable, and generates a homogeneous tradable consumption good. No labour input is involved. No new production of the asset is possible (so the analysis is essentially short-run). It follows that the physical capital stock in each country is adjustable only when the real asset is mobile. It is assumed to begin with that the real asset is immobile; mobility is discussed in Section 6.3.

All individuals in the same country have identical endowments and identical preferences; furthermore, there are the same number of individuals in each country. These assumptions are somewhat more restrictive than are really necessary but they have the advantage of providing a simple intuitive basis for the model. Given these assumptions, international economic relations between the two countries may be analysed in terms of the relations between two representative individuals, one from each country.

Each country has a given initial endowment of the real asset; each unit of the asset yields a known output in the current period, and in the future an uncertain perpetual flow of output. Both current and future output will normally differ according to the location of the output. Residents of the two countries have (possibly different) perceptions of the two future output streams; these perceptions relate to their means and standard deviations, and to the correlation between them.

Each unit of the asset is owned by a separate firm, which offers both equity and debenture claims secured against it. A debenture offers a certain future real income; inflation risk, exchange risk and the risk of default are all ignored. The residual income accrues to the equity-holders. This is a very strong assumption. It would be justified if all equity-owners had unlimited liability, and had sufficient debenture income to guarantee that they could make good any losses for which they were liable. Alternatively, it would be justified if the level of debenture income were so low relative to the expected product of the asset (for example, giving a margin of at least twice the standard deviation of the product) that the probability of equity losses was negligible.

Individuals hold not only equity and debenture claims, but also claims against current output. These claims may be regarded as interest and dividend payments distributed during the current period. Each individual can either use up his claims on consumption or invest them by purchasing equities or debentures (ex-dividend, of course). Individuals cannot hold any of the three claims in negative amounts; in particular, individuals cannot increase their equity holdings by issuing their own debentures once their holdings of corporate debentures are exhausted.

The representative individual's preferences in each country are given by a well-behaved utility function defined over current consumption, expected future consumption and the standard deviation of future consumption (a 'bad'). There is a uniform and parametric price for each claim, the claim on current output being *numéraire*. Given these prices and his initial endowments, the individual's demands for equities and debentures issued in each of the two countries are determined by the maximisation of utility subject to a budget constraint. The resulting demands are functions of equity and debenture prices, initial endowments and perceptions of the uncertain equity income streams.

It is often convenient to express these demands not in terms of debenture price but in terms of the capitalisation rate. The capitalisation rate for a given debenture is the rate of discount which when applied to the income stream values the stream at its prevailing price. To a first approximation the capitalisation rate is equal to the ratio of the debenture payment to the debenture price (the equation would be exact if the income stream began in the current period rather than the next period). It should be noted that because both types of debenture offer risk-free incomes, when debentures are internationally tradable the demand for each type of debenture will be infinitely elastic whenever the capitalisation rates are equal.

In deriving the supply functions it is assumed that there is no change over time in the global stock of real assets. The actual form of the supply conditions depends upon whether or not the real asset is internationally mobile. If it is immobile then each type of equity is in completely inelastic supply. This gives a total of four market equilibrium conditions: for current output, for total debenture income and for each type of equity. However, only three of these equations are independent because of Walras Law (which is obtained by summing the budget constraints of all individuals). This gives three independent equations in three unknowns: the international capitalisation rate, and the prices of each country's equity. Under the usual conditions these equations have a unique solution.

Substituting the equilibrium values into the demand functions and comparing these demands with the initial endowments determines the international pattern of ownership and finance. Net international investments in equities and debentures are functions of the initial international endowment of claims (which in turn reflects the underlying endowments of real assets), and the perceptions of equity income streams.

6.3 IMPLICIT RENTALS AND THE MOVEMENT OF REAL ASSETS

The pattern of equity and debenture ownership described does not indicate precisely the functional specialisation between risk-bearing and finance. While the debenture-holder provides only finance, the equity-holder provides a mixture of the two. The equity-holder becomes a pure risk-bearer only at the point where his expected income is just sufficient to compensate him for the risks involved; with a perfect equity market this point is reached when the price of the equity is zero. To obtain a pure division between finance and risk-bearing it is therefore necessary to set the debenture incomes so that the equilibrium equity prices are zero.

The critical values of debenture income are the certainty equivalents of the uncertain income streams yielded by the real assets in the two locations. They represent the competitive long-term rentals that the risk-bearers would be willing to pay if they were obliged to rent the assets instead of purchasing them outright with borrowed resources. When the real asset endowments in each country are fixed the implicit rentals are essentially quasi-rents, and will normally differ between the two locations.

When the real asset is mobile it will move internationally until either the implicit rentals have been equalised or stocks of the real asset have become concentrated entirely in one location. In this case the implicit rental will normally exceed the rental that prevailed in the other location. This is a familiar neoclassical result, which is exemplified by other theories, such as that of MacDougall (see Section 6.5).

6.4 THE FORMAL MODEL OF FINANCE AND OWNERSHIP

This section presents the formal model underlying the preceding discussion, and Sections 6.5–6.8 provide a graphical illustration of some special cases of it. The main theme is taken up again in Section 6.9, where the distinction between ownership and utilisation is discussed.

Let the country in which the asset is located be indexed by $i = 1, 2$, and the country in which the individual is resident be indexed by $j = 1, 2$. Let

a_i be the current output generated by a unit of the real asset located in country i

b_i the amount of the real asset located in country i

φ_i the future real income offered by a debenture issued in country i

μ_{ij} the mean future output of an asset located in country i as perceived by a resident of country j

σ_{ij} the standard deviation of future output of an asset located in country i as perceived by a resident of country j

γ_j the correlation between the two streams of output, as perceived by residents of country j

$\xi_{ij} = \mu_{ij} - \varphi_j$ the mean of the residual income offered by an equity issued in country i as perceived by a resident of country j

w_j the number of units of current output claimed by a resident of country j

x_{ij} the number of debentures (one per asset) issued in country i and held by a resident of country j

$x_j = \Sigma_i \varphi_i x_{ij}$ the total debenture income received by a resident of country j

y_{ij} the number of units of equity issued in country i and held by a resident of country j

p_i the price of debenture issued in country i

q_i the price of equity issued in country i

$c_i = \varphi_i(1 - c_i)/p_i$ the capitalisation rate of debenture issued in country i

m_j the mean of the future consumption stream anticipated by a resident of country j

s_j the standard deviation of the future consumption stream anticipated by a resident of country j.

A bar indicates a fixed endowment, and a prefix Δ the excess of the actual amount over the initial endowment; superscripts d, s and e represent respectively, demand, supply and equilibrium value. Suppression of a subscript indicates summation over it.

The representative individual in country j maximises utility

$$u_j = u_j(w_j, m_j, s_j) \tag{6.1}$$

where from the laws of probability

$$m_j = \Sigma_i(\varphi_i x_{ij} + \xi_{ij} y_{ij}) \tag{6.2}$$

$$s_j = \{\Sigma_i \sigma^2_{ij} y^2_{ij} + 2\gamma_j \sigma_{1j} \sigma_{2j} y_{1j} y_{2j}\}^{1/2} \tag{6.3}$$

subject to the budget constraint

$$\Delta w_j + \Sigma_i(p_i \Delta x_{ij} + q_i \Delta y_{ij}) = 0 \tag{6.4}$$

Transforming from the debenture price to the capitalisation rate and imposing the restriction

$$c_i = c \qquad (i = 1,2) \tag{6.5}$$

gives the demand functions

$$
\left.
\begin{aligned}
w^d_j &= w^d_j \\
x'^d_j &= x'^d_j \\
y^d_{ij} &= y^d_{ij}
\end{aligned}
\left(
\begin{aligned}
&c, \quad q_1, q_2, \\
&\bar{w}_j, \bar{x}^!_j, \bar{y}_{1j}, \bar{y}_{2j} \\
&\xi_{1j}, \quad \xi_{2j}, \sigma_{1j}, \gamma_j
\end{aligned}
\right)
\right\} \quad (j = 1,2) \tag{6.6}
$$

Summation over j yields the aggregate demands w^d, x'^d, y^d_i as functions of f, q_i, $\bar{w}_j$, $\bar{x}_j$, $\bar{y}_{ij}$, ξ_{ij}, σ_{ij}, γ_j $(i, j = 1, 2)$.

When the real asset is immobile the supplies are

$$
\begin{aligned}
w^s &= \Sigma_i a_i \bar{b}_i \\
x'^s &= \Sigma_i \varphi_i \bar{b}_i \\
y^s_i &= \bar{b}_i
\end{aligned}
\tag{6.7}
$$

The equilibrium conditions

$$w^d = w^s, \ x'^d = x'^s, \ y^d_i = y^s_i \quad (i = 1, 2) \tag{6.8}$$

constitute four equations, any one of which can be obtained from the others by summing (6.4) over j. This leaves three independent equations to determine c^e, $q^e_i(i = 1, 2)$. Substituting the equilibrium values back into the demand functions (6.6) and comparing these demands with the initial endowments determines the pattern of international financial transactions:

$$\left.\begin{array}{l} \varDelta w_j = \varDelta w_j \\ \varDelta x'_j = \varDelta'_j \\ \varDelta y_{ij} = \varDelta y_{ij} \end{array}\right\} \bar{w}_j,\ \bar{x}'_j,\ \bar{y}_{ij},\ \xi_{ij}\sigma_{ij},\ \gamma_j \quad (i,j=1,2) \right\} \tag{6.9}$$

The implicit rentals may be determined by endogenising the debenture incomes $\varphi_i(i=1,2)$. This adds two new unknowns to the model, but at the same time the equity price condition

$$q_i = 0 \quad (i=1,2) \tag{6.10}$$

adds two new constraints. The net effect is a switch of endogeneity from q_i to φ_i. Individual asset demands are now a function of the three variables, c, $\varphi_i(i=1,2)$, and their equilibrium values are obtained as before from the equilibrium conditions for the equity and debenture markets.

In the case where the real asset is mobile the supply conditions (6.7) become instead

$$\begin{aligned} w^s &= \Sigma_i a_i b_i \\ x'^s &= \Sigma_i \varphi_i b_i \\ y^s_i &= b \end{aligned} \tag{6.11}$$

where

$$\Sigma_i b_i = b \tag{6.12}$$

There is now an additional unknown, say b_1, but assuming incomplete concentration of the asset in any one location, there is an additional restriction

$$\varphi_i = \varphi \tag{6.13}$$

This gives three indepenent equations in the three unknowns c, φ, b, which can be solved as before to determine simultaneously the international allocation of finance and risk-bearing, and the international allocation of the real asset.

6.5 INTERNATIONAL CONSUMPTION-LOANS

The properties of the model may be examined by considering a number of special cases. Setting

$$\begin{aligned} \sigma_{ij} &= y_{ij} = \bar{y}_{ij} = 0 \\ a_i &= \mu_i = \varphi_i = 1 \end{aligned} \quad (i,j=1,2) \tag{6.14}$$

gives a pure consumption-loan model of international investment. There is no uncertainty. Each asset is entirely financed by debentures, and to simplify matters units of the consumption good are normalised so that each asset generates just one unit of the consumption good; the productivity of the asset is assumed to be the same both now and in the future. There is just one type of debenture.

The allocation of finance between the two countries is illustrated in Figure 6.1. The square $QRST$ measures the global *per capita* real capital stock QR horizontally and the corresponding *per capita* global output QT vertically. Suppose that initially the residents of each country own all their own indigenous assets; then the representative resident of each country will have equal endowments of current consumption claims and debentures, reflecting the *per capita* real asset endowment of his country. This allocation is represented by the point J which lies on the diagonal QS.

The indifference map for the resident of country 1 emanates from the origin Q and the map for the resident of country 2 from the origin S. At

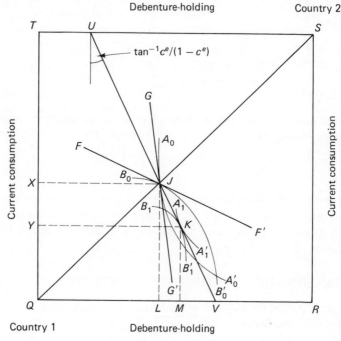

FIGURE 6.1   *International equilibrium in the pure consumption-loan model*

the initial allocation J the indifference curves A_0A_0', B_0B_0' intersect, indicating different marginal rates of substitution between present and perpetual future consumption. This implies that in an autarkic state, with no international transactions, the equilibrium capitalisation rates in the two countries will differ, as indicated by the different slopes of the tangents FF' and GG' at J.

Once markets are opened up, equilibrium is achieved at K where the indifference curve A_1A_1' is tangent to the indifference curve B_1B_1'. The equilibrium capitalisation rate is determined by the slope of the tangent UKV. The flow of finance from country 1 to country 2 involves LM units of capital, valued at XY in terms of output (both on a *per capita* basis).

As illustrated, the residents of country 2 are more impatient for consumption than are the residents of country 1. Prior to trading, the capitalisation rate is lower in country 1, so that when markets open, residents of country 1 acquire debentures from residents of country 2. The price of debentures is bid up in country 2 and bid down in country 1 until the capitalisation rates are equalised. A net acquisition of debentures is made by country 1, enabling the residents of country 2 to finance their consumption from country 1. Each resident of country 1 makes a consumption loan XY to a resident of country 2, as a result of which the resident of country 2 effectively mortgages an amount LM of his indigenous capital stock. If real assets are immobile then an amount LM in consumption units is remitted internationally in each subsequent period as interest on this loan. If real assets are mobile then an alternative is for LM units of real assets to be moved once and for all from country 2 to country 1.

It should be noted that the value of debentures owned by the host-country (country 2) does not necessarily diminish, even though both the number of debentures owned and total debenture income are lower than before. This is because the price of debentures in country 2 has risen as a result of the international equalisation of the capitalisation rates. Whether the value of debentures rises or falls depends upon the price elasticity of demand for debentures. Similar reasoning shows that the value of debentures owned by the source country (country 1) does not necessarily increase.

Once the international financial market has been opened up, subsequent flows of finance will be generated by differential changes in intertemporal preferences between the two countries. For example, if the residents of country 2 become even more impatient than before, relative to residents of country 1, then their demands for finance will increase, and a further flow of investment into 2 will occur.

6.6 SPECIALISATION OF RISK-BEARING

Setting

$$a_i = w_j = \bar{w}_j = 0 \qquad (i, j = 1, 2) \qquad (6.15)$$
$$\sigma_{ij} = \mu_{ij} = \mu, \ \gamma_j = 1$$

gives a simple model illustrating the specialisation of risk-bearing. There is no current consumption. The only choice is whether to hold claims on future consumption in the form of equity or debenture. There is just one type of equity and one type of debenture. The most risk-averse individuals hold debentures, the least risk-averse hold equity.

Figure 6.2 illustrates the equilibrium of the individual investor choosing between equity and debenture. His initial endowments are

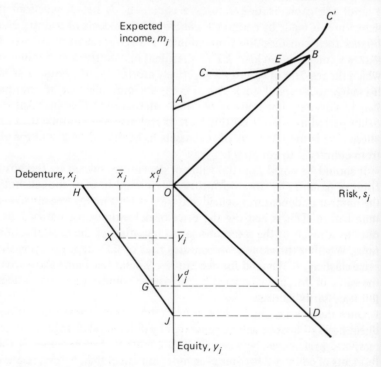

FIGURE 6.2   *Derivation of individual demands for equity and debentures*

represented by the point X in the lower left-hand quadrant. If residents of each country initially own and finance their own indigenous assets, then the representative investor will have equal endowments of equity and debenture, as indicated by the position of X in the figure. The relative price of equity and debenture determines the slope of the budget line HJ passing through X. If the individual concentrates his portfolio entirely on debenture then he obtains a risk-free real income represented by the point A in the top left-hand quadrant. As the amount of equity in the portfolio is increased both the expected income and risk increase at a fixed rate, until the entire portfolio consists of equity, at which point the combination of expected income and risk is represented by the point B. Individual preferences, illustrated by the sample indifference curve CC', are maximised at E where the indifference curve is tangent to the straight line AB. The optimum E is achieved by a mixture of equity and debenture represented by G. The point G represents the individual's demands for equity and debenture, given the prevailing relative price of equity.

This analysis can be applied to the representative individual in each country to derive the aggregate demands for equity and debenture as a function of the relative price of equity. Global equilibrium is illustrated in Figure 6.3. The square $O'JOK$ has dimensions equal to the global endowment of real assets. Equity and debenture held in country 1 are measured from the origin O, which corresponds to the origin in Figure 6.2. Equity and debenture held in country 2 are measured from the origin O'. The initial allocation of equity and debenture is fixed at X, and the equilibrium allocation is at G, where the plans of the residents of the two countries are harmonised. The equilibrium relative price of equity is measured by the reciprocal of the slope of the line $J'K'$ passing through G and X. The extension of the axis OJ to OJ' allows the distribution of wealth to be illustrated geometrically. In debenture units, the wealth of country 1 is OL and the wealth of country 2 is $O'K'$; alternatively, in equity units, the wealth of country 1 is measured by OM and the wealth of country 2 by $O'J'$.

As illustrated in the figure, the residents of country 2 are more risk-averse than the residents of country 1, and so they concentrate their portfolio on debentures. Risk-bearing is specialised (incompletely) with residents of country 1 who hold a relatively high proportion of equity in their portfolio.

The opening up of international financial markets induces a two-way flow of capital, as residents of country 1 sell GS debentures in order to buy GR equities. Once the markets have been opened, subsequent flows

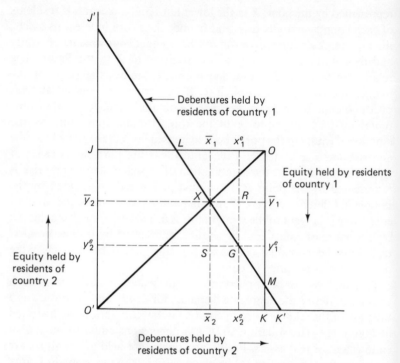

FIGURE 6.3 *International equilibrium in the equity and debenture markets*

will occur mainly as a result of relative changes in risk-aversion among residents of the two countries. For example, if risk-aversion increases further in country 2 then the residents of 2 will dispose of equity to residents of 1, in return for additional debentures.

It should be emphasised that changes in risk-aversion do not involve any net flows of investment, only two opposite but equal flows, consisting of a purchase of equity financed by a sale of debenture, or a purchase of debenture financed by a sale of equity. However, because of the risk involved, an equity claim of equal market value to a debenture claim carries a higher expected income, and so on average there will be a net flow of income to the country which specialises in equity-holding. This net flow of income represents a premium payable for risk-bearing, that is, a premium implicitly paid by the debenture-holders to the equity-holders for the insurance of their income.

6.7 INTERNATIONAL DIVERSIFICATION OF EQUITY OWNERSHIP

Setting

$$a_i = \varphi_i = w_j = \bar{w}_j = x_j = \bar{x}_j = 0$$
$$\mu_{ij} = \mu_i,\ \sigma_{ij} = \sigma_i,\ \gamma_j = \gamma < 1$$
$$(i, j = 1, 2) \tag{6.16}$$

gives a variant of the Grubel model of international diversification. The model shows that when the risks associated with assets differ according to the location of the asset, risk-averse investors will gain from holding internationally diversified equity portfolios. To simplify the diagrammatic analysis, debentures are ignored.

The portfolio equilibrium of the individual investor is exhibited in Figure 6.4. The figure has the same format as Figure 6.2 with the

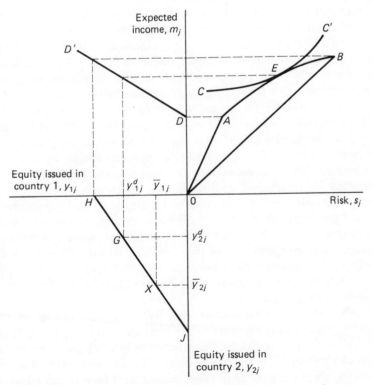

FIGURE 6.4   *Derivation of individuals' demands for two types of equity*

budget constraint *HJ* in the lower left-hand quadrant passing through the representative point of the initial endowment, *X*, and the upper right-hand quadrant showing the trade off *AB* between expected income and risk. As before, the diagram refers to the representative resident of a single country. However, the individual's endowments now refer to two different types of equity, instead of to a homogeneous equity and a homogeneous debenture as before. Because each equity carries with it some risk, the point *A* no longer lies on the vertical axis, but to the right of it. Also, because there is less than perfect correlation between the income fluctuations of the two types of equity, the locus *AB* is not a straight lne, but is convex to the vertical axis. The degree of convexity is greater the lower (or more negative) is the correlation between the two income streams; the greater the degree of convexity the greater are the gains from portfolio diversification.

The point of tangency between the indifference map and the locus *AB* is at *E*, where the indifference curve *CC'* is tangent to *AB*. Transforming back via *DD'* shows that this combination of expected income and risk is achieved by a portfolio mix represented by *G*.

If real assets are immobile then global equilibrium in portfolio choice may be represented using a diagram similar to Figure 6.3. It is sufficient merely to relabel the axes in this figure in order to achieve the desired interpretation. The efficiency gains from diversification mean that there will be a tendency for all individuals to hold some of each asset. However, individuals with the highest degree of risk-aversion will tend to hold the equity which offers the lowest risk for a given level of expected income. This last result, though, no longer applies once debentures are introduced into the analysis, for then risk can be avoided by trading off equities against debentures, instead of one equity against another. Once debentures are introduced, equity choice is influenced purely by the gains from diversification and not by the avoidance of risk. Individuals will hold the two equities in the same proportions independently of their attitudes to risk. Thus, when the international equity markets are opened up, individuals in each country will buy the other's equity until the composition of their equity portfolios is the same.

When real assets are mobile, they will move in order to equalise international rentals. So long as the same asset commands a different rental at different locations, there are gains to arbitrage to be had by switching the asset to the higher-rental location. As explained earlier, arbitrage will continue until either rentals have been equalised, or all stocks of the real asset are concentrated at the same (high rental) location.

When there is mobility, the portfolio model of equity choice determines both the ownership and the location of assets. Location is determined by the maximisation of equity valuation, while ownership is governed by efficient diversification, conditional upon the prevailing equity values.

6.8 INTERNATIONAL SPECULATION

Setting

$$a_i = \varphi_i = w_j = \bar{w}_j = x_{ij} = \bar{x}_{ij} = 0 \qquad (i, j = 1, 2) \qquad (6.17)$$
$$\gamma_j < 1$$

gives a weaker variant of the preceding model in which investors may take speculative positions in the equity markets. The preceding model assumes that all individuals have the same perception of the mean income, standard deviation and correlation between the future income streams. Implicitly this assumes that all individuals have access to similar information. However, there are good reasons to suppose that access to information is unequal between individuals. Some individuals may have better knowledge of the past income stream generated by an asset, or better forecasts of the 'states of nature' which are relevant to its future performance. This will lead to a difference of opinion among individuals about expected incomes, standard deviations, and correlations (Gonedes, 1976; Grossman, 1976).

Risk may involve not just an objective estimate of a standard deviation, but also an explicitly subjective element reflecting the individual's confidence in his own judgement. Confident individuals act on hunches and judgements as though they were founded on fact, while timid individuals doubt even apparently reliable information. Given unequal access to information, confident individuals may form estimates of expected income which vary considerably among themselves, while at the same time making subjective estimates of risk which are very low. On the other hand, timid individuals will form estimates of expected income which cluster round a 'consensus' view, while at the same time making subjective estimates of risk which are very high.

There will be a tendency for confident individuals to concentrate their portfolios on assets they believe to be undervalued. They will specialise in 'taking a position' in cases where they believe that 'the market has got it wrong'. Because they perceive low risks, they will concentrate their portfolios on equities whose expected return (that is, the expected income normalised with respect to equity price) is relatively high, and avoid altogether equities whose expected return is low. Because their perception of risk is low they will anticipate only small gains from risk-reduction and so they will neglect to diversify. Timid individuals, on the other hand, will continue to follow the precepts of the Grubel theory, with total emphasis on risk-minimisation.

It can be argued that in a world of imperfect information, foreigners will perceive greater risks than domestic residents with respect to any given asset. Given that the costs of gathering information normally increase with distance from the subject, foreigners will obtain less information per unit expenditure on search than will residents of the country where the asset is located. Having less information they will be faced with more imponderables and so perceive greater risks. Another contributory factor may be that foreign-owned assets are more liable to expropriation (a similar point applies to the repudiation of foreign-owned debentures, but this is a complication that will be ignored).

The bias against foreigners in risks will tend to reduce the international diversification of equity ownership. Since they are disadvantaged in terms of information costs, few investors are likely to take a position in foreign assets – and they are unlikely to survive for long as investors if they do.

6.9 DIVISION OF RISK-BEARING BETWEEN OWNERS AND UTILISERS

Separation of ownership and utilisation is effected by a contract of hire. The utiliser normally pays a fixed rent over a fixed period of time, at the end of which it is liable for renegotiation. In return the utiliser acquires temporary discretion over the use of the asset, and ownership of the product generated by its use. This creates a division of risks between owner and utiliser.

The utiliser bears the risks associated with temporary disturbances which affect the productivity of the asset during the rental period. The owner continues to bear the risks associated with long-term or permanent changes in the productivity of the asset. More specifically, an owner who repeatedly hires out an asset bears the risk that permanent changes will occur which, once they are recognised, will affect in perpetuity the future rental that the asset will command. On the other hand, a person who repeatedly hires an asset bears the risks associated with a succession of transitory changes which could not be foreseen at the times the contracts of hire were negotiated.

The division of risk will be reflected in a division of powers of control over the asset. The division of powers between owner and utiliser is fixed by the contract. In an efficient contract, the owner will reserve for himself control over things which affect the long-term viability of the asset, while the utiliser will control things whose effects are of a purely transitory nature. In total, the amount of discretion will tend to be less than where the owner himself utilises the asset. This is because a contract of hire normally imposes obligations on the two parties from which they cannot escape. These obligations are a form of mutual insurance necessitated by the distrust between the two parties. These constraints imposed by the contract create contractual costs over and above those involved in negotiation. In certain cases they may be sufficient to eliminate the market for hire completely.

Suppose, however, that there is an efficient market for hire. If the income streams of the owner and hirer are compared it will be seen that the former consists of low-frequency fluctuations, in which all cycles of frequency less than the contract period have been filtered out, while the latter consists of high-frequency fluctuations in which all cycles of frequency greater than the contract period have been filtered out. It follows that the two streams have non-overlapping frequencies, and that as a result the correlation between them is zero.

It is convenient at this stage to introduce two types of firm. The producing firm only utilises assets – it does not own them – while the property firm owns assets, but does not utilise them. The property firm issues both equity and debenture, just as before, but the producing firm issues only equity. The producing firm pays for hire on a daily basis (even though the contract period may be longer) and so has no need of finance (except for production lags, which are ignored). There is free entry into production, which means that the value of each producing firm's equity at the beginning of each contract period is zero. By convention, each producing firm utilises one unit of the asset. It is assumed that investors hold stationary expectations about the rental in each location, so that as competition between producers adjusts the rental, expectations of the average future rental alter by the same amount. However, the future rental stream is regarded as uncertain, so that an equity stake in a property firm still carries risk.

The determination of equilibrium is discussed formally in the following section. The most important result is simply that differences between investors in their perception of risk may lead some to specialise in bearing ownership risks, by holding the equity of property firms, while others may specialise in bearing utilisation risks, by holding the equity of producing firms. Some further consequences of the separation of ownership and utilisation are considered in Section 6.11.

6.10 EQUILIBRIUM OF RISK-SHARING WHEN ASSETS ARE HIRED

Since there continues to be just one kind of real asset, and one kind of debenture issued in each country, the variables a_i, b_i, φ_i, w_j, x_{ij}, x'_j, p_i, c_i may be defined exactly as before. Also utility, mean income and the standard deviation of income continue to be denoted by u_j, m_j, s_j respectively. Let

r_i be the rental in location i,

g_i the price of equity issued by property firms in country i,

h_i the price of equity issued by producing firms in country i,

y_{ij} the amount of property-firm equity issued in country i and held by a resident of country j,

z_{ij} the amount of producing-firm equity issued in country i and held by a resident of country j,

$\eta_i = r_i - \varphi_i$ the mean income offered by property-firm equity issued in country i,

μ_{ij} the mean future output of an asset located in country i as perceived by a resident of country j,

$\theta_{ij} = \mu_{ij} - r_i$ the mean income offered by producing-firm equity issued in country i, as perceived by a resident of country j,

a_{ij} the standard deviation of the income offered by property-firm equity issued in country i, as perceived by a resident of country j,

β_{ij} the standard deviation of the income offered by producing-firm equity issued in country i, as perceived by a resident of country j,

γ_j the correlation between the property income streams, as perceived by a resident of country j, and

δ_j the correlation between the production income streams, as perceived by a resident of country j.

The correlation between property income and production income streams is correctly perceived by all individuals to be zero.

It is assumed that although there are now income streams of different frequency, individual preferences continue to be based only on the first and second moments of the total income stream. The representative individual in country j therefore continues to maximise (6.1) subject to

$$m_j = \Sigma_i(\varphi_i x_{ij} + \eta_i y_{ij} + r_{ij} z_{ij}) \tag{6.18}$$

$$s_j = \{\Sigma_i(a_{ij}^2 y_{ij}^2 + \beta_{ij}^2 z_{ij}^2) + 2\gamma_j a_{1j} a_{2j} y_{1j} y_{2j} + 2\delta_j \beta_{1j} \beta_{2j} z_{1j} z_{2j}\}^{1/2} \tag{6.19}$$

$$\Delta w_j = \Sigma_i(p_i \Delta x_{ij} + g_i \Delta y_{ij} + h_i \Delta z_{ij}) = 0 \tag{6.20}$$

This determines the individual demand functions

$$\left.\begin{aligned} w_j^d &= w_j^d \\ x_j'^d &= x_j'^d \\ y_{ij}^d &= y_{ij}^d \\ z_{ij}^d &= z_{ij}^d \end{aligned}\right\} \left(\begin{array}{c} c, g_1, g_2, h_1, h_2, r_1, r_2 \\ \bar{w}_j, \bar{x}_j, \bar{y}_{1j}, y_2, \bar{z}_{ij}, z_{2j}, \\ a_{1j}, a_{2j}, \beta_{1j}, \beta_{2j}, \gamma_j, \delta_j \end{array}\right) \tag{6.21}$$

Aggregating the demands and comparing them with the supply conditions

$$\begin{aligned} w^s &= \Sigma_i a_i \bar{b}_i \\ x^s &= \Sigma_i \varphi_i \bar{b}_i \\ y_i^s &= \bar{b}_i \quad (i=1, 2) \\ z_i^s &= \bar{b}_i \quad (i=1, 2) \end{aligned} \tag{6.22}$$

gives six market-clearing conditions

$$w^d = w^s, \; x'^d = x'^s, \; y_i^d = y_i^s, \; z_i^d = z_i^s \quad (i=1, 2) \tag{6.23}$$

of which five are independent. Using the fact that

$$h_1 = h_2 = 0 \tag{6.24}$$

gives five equations for the five unknowns c, g_1, g_2, r_1, r_2. Substituting the equilibrium values back into the demand functions determines the international allocation of finance, ownership risk, and utilisation risk.

The case in which the real asset is mobile may be dealt with in the same way as before.

6.11 RATIONALE OF THE FIRM

So far the only function of the firm has been to issue equities and debentures and to hire out (or hire in) assets. It has been assumed that each firm owns a single homogeneous real asset; this however is only a convention, without which the size of the firm would be indeterminate.

The firm is essentially a unit of utilisation. When assets are small, or divisible, the rationale for the firm is that economies are achieved by arranging that several different assets share the same utiliser. The size of the firm is set at the margin where the advantage to the utiliser of adding a further asset to this pool is just outweighed by the cost of doing so. Where assets are indivisible there is a further complication, because the size of the firm is also influenced by the economies of sharing the use of the same asset. Assets are shared up to the margin where the benefits of introducing an additional utiliser are just outweighed by the costs involved.

Firm economies are of four main kinds. The first two – plant and multiplant economies – are technological in origin, though it is their organisational implications that are crucial. The other two are marketing economies – which are strongly influenced by costs of communication and physical distribution – and economies of transfer-pricing, induced by fiscal intervention.

Plant Economies

Plant economies are themselves of three kinds. Economies of complementarity are achieved by placing assets of different types together (a fixed-proportions joint-input production technology is the simplest example of this). Economies of agglomeration are achieved by placing assets of the same type (or similar groups of assets) together. Economies of indivisibility are achieved by using large indivisible assets in place of smaller ones.

Economies of agglomeration and indivisibility are usually lumped together under the heading of economies of scale. However in the present context it is more convenient to consider economies of complementarity and agglomeration together under the heading of economies of combining assets, and to consider economies of indivisibility separately.

Economies of combination arise both from the exploitation of productive externalities between the assets within the plant, and the removal of unproductive externalities between these assets and other assets outside the plant. Thus the firm gains from both the internal contiguity and the external isolation of assets.

In principle each asset within the plant could be utilised by someone different. The output of each asset would be individually metered and valued, and its utiliser would have discretion over how it was deployed. Externalities between assets would be 'internalised' through contract – generally a multilateral contract between all the utilisers involved in the plant. The contract would involve an exchange of obligations, perhaps accompanied by side payments (for a discussion of side payments see Bacharach, 1976). In practice, the efficient deployment of each asset would be contingent on the prevailing 'state of nature' (Arrow, 1970). The contract would therefore have to stipulate contingent obligations, and the utilisers would need to collect information on the state of nature so that they could honour their obligations. Given the costs of collecting information, and its public good characteristics, it would benefit the utilisers to form a club to collect the information, and perhaps to arrange for the implementation of the appropriate responses. Thus even if they did not jointly utilise the assets it would still pay them to share the cost of managing the plant.

In practice, however, long before this point is reached, the difficulties of auditing individual outputs and the costs of negotiating and enforcing a multilateral contract are likely to lead to the plant being brought under a single utiliser. The other utilisers may continue to be involved with the plant as equity shareholders in the utilising firm. The only possible disadvantage of such an arrangement is that where many shareholders are involved, the incentive for any one shareholder to monitor the management is reduced. This problem is avoided if one individual becomes sole owner of the equity in the utilising firm, by buying out all the owners. Whether one individual is willing to bear all the risk of the plant will depend upon its size.

The same sort of arguments apply, with even greater force, to sharing the use of an indivisible asset (Loasby, 1976). It may be impossible even to conceptualise how the asset could be resolved into distinct parts utilised by different individuals, how the outputs of these parts could be metered or valued, and what sort of provisions would be involved in a contract which co-ordinated their use. It is true that some indivisible assets are designed specifically for sharing, but these are usually shared not through simultaneous utilisation, as defined above, but through a single utiliser selling a carefully specified service whose provision remains under his own control. Sharing can also be effected by alternating use of the asset frequently, but in this case each utiliser normally has exclusive use of the asset, even though it is only temporary. Such sharing is equivalent to a succession of short-term hirings which circulate among the parties concerned. At any one time the asset still has a single utiliser.

Multiplant Economies

Multiplant economies most commonly arise where there are intermediate product flows linking the plants, or where all plants share access to a common resource (in particular, an intangible resource such as proprietary know-how). Here the externalities between the assets operate at a distance, via trade routes or communication channels. Internalisation of the externalities through contract is often difficult, because of the problems of devising a contract which is simple and easily enforceable and yet does not distort interplant co-ordination (licensing contracts are a good example of the problems involved). The alternative to internalisation by contract is internalisation through a common utiliser, and it is this that creates the multiplant firm.

The most common example of intermediate product flows is in multistage production, and in this case internalisation through common utilisation creates vertical integration. The most frequently cited example of proprietary know-how is production technology. The internalisation of technology transfer generates a horizontal integration of production based on a vertical integration of production and R & D. If the know-how is of a more general kind, consisting of marketing or organisational skills, then internalisation of transfers of know-how may result in a form of conglomerate integration of production based on an innovative management team.

Marketing Economies

The negotiation and enforcement of a contract involves significant fixed costs, that is, costs which are independent of the amount or value of the transation. This creates an incentive both to increase the volume traded between any two parties within a given period and also to negotiate long-term contracts for recurrent trade. The two strategies complement one another in reducing the average fixed contractual cost per unit time.

A producer can only benefit from high-volume transactions if his scale of production is large, which in turn implies that he is utilising a large number of assets. By hiring the assets in bulk, the average contractual cost of the producer is minimised.

Similar considerations imply that assets should be hired and output sold using long-term contracts. A long-term contract for hire is asymptotically equivalent to outright ownership, in the sense that as the length of the contract period approaches the economic lifetime of the asset, the owner's risk tends to zero, as the asset is bound to have no further use when it is returned to him. The only uncertainty that remains relates to its scrap value. In view of this it may be economic to avoid altogether the costs of the contract of hire by arranging that the utiliser owns his own assets outright. In this case the existence of contractual costs leads to the integration of ownership and utilisation. The economies of utilising assets in common then translate into economies of owning assets in common.

There is however an important limitation to this strategy arising from the fact that there is one major asset – namely labour – for which ownership is inalienable, and for which long-term contracts equivalent to alienation are unenforceable in law. The inability of producers to secure future supplies of labour on fixed terms involves them in considerable risks if they attempt to sell their output forward on fixed terms, and this means that the scope for long-term contracts in output is considerably reduced. This in turn feeds back on the risks involved in the outright ownership of alienable assets such as producer goods, particularly those which are not easily transferred to alternative uses should inputs of the complementary types of labour become very scarce in the future. Thus the inalienability of labour contributes to the illiquidity of other assets. By increasing the level of risk relative to contractual costs, it encourages the specialisation of risk through the contract of hire, and the sharing of these risks through the diversification of equity-ownership in the owning and utilising firms.

Economies of Transfer-pricing

Where assets located in different fiscal areas have the same owner or utiliser it becomes possible for the owner to exploit a lack of fiscal harmonisation to reduce his tax liabilities. The owner creates notional transactions which reallocate income from higher-tax areas to the lowest-tax area. It may also be possible for him to bypass capital controls by disguising capital transfers as income payments, using the same principle. Notional transactions are less detectable if they are disguised by overvaluing or undervaluing actual trade flows of intermediate products (a strategy often used in both internal and external transfers of technology, where politically sensitive royalty payments are disguised as overvalued flows of tied inputs; see Vaitsos, 1974). Because of this, utilisers have more scope for transfer-pricing than do owners. Owners who wish to minimise their tax liabilities, or to bypass capital controls may therefore find it advantageous to integrate ownership and utilisation, as described earlier.

Taken together, the firm economies described above provide a reasonably comprehensive account of the factors responsible for the creation of the firm. These factors explain first and foremost why assets should have a common utiliser, but they also demonstrate why utilisers may wish to become owners (to economise on transaction costs) and why owners may wish to become utilisers (to benefit from transfer-pricing). Thus the theory provides a reasonable account of the firm both as a unit of ownership and a unit of utilisation.

6.12 MANAGEMENT OF THE FIRM

In a world of change, where new information is always becoming available, efficient utilisation of assets demands active control. It is necessary to review options continuously in the light of new information, so that decision-making becomes a continuous and resource-intensive process.

In practice, utilisers normally delegate control to professional managers who have a comparative advantage in the supply of the skills and the effort involved. Indivisibilities in management encourage the growth of large firms, while diseconomies of bureaucracy inhibit it. The latter are often associated with a loss of managerial accountability consequent upon highly diversified share ownership.

This section considers those aspects of management which have a bearing on the nationality of the firm, as discussed in the introduction. Four aspects are considered:

(1) the country in which the parent firm is registered
(2) the location of group headquarters
(3) the national culture on which the informal relations between managers (and among employees generally) are modelled
(4) the nationality from which most of the top management is recruited.

These decisions are initially made by the founder of the firm, but they may be reviewed at any time. However, the consequences of changing any one of them are so momentous that changes are likely only at critical stages in the growth of the firm, such as the point at which the founder relinquishes *de facto* control. Because the changes are so momentous, the owners of the firm are unlikely to give the management much discretion in the matter. It may therefore be assumed that the decisions will be made in accordance with the owners' primary objective, namely the maximisation of the value of the firm's equity.

Suppose to begin with that each of the four decisions is separable, in the sense that the choice of country of registration has no effect on costs of alternative headquarters locations, and so on. This is a counterfactual assumption which is relaxed below.

Let the nationality of the firm in any one of these aspects be indexed by $i = 1, \ldots, m$. The set of possible nationalities of the firm embraces the set of countries in which the firm plans to produce (the set of production locations is assumed to be independent of the economics of managerial organisation). The set of countries of production is indexed by $j = 1, \ldots, n$, where $n < m$. Let c_{ij} be the total cost of operating in country j when the firm is registered in country i. Then in each case the optimal nationality of the firm is determined by the minimisation of

$$c_i = \sum_{j=1}^{n} c_{ij} \qquad (6.25)$$

with respect to $i = 1, \ldots, n$.

Note that the solution depends not only on the elements c_{jj} – that is, on the costs of producing in the firm's own country – but on the elements $c_{ij} (i \neq j)$ as well. These elements reflect the attitudes of the host countries to foreign firms of different nationalities. The attitudes of the host-government, customers, workers and suppliers of services will all affect the production costs of the foreign firm. The most attractive nationality is one that is not only cost-effective for production at home, but provides favoured treatment abroad, or at least a minimum of adverse discrimination. So far as the host-government is concerned this means that to attract firms not only must the domestic climate be right, but political and economic relations with the favoured locations for overseas production must be good as well.

In the case where the various decisions are inseparable, the analysis may be generalised by redefining the cost c_{ij} as the cost of production in country j for a national of country i, assuming that the three other nationality decisions have already been made to achieve a minimum of cost, conditional upon i and j. The total cost criterion (6.25) then applies just as before.

In many cases the nationality of the firm in each of the four respects will be the same; this will be particularly true of small firms, which remain much as the founder originally organised them. This is by no means the case for all firms however. Large firms in particular will be attracted to register in countries which have a liberal attitude toward company reporting of sensitive items, and which have governments who are willing to use their political power in support of business interests overseas. Conversely, governments anxious to acquire international political power will be keen to attract registration by large and economically powerful firms. The result will be a compact between firms and governments to further their mutual interests overseas.

The location of group headquarters will be influenced by communication costs. Easy access to the home government will be desired, especially by large firms. This suggests that headquarters will normally be located in the country where the firm is registered. Access to supplies of skilled management will also be important, but this is unlikely to be a crucial influence, as we shall see later.

The choice of corporate culture is a much more complex matter. Culture is not purely a question of nationality – it also has religious and ethnic dimensions. In the present context, a culture may be defined as a set of rules for individual and group behaviour within the firm which are widely recognised and are enforced by spontaneous expressions of approval or disapproval from others. A firm needs a culture to complement the formal rules which are enforced hierarchically through discipline and reward. Cultural sanctions encourage the individual to co-operate in situations where formal sanctions would be too expensive to enforce.

It is reasonable to suppose that, from an economic standpoint, some cultures are more viable than others. It is widely accepted, for example, that cultural factors are very important in explaining productivity differentials (Jaques, 1951; Krimpas, 1975). Most studies have focused on an international comparison of plants, but it would be surprising if the same factors did not apply at the firm level as well.

Cultures which emphasis self-discipline and the subjection of the 'individual will' to the 'corporate will' should lead to higher productivity than cultures which emphasise the opposite characteristics. A culture with these characteristics is likely to be associated with militaristic ideals; thus nations with militaristic attitudes are most likely to provide a model for corporate culture.

Professional managers tend to be internationally mobile, which means that the supply of management may well be separable from issues such as the registration of the company and the location of its headquarters. Management will be recruited from wherever educated and skilled labour is most abundant. However the productivity of individual managers will also depend on their compatibility with the corporate culture; although the culture may on average raise productivity, it may reduce the productivity of a minority of employees who do not fit into it. The efficient firm will minimise the size of this minority by biasing its recruitment in favour of managers who are already familiar with the culture, that is, by recruiting predominantly from the nation on whose culture the firm is modelled.

Overall, therefore, there will be a tendency for headquarters to be located in the country of registration, and for management to be recruited from the country on whose culture the firm is modelled. Firms will tend to register in countries which have lenient rules on disclosure and which aggressively promote their economic interests overseas. They will model their culture on nations in which there is a propensity toward militaristic ideology. To the extent that this ideology is reflected in respect for business secrets and in economic expansionism overseas, the countries which are most suitable for registration may also provide the most attractive models for corporate culture. In this case the four aspects of corporate nationality may coalasce: the countries which offer suitable cultural models will become the countries in which firms register and locate their headquarters and from which they recruit their senior management.

6.13 AN INTEGRATED THEORY OF FDI

As noted earlier, the theory of FDI is obtained by integrating the theory of international capital markets, the theory of the firm and the theory of trade. The results of this integration may be discussed most easily by considering in turn the various pair-wise combinations of the theories.

The integration of the theory of international capital markets with the theory of the firm is quite straightforward. The firm is an intermediary through which the income generated by various assets is channelled to the individual investor. The firm holds a portfolio of claims to the income obtained by owning or utilising the various assets. The nature of each firm's portfolio is determined chiefly by the economies which arise when particular groups of assets share the same utiliser. The individual investor holds a portfolio of claims against the firms. The composition of this portfolio reflects the investor's attitude to risk, the potential gains from diversification, and his confidence in taking a position with respect to particular firms. It should be noted that taking a position with respect to a particular firm is not quite the same thing as taking a position with respect to a particular asset. Most firms utilise several different types of asset and so the risks associated with the different assets are consolidated in the risks associated with any particular equity.

The factors which influence the sources of finance and risk-bearing are largely independent of the factors which influence the nationality of the firm. However, the nationality of the firm may well be influenced by individual investors' perceptions of the risks associated with corporate debt. In practice perceptions of equity-risk will depend not only upon the location of the real assets utilised by the firm, but on investors' confidence in the management's ability to manage. This confidence may well depend upon the nationality of the corporate culture and the country from which the management is mostly recruited. Investors' perceptions of both equity- and debenture-risk will depend on their confidence that corporate debt will not be repudiated. Their degree of confidence will depend on the country in which the firm is registered. Since most investors have confidence in their own nationality, there will be a tendency for firms to adopt the nationality of countries which offer the largest supplies of finance and risk-bearing. The nationality of these firms, as reflected in the ownership of their shares, will coincide with their nationality as represented by their country of registration and the affiliation of their management generally.

The integration of the theory of international capital markets with the theory of trade poses no major problems of principle. Specific aspects of the two theories have already been integrated, though a full analysis would be relatively complicated and lies well beyond the scope of this chapter.

The integration of the theory of the firm with the theory of trade is more problematic. The relevant theory of the firm is an institutional one in which market imperfections have a central role, while the theory of trade, in its simple variants at least, assumes efficient markets. Integration is achieved most easily by assuming that while alternative institutional arrangements differ in their efficiency, for each co-ordination problem there is just one institutional arrangement which is best, and this arrangement is perfectly efficient (Casson, 1979). The type of institution that is used in each instance is determined by relative efficiency, as described by the institutional theory, while the allocation of resources effected by the chosen institution can be predicted from the theory of efficient markets. The implication of this approach is that the growth of firms by the internalisation of markets proceeds only so long as internalisation increases efficiency, and that the allocation of resources effected by firms is always efficient.

The integration of all three theories provides answers to a complex of issues connected with FDI. These issues are listed in Table 6.1. The list is only preliminary and there are many other issues which could be added to it. The various issues are of course interdependent, but in each case there is one theory which could be used on its own to provide a partial analysis of the issue; this theory is indicated in the right-hand column of the table. The justification for the theory of FDI lies in the fact that a general analysis based on the integrated theory may yield different predictions than would a series of partial analyses of each issue.

TABLE 6.1   *Issues in FDI*

Issue	Relevant theory

Origins of finance
  Funding
  Risk-bearing
    Ownership risks
    Utilisation risks
	Theory of international capital markets

Location of control
  Country of registration
  Location of headquarters
  Cultural affiliation
  Source of management
	Theory of the firm

Location of production
  (includes the location of each
  individual asset)
	Trade theory

Destination of final sales
  (taken as given in the market
  servicing decision)	

7 Multinationals and Intermediate Product Trade

MARK CASSON

7.1 INTRODUCTION

Dunning (1981) suggests that the behaviour of multinational enterprises (MNEs) can be analysed in terms of three groups of factors: ownership advantages, location advantages, and internalisation. Buckley (1983) notes that of these three, location advantages have received least attention in recent years, despite the fact that, historically, location advantages have strongly influenced the growth of international production (Dunning, 1982). This chapter is an attempt to make good this deficiency.

The theory of location developed below has four main objectives:

(1) To provide an integrated analysis of the three main types of international investment and to explain the relation between them; these are (i) import-substituting investment in the high-technology industries of developed countries, (ii) 'export-platform' manufacturing investment in cheap-labour countries, and (iii) agricultural- and raw materials-based investment in land- and mineral-rich countries.
(2) To provide a framework for analysing the post-war growth of intermediate product trade and in particular to explain intra-firm trade in components and semi-processed materials.
(3) To examine the influence of transfer-pricing on the international rationalisation of production within an MNE, and in particular to analyse how the location of production by an MNE will differ from location of production by independent competitive producers in the same industry.

(4) To analyse in a comparative static framework the impact of technical progress, trade liberalisation and tax harmonisation on the location of production with an MNE.

The conventional theory of international location is based upon the Heckscher–Ohlin (HO) theory of trade. However attempts to apply the HO theory to the MNE (for example Casson, 1979, Chap. 4) have had only limited success. The HO theory seems to be a blind alley, and there are three main reasons for this:

(1) The HO theory overemphasises the role of factor substitution in the location of production. Factor substitution introduces analytical complications which impede the consideration of other important issues. As a result other influences on location – in particular transport costs and economies of scale – are often assumed away.
(2) The theory focuses upon the specialisation of production between industries rather than on the division of labour within an industry. It is therefore ill-adapted to the analysis of intra-industry intermediate product trade.
(3) The theory takes a very narrow view of technology in general and of technical progress in particular. It ignores the fact that much modern technology is proprietary, with imperfect competition being the norm in markets for new products. The analysis of technical progress also reflects the biases of the theory as a whole: it is preoccupied with the classification of technical progress in terms of factor savings and ignores technical progress which reduces transport costs, stimulates economies of scale and promotes the intra-industry division of labour.

7.2 AN ALTERNATIVE TO THE HO THEORY

This paper begins from a standpoint quite different from the HO theory. It is inspired by geographical theories of industrial location, and in particular by Norman (1979). This alternative standpoint may be set out in terms of three broad principles.

(a) *Factor substitution has a very limited role in the location of production.* In the HO theory the inputs to production are immobile factors which are continuously substitutable. Differences between locations in relative endowments of the factors generate differences in comparative cost and these differences in cost govern the location of production. It can be argued, however, that factors are not so immobile as the HO theory assumes, and that substitution possibilities are discontinuous, and in some cases negligible. On these grounds it may be argued that the HO approach is less plausible than the much simpler Ricardian theory of comparative labour cost.

Capital, for example, is not so immobile as alleged by the HO theory (MacDougall, 1960). Post-war capital markets are probably better integrated between the metropolitan centres of different countries than they are between metropolitan and non-metropolitan areas of the same country. Furthermore, the MNEs' ability to bypass exchange controls through transfer-pricing creates an internal market within which the cost of capital is equalised across locations (Rugman, 1981, Chap. 4). The availability of capital at a particular location does not, therefore, directly influence the decision to produce there. Rather the availability of capital to the firm as a whole determines to what extent it is economic to divert capital to a particular location to substitute for other factors with which that location is poorly endowed. It is only in this very limited sense that capital substitution influences the extent to which one location is more attractive than another.

Another point is that in practice opportunities for technical substitution between factors are probably less than is assumed by the HO theory. Historically, the most important immobile inputs to production have been labour and environmental services, where environment includes land, soil-quality, weather, geological features such as mineral deposits and so on. Casual empiricism suggests that technical substitutability between environmental services and other factors is much lower than the substitutability between labour and capital. Thus it may be more reasonable to assume that immobile inputs must be combined in fixed proportions than to assume the existence of a continuum of alternative production techniques.

Next, it can be argued that the margin is of little significance in the supply of environmental services. This is because the environment often has the characteristics of a public good. In many cases – for example, the weather – an environmental service is either not available, or is available in such abundance that environmental capacity far exceeds user demand. If an environmental service is not available then – because of limited substitution possibilities – production which normally requires this service cannot take place at all. If the service is available then its opportunity cost is zero and input requirements for this service exert no influence on the level of output. Thus the local environment determines whether or not production is feasible at a given location, but when production is feasible it does not influence the scale on which production occurs.

It is, of course, often possible to discover a margin which influences production – a margin determined by the level of pollution, for example, or by the depletion of some non-renewable resource. The basic point is not that such margins do not exist, but that they are of secondary importance in the location of international production.

It is a consequence of the propositions above that, given a set of locations at which production is feasible, marginal production cost varies between these locations mainly on account of differences in labour costs. These differences reflect differences between locations in the comparative advantage of labour in different industries. Once the impact of environment on the feasibility of production has been taken into account therefore, the influence of international factor endowments on the location of production can be analysed using the Ricardian theory of comparative labour costs.

To express this conclusion another way, it can be said that if capital is mobile, technical substitution is limited and environmental services have public good characteristics then the only margin of significance is the margin at which labour is allocated between industries. It is the position of this margin at different locations which is crucial to international production.

(b) *Technical progress has more to do with reducing transport costs, stimulating economies of scale and promoting the division of labour than it has to do with conventional factor-saving advances in production technology.*

The HO theory is preoccupied with labour-saving and capital-saving technical progress in production – reflecting the emphasis of the theory on factor substitution. The complications introduced by factor substitution make it necessary to simplify by ignoring transport costs and economies of scale. It is obvious, however, that technical improvements in transport have done much to widen the scope for international trade. The HO theory can analyse easily only the extreme case in which a hitherto untradeable product becomes perfectly tradeable. A satisfactory theory must include transport costs at the outset.

The HO assumption of constant returns to scale in production makes it difficult to analyse the consequences of innovations which alter returns to scale. The most obvious case of this is the introduction of a continuous-flow production technique. Establishing continuous-flow production usually incurs a set-up cost, which affords economies to the length of the production run. More important in the present context is that economies of speed and size in machinery often mean that set-up costs increase less than proportionately to capacity. Furthermore, large size may offer economies not only in set-up costs but in running costs – for example, heat loss per unit throughput diminishes continuously with respect to the size of a boiler, pipeline, etc. Thus with continuous flow technology, marginal set-up cost and marginal running cost normally both diminish with respect to the capacity of the plant and therefore generate long-run economies of scale with respect to the rate of output. The exploitation of these economies is limited only by transport costs and the size of the market.

Another form of technical progress overlooked by the HO theory is an increase in the division of labour within an industry. Each subdivision of a productive activity creates a market for an intermediate product. The resolution of an activity into a sequence of two independent activities creates a market in a semi-processed material linking the first activity to the second. (The sequence may, of course, involve more than two activities, in which case there are several intermediate product markets.) In some cases, the division of labour creates a pyramid of activities in which both vertical and horizontal specialisation occurs; the activities at the bottom of the pyramid produce 'components' which are then combined in an 'assembly' process higher up. In some cases the intermediate products may not be tradeable, in which case the subdivision occurs within the plant and may appear simply as a factor-saving shift in the plant production function. When an intermediate product is tradeable, however, it is possible to separate spatially the activities which it links and so replace a single plant by two different ones.

In certain cases the opportunity for spatial separation may increase overall efficiency even though there is no actual factor-saving in either activity. If each activity makes intensive use of a different immobile input then without division of labour each activity must take place at a location where both the inputs are available. With division of labour each activity can take place at a location where only one of the inputs is available. This reduces the pressure on factor use at well-endowed locations and increases efficiency through international specialisation. Alternatively it may simply allow one of the activities to be moved nearer to the final market, and thereby economise on overall transport costs.

(c) *Technology is normally proprietary and firm-specific at the time of innovation. Access to know-how constitutes an important barrier to entry encouraging monopoly or oligopoly in the supply of new products. It is often advantageous for the monopolist to integrate backward into the supply of inputs or components embodied in the final product. This leads to international production of new products being controlled by vertically integrated monopolistic MNEs.*

Many new products are designed specifically to economise upon transaction costs. For example, the introduction of a versatile good which substitutes for several more specific goods enables buyers to economise on transaction costs in the final product market. The typical versatile good is a multi-component good which can be adapted to different uses by utilising different subsets of components. Each sub-set of components substitutes for some specific good. This allows the buyer of a multi-component good to obtain several different services through a single transaction (Casson, 1982, Chap. 10).

The production of a multi-component good, of course, creates transactions between the component producers and the assembler of the good. The cost of these additional transactions is, however, low compared with the savings that are effected in the final product market. Costs are high in the final product market whenever atomistic buyers with little knowledge of the product make irregular purchases. By contrast, component transactions normally involve regular bulk transactions among a few well-informed parties.

New products are also designed to economise on transport costs. Improvements in product design may reduce the bulk or weight of the product, or make it easier to 'stack' in transit. A final product is normally bulkier than the individual components from which it is assembled. Economies in transport costs can therefore be achieved by moving the point of assembly closer to the final user – for example, the product is shipped in 'kit' or 'knocked-down' form to the wholesaler or retailer – in some cases even to the final purchaser. These economies are achieved by designing the product so that its assembly is relatively trivial. The sophistication of the product is built into its components. The result is that economies of scale are likely to predominate in component production and to be relatively insignificant at the assembly stage.

The designer of a product will normally wish to control the marketing of it. The incentive is greatest when the design cannot be patented, for then licensing is problematic (see Chapter 3). Complexity of the specification also discourages licensing because of the need for accuracy in the claims that are made for the product. Licensing is also more difficult if the final product is easily transported for then it is difficult to prevent licensees from invading one another's markets and reducing the world-wide monopoly rent that is earned.

The designers will also wish to control component production. If component design embodies know-how then the designer will be reluctant to subcontract production for reasons of secrecy (see Chapter 2). Control of component production is also important when the tolerances allowed for components in the assembly process are very tight. This is particularly important when the product is durable, for maintenance costs can them be kept down by using interchangeable replacement parts. Precision is therefore vital in component manufacture and this creates a quality problem. Since the costs of poor quality are borne by the assembler he has a vested interest in supervising production, and one way of exercising supervision is to integrate backward into component production.

7.3 A MODEL OF THE LOCATION OF INTERNATIONAL PRODUCTION

This section presents a general equilibrium model of the world economy. In some respects it can be regarded as the development of an intuitive model used by Dunning (1972) in which there are just two consumer products: one product is competitively supplied and the other is monopolised by an MNE. The monopoly good is sold internationally and is produced using an integrated sequence of component manufacture, assembly and marketing. The model allows for both international and inter-regional trade in components and the assembled product. Goods move along paths connecting the nodes of a transport network. The routing of goods is modelled, as well as the origin and final destination of each consignment. Environmental endowments determine the locations at which production of each good is feasible. Within these constraints the exact location of production is determined by comparative labour costs. Profit taxes and tariffs are included to allow scope for transfer-pricing. The analysis takes full account of the distributional implications of wages, profits, taxes and tariffs for the demand side of the economy – though very strong assumptions are made in this respect.

This section outlines the general structure of the model. The profit-maximising MNE location strategy is analysed in Section 7.4. The computation of the general equilibrium is illustrated in Section 7.5. The conclusions are summarised in Section 7.6.

Let there be a fixed number of point locations, indexed $i = 1, \ldots, L$, each of which is a potential site for production and a potential source of demand. The ith location has a fixed endowment of homogeneous labour, $N_i \geqslant 0$. Labour is the only variable factor of production and is measured in an internationally standardised efficiency unit (as shown later). Labour is geographically immobile, though perfectly mobile between different industries at the same location.

There are $H + 4$ distinct activities that can, in principle, be carried on at each location. Activity zero is the marketing of a monopolised consumer good produced by a (potential) MNE. Activity 1 is the assembly of the monopolised good from components; the term 'component' designates any tradeable raw material or intermediate product; likewise the term 'assembly' designates any activity which processes one or more of the 'components' to produce the final product. The H activities 2 to $H + 1$ involve the production of different components. It is assumed that each of the foregoing activities, indexed $h = 0, 1, \ldots, H + 1$, are carried on by the same firm; the output of the hth activity at location i is $x_{hi} \geqslant 0$. The firm is thus vertically integrated from component production through assembly to marketing, and is horizontally integrated across locations.

The remaining two activities are carried on only by independent competitive producers. One activity is the production of a consumer good which is an imperfect substitute for the monopolised good; output of this good at location i is $y_i \geqslant 0$. The competitive consumer good can be traded costlessly but the monopolised consumer-good and its components cannot. The remaining activity is a transport service, whose output at location i is $t_i \geqslant 0$. The transport service is an intermediate product, hired exclusively by the monopolist for the physical distribution of the components and the assembled product.

Some of the monopolised activities require inputs of non-tradeable environmental services. It is assumed that locations either have abundant endowments of these inputs – in which case they are available free – or none at all. If a location has suitable endowments then production can proceed, otherwise it cannot. The variable γ_{hi} assumes a value of unity when the hth activity can proceed at location i and zero when it cannot.

The competitive consumer good and the transport service are perfect substitutes in production and are produced under constant returns to scale. At each location labour-productivity in transport is the same constant proportion of labour-productivity in the competitive consumer-good industry. The efficiency unit of labour at each location is set so that one unit of labour generates one unit of the competitive consumer-good. Since the consumer-good is freely tradeable the efficiency unit is standardised across locations. The unit of transport service is chosen so that one efficiency unit of labour generates one unit of the transport service. Thus differences between locations in labour productivity in the two competitive activities are reflected entirely in differences between the locations in their endowments of efficiency units per head of working population.

The production technology for the hth monopolised activity may be expressed indirectly using the input demand function

$$n_{hi} = n_h(\eta_{hi} x_{hi}, \gamma_{hi}) \qquad\qquad (h = 0, 1, \ldots, H+1) \qquad (7.1)$$

where $n_{hi} \geqslant 0$ is the input of labour to the hth activity at the ith location and $\eta_{hi} > 0$ is a cost parameter indicating the *comparative disadvantage* of labour at location i in the hth activity (relative to the production of the competitive consumer good). The input function $n_h(.)$ allows no free production, is twice differentiable and everywhere increasing with respect to output, but is otherwise unrestricted and so is compatible with either increasing, constant or decreasing returns to scale. Aggregate employment in monopoly production at location i is

$$n_i = \sum_{h=0}^{H+1} n_{hi} \qquad\qquad (7.2)$$

As already noted, the monopolist's activities embrace three stages: component production, assembly and marketing. Assembly combines components in fixed proportion while marketing requires a unit input from assembly for every unit sold. Let $z_{hi} \geqslant 0$ be the input of the hth component into assembly at location i, and let $b_h > 0$ be a fixed input–output coefficient for the assembly process; then

$$z_{hi} = b_h x_{1li} \qquad\qquad (h = 2, \ldots, H+1) \qquad (7.3)$$

Let z_{0i} be the input of the assembled product to the marketing activity at location i. Recalling that x_{0i} is the output of marketing, that is, the quantity sold, we have

$$z_{0i} = x_{0i} \qquad\qquad (7.4)$$

It is assumed that at each location there is a perfectly competitive labour market. Since the two competitive activities operate under constant returns to scale the whole of the income from them accrues to the sole variable factor, labour. Each location is sufficiently well endowed with labour for its specialisation in the marketing, production and transport of the monopoly good and its components to be always incomplete. Thus at each location the monopolist faces an infinitely elastic supply of labour at a unit wage.

It is assumed that the recipients of monopoly profit do not work and that only workers demand the monopoly consumer good. Since full employment wage income in each location is equal to the exogenous endowment of labour efficiency units, the income out of which the monopoly product is purchased is independent of the profit earned by the monopoly. Furthermore because no monopoly shareholders wish to purchase the monopoly good, the real income of the shareholders can be evaluated without reference to the price they must pay at their location as consumers of the monopoly good. Monopoly shareholders are therefore unanimous that management should maximise profit in units of the competitive consumer good.

The monopolist can discriminate between buyers at different locations but not between buyers at the same location. It may be assumed, for example, that the monopolist can costlessly introduce minor differentiations of the product which make it suitable for use at just one particular location. Potential arbitragers can only reverse these differentiations at prohibitive cost. It follows that the monopolist must charge a uniform price at each location but can set prices at different locations quite independently.

Analysing the consumer choice of the typical worker at a given location shows that when his preferences are smooth and strictly quasi-concave his demand for the monopolised product will normally be a continually increasing function of his wage income and a continuously decreasing function of its relative price. Since a worker's wage income is determined by his exogenous endowment of efficiency units, the aggregation of consumer demand across workers poses no problems. Thus for any set of workers' endowments at any location i there exists an aggregate demand d_i for the monopoly product which diminishes continuously with respect to its relative price p_i; this may be expressed in the indirect form.

$$P_i = p(d_i, N_i, f_i) \tag{7.5}$$

where N_i is the aggregate endowment of efficiency units and f_i is a paramenter governing the intensity of demand; f_i reflects a complex of factors, including the tastes of the different workers and the distribution of the efficiency units between them. It is assumed for simplicity that an input of marketing services in excess of the minimum prescribed by (7.1) has no effect whatsoever on the intensity of demand. It is assumed that the monopolist maintains the product market in equilibrium by meeting all the demand forthcoming at the price he has set; thus

$$d_i = z_{0i} \tag{7.6}$$

The gross quantity of the hth monopoly product ($h = 1, \ldots, H+1$) shipped from location i to location j is $m_{hij} \geqslant 0$ (the amount produced at location i for the local market is thus m_{hii}). Shipments to a location i include not only consignments destined for customers at i but also consignments being routed through i to other destinations. Let $x_{hij} \geqslant 0$ be the amount of the hth monopoly product consigned from production at i to customers at j ($x_{hii} = m_{hii}$), and let e_{hi} be the amount of the hth product routed through i for onward shipment to some other destination.

It is assumed that monopoly products can be freely disposed of either at the point of production, or at the point of delivery, but not during shipment. It is a consequence of this that (i) the total outward consignment from a location cannot exceed the local production:

$$\sum_{j=1}^{L} x_{hij} \leqslant x_{hi} \qquad (h = 1, \ldots, H+1) \tag{7.7}$$

(ii) the total inward consignment cannot be less than the local input:

$$\sum_{j=1}^{L} x_{hji} \geqslant z_{hi} \qquad (h = 1, \ldots, H+1) \tag{7.8}$$

(iii) the total outward shipment is equal to the sum of total outward consignments and the shipments being routed through the location on the way to somewhere else:

$$\sum_{j=1}^{L} m_{hij} = \sum_{j=1}^{L} x_{hij} + e_{hi} \qquad (h = 1, \ldots, H+1) \tag{7.9}$$

(iv) the total inward shipment is equal to the sum of total inward consignments and the shipments destined for re-export:

$$\sum_{j=1}^{L} m_{hji} = \sum_{j=1}^{L} x_{hji} + e_{hi} \qquad (h = 1, \ldots, H+1) \tag{7.10}$$

The input of transport services to trade between two locations i and j varies according to the product concerned, but is always directly proportional to the quantity exported:

$$t_{hij} = a_{hij} m_{hij} \qquad (h = 1, \ldots, H+1) \tag{7.11}$$

where $a_{hii} = 0$. The size of the parameter $a_{hij} \geqslant 0$ reflects the bulk, weight and fragility of the commodity h and the geographical relation between the locations i and j. If direct transit from i to j is difficult, it may be easier to route exports through one or more intermediate locations; for example, if $a_{hij} > a_{hil} + a_{hlj}$ then it is efficient to route exports from i to j *via* l (as shown later).

Because of the earlier assumption that at each location labour productivity in transport stands in exactly the same constant relation to labour productivity in the consumption good industry, no location has a comparative advantage in the supply of transport services. It is assumed, however, that transport services on a given route can be supplied only from the two terminal locations and that the supply of services must be shared equally between them. Thus the total requirement of transport services at location i is

$$t_i = \tfrac{1}{2}\sum_{h=1}^{H+1}\sum_{j=1}^{L}(t_{hij} + t_{hji}) \tag{7.12}$$

Locations are distributed across countries – though no fixed pattern is assumed. Each country has a sovereign government which levies tariffs and taxes. Countries may in turn be affiliated to free trade areas, customs areas or to international conferences which attempt to harmonise tariffs or taxes.

Let imports of the hth product at location i, originating from location j, be subject to an *ad valorem* tariff $s_{hji} \geqslant 0 (s_{hii} = 0)$. It is often asserted that the impact of tariffs is analogous to that of transport costs but this is true only in respect of consignments and not in respect of shipments. The reason is that tariffs are not normally levied on goods in transit through a location but only upon goods finally destined for it; goods imported to a location for immediate re-export can normally remain in bond and avoid customs duties. Thus while transport costs are incurred over every segment of a route taken by a consignment, tariffs are levied only at the final destination.

Tariffs are often specified according to country of origin and this clearly affords importers an opportunity for 're-originating' goods for tariff purposes at selected points on their route. This complication will, however, be ignored. It is assumed that tariffs are levied according to origin irrespective of the route, and that importers are honest when declaring origin.

Let q_{hi} be the transfer price for the hth product delivered to location i. The transfer price is identified with the internal 'invoice price' upon which tariffs are based and upon which the international allocation of profit is calculated. It is assumed that there are upper and lower bounds upon transfer prices based upon what the monopolist thinks the fiscal authorities will tolerate. In assessing these bounds the monopolist must take account of the attitudes of both the importing and exporting countries, as well as the attitude of the country in which the parent company is domiciled. If the lower bound for the hth commodity at location i is $Q_{hi} > 0$ and the upper bound is $Q_{hi}' \geq Q_{hi}$, then

$$Q_{hi} \leq q_{hi} \leq Q_{hi}' \qquad (h = 1, \ldots, H+1) \qquad (7.13)$$

The tariff payments collected at location i are

$$v_i = \sum_{h=1}^{H+1} \sum_{j=1}^{L} s_{hji} q_{hi} x_{hji} \qquad (7.14)$$

and so using equation (7.6), the accounting profit imputed to location i is

$$\pi_i = p_i d_i + \left(\sum_{h=1}^{H+1} \sum_{j=1}^{L} q_{hj} x_{hij} - \sum_{h=1}^{H+1} \sum_{j=1}^{L} q_{hi} x_{hji} \right) - n_i - t_i - v_i \qquad (7.15)$$

The first term in (7.15) is the revenue from local sales of the final product, the second term is the imputed revenue of intra-group exports net of the imputed value of intra-group imports, and the third term is the local wage bill. The two remaining terms are transport expenditure and tariff payments. It is assumed that at each location it is always the local subsidiary that hires the local transport services; there is no internal manipulation of payments for transport services. Similarly it is assumed that it is always the local subsidiary that pays the import tariff.

When accounting profit is aggregated across locations the imputed values of intra-group transactions cancels out and gives a global profit

$$\pi = \sum_{i=1}^{L} \pi_i = \sum_{i=1}^{L} (p_i d_i - n_i - t_i - v_i) \qquad (7.16)$$

Let profit taxation in location i be levied at a constant proportional rate $\tau_i (0 \leq \tau_i < 1)$ on the profits of the local subsidiary. Tax revenues and tariff payments collected at each location are distributed to local residents in transfer payments. The payments, it is assumed, accrue to profit-recipients rather than to wage-earners, and so have no distributional impact on the demand for the monopolised product. Profit recipients do not, however, 'endogenise' their income from taxes and tariffs when considering the optimal pricing strategy of the monopoly management.

The monopolist maximises global post-tax profit

$$\pi' = \sum_{i=1}^{L}(1 - \tau_i)\pi_i \tag{7.17}$$

which simplifies to

$$\pi' = (1 - \tau)\pi \tag{7.18}$$

when tax rates are harmonised

$$\tau_i = \tau \; (i = 1, \ldots, L) \tag{7.19}$$

When tax rates are harmonised transfer prices enter into post-tax profit only through the impact of tariff payments on pre-tax profit. Consequently a maximum of post-tax profit π' implies a maximum of pre-tax profit π and vice versa.

The residents of location i own a fixed proportion $g_i \geqslant 0$ of the monopoly equity, where

$$\sum_{i=1}^{L} g_i = 1 \tag{7.20}$$

Let π^* be the global maximum of profit and let π^*_i be the imputation of profit to location i associated with this maximum. Budgetary balance for the residents of location i requires that

$$c_i + p_i d_i = N_i + g_i \pi'^* + \tau_i \pi_i^* + v_i \tag{7.21}$$

which determines c_i, the consumption of the competitive consumer good as the balancing item in household budgets. Equilibrium in the labour market at location i requires that

$$y_i + n_i + t_i = N_i \tag{7.22}$$

which determines y_i, the production of the competitive good. Comparing (7.21) and (7.22) determines the 'balance of trade' created by the production, transport and consumption of the monopolised goods. The balance is equilibrated by a net import at location i of

$$u_i = c_i - y_i \tag{7.23}$$

units of the competitive consumption good. Since the competitive consumption good can be freely traded, the actual network of trade in the competitive good is indeterminate. However, adding (7.21), (7.22) and (7.23), summing over i and using (7.16), (7.17) and (7.20) shows that

$$\sum_{i=1}^{L} u_i = 0 \tag{7.24}$$

which demonstrates that the trading system as a whole is consistent.

7.4 MULTINATIONAL LOCATION STRATEGY

The behaviour of the MNE monopolist may be deduced in the usual way from the first order conditions for a maximum of profit. Substituting equations (7.1), (7.2), (7.5), (7.6), (7.11), (7.12), (7.14) and (7.15) into the maximand (7.17) and simplifying the constraints (7.3), (7.4) and (7.7) – (7.10) through the elimination of terms in e and z gives the Lagrangian:

$$
\begin{aligned}
L = \sum_{i=1}^{L}(1-\tau_i) & \left\{
\begin{array}{l}
p_i(d_i)d_i + \sum_{h=1}^{H+1}\sum_{j=1}^{L}q_{hj}x_{hij} - \sum_{h=1}^{H+1}\sum_{j=1}^{L}q_{hi}x_{hji} \\
- \sum_{h=0}^{H+1}n_{hi}(x_{hi}) - \tfrac{1}{2}\sum_{h=1}^{H+1}\sum_{j=1}^{L}(a_{hij}m_{hij}+a_{hji}m_{hji}) \\
- \sum_{h=1}^{H+1}\sum_{j=1}^{L}s_{hji}q_{hi}x_{hji}
\end{array}
\right\} \\
& + \sum_{h=1}^{H+1}\sum_{i=1}^{L}\xi_{hi}\Big(\sum_{j=1}^{L}m_{hji} - \sum_{j=1}^{L}m_{hij} - \sum_{j=1}^{L}x_{hji} + \sum_{j=1}^{L}x_{hij}\Big) \\
& + \sum_{i=1}^{L}v_{1i}\Big(\sum_{j=1}^{L}x_{1ji} - d_i\Big) \\
& + \sum_{h=2}^{H+1}\sum_{i=1}^{L}v_{hi}\Big(\sum_{j=1}^{L}x_{hji} - b_h x_{1i}\Big) \\
& + \sum_{h=1}^{H+1}\sum_{i=1}^{L}\mu_{hi}\Big(x_{hi} - \sum_{j=1}^{L}x_{hij}\Big) \\
& + \sum_{h=1}^{H+1}\sum_{i=1}^{L}\lambda_{hi}(q_{hi}-Q_{hi}) \\
& + \sum_{h=1}^{H+1}\sum_{i=1}^{L}\lambda_{hi}{}'(Q_{hi}{}'-q_{hi})
\end{aligned}
\tag{7.25}
$$

where v_{hi}, ξ_{hi}, μ_{hi}, λ_{hi}, λ_{hi}' are undetermined multipliers whose significance is explained later.

The Kuhn–Tucker necessary conditions for a local maximum (Intriligator, 1971) are as follows:

(a) The component production decision

Let μ_{hi} be the shadow cost of producing the hth monopolised good at location i. For each component the shadow cost of production at any location cannot exceed the marginal cost of local production, net of tax relief. If the component is locally produced then the shadow cost of component production is equal to the marginal net cost of local production. Thus for $h = 2, \ldots, H+1$

$$\mu_{hi} \leqslant (1 - \tau_i) \partial n_{hi} / \partial x_{hi} \tag{7.26}$$

with equality if $x_{hi} > 0$

(b) The assembly decision

The shadow cost of producing the assembled product at any location cannot exceed the sum of the shadow expenditure on component inputs and the marginal net cost of local assembly, and is equal to this sum if the product is assembled locally. Let v_{hi} be the shadow cost of the hth monopoly product at location i; then

$$\mu_{1i} \leqslant \sum_{h=2}^{H+1} v_{hi} b_h + (1 - \tau_i) \partial n_{li} / \partial x_{li} \tag{7.27}$$

with equality if $x_{1i} > 0$.

(c) The routing decision

Let ξ_{hi} be the shadow price of a shipment of the hth product at location i and define

$$\varphi_{hij} = \xi_{hj} - \xi_{hi} \tag{7.28}$$

as the shadow value of transport for the hth product from i to j. It is an immediate consequence of the definition (7.28) that

$$\varphi_{hii} = 0, \ \varphi_{hij} = -\varphi_{hji} \tag{7.29}$$

For all the components, and the assembled product too, the shadow value of transport from i to j cannot exceed the unit transport cost, net of tax relief; if the good is actually shipped from i to j then the shadow value and the unit cost are equal. Thus for $h = 1, \ldots, H+1$

$$\varphi_{hij} \leqslant [1 - \tfrac{1}{2}(\tau_i + \tau_j)] a_{hij} \tag{7.30}$$

with equality if $m_{hij} > 0$.

(d) The transfer-pricing decision

The shadow value of a transfer price constraint is non-zero only if the constraint itself is binding. When the lower bound on the transfer price for the hth product at location i is binding then the shadow value of the constraint is equal to the excess of the saving in tariff payments at i induced by a marginal lowering of the transfer-price over the additional tax obligations incurred by the reallocation of profit to location i. Likewise when the upper bound on the transfer price is binding, the shadow value of the constraint is equal to the excess of the saving in tax obligations incurred by a marginal reallocation of profit from location i over the additional tariff liability incurred.

Let λ_{hi} be the shadow value of the lower bound on the transfer price of the hth commodity at location i, and let λ'_{hi} be the shadow value of the corresponding upper bound. Define the shadow value of the combined transfer price constraints as

$$\delta_{hi} = \lambda_{hi} - \lambda'_{hi} \tag{7.31}$$

The lower bound is binding if $\lambda_{hi} > 0$ and the upper bound is binding if $\lambda'_{hi} > 0$. For each component, and for the assembled product, the shadow value of the combined transfer-price constraints at location i is

$$\delta_{hi} = (1-\tau_i)\sum_{j=1}^{L} s_{hji} x_{hji} + \sum_{j=1}^{L} (\tau_i - \tau_j) x_{hji} \tag{7.32}$$

for $h = 1, \ldots, H+1$. Note that in (7.32) the expressions for tariff savings and tax savings are weighted sums of the tariff rates and tax rates, with the weights being the quantities consigned from the different locations.

(e) The disposal decision

If the shadow cost of production of the hth product at the ith location is positive then there is no disposal of output, that is, if $\mu_{hi} > 0$ then the output constraint (7.7) is binding. If the shadow value at the ith location is positive then there is no disposal of supplies, that is, if $\nu_{hi} > 0$ then the inward consignment constraint (7.8) is binding.

(f) The assembly sourcing decision

Consider any assembly point j and any potential component source i. The shadow cost of the hth component at j cannot exceed the sum of its shadow cost of production at i, the shadow value of its transport from i, the tariff payable at j and the additional tax attributable to the reallocation of cost from j to i. If the component is actually consigned from i to j then the shadow cost is equal to this sum. Thus for $h = 2, \ldots,$ $H + 1$

$$v_{hj} \leqslant \mu_{hi} + \varphi_{hij} + [(1 - \tau_i)s_{hij} + \tau_i - \tau_j]q_{hj} \qquad (7.33)$$

with equality if $m_{hij} > 0$.

(g) The market sourcing decision

The shadow value of the assembled product at any location j cannot exceed the sum of the shadow cost of assembly at any location i, the transport and tariff costs incurred in its consignment from i to j, the additional tax attributable to the reallocation of profit from j to i and the marginal net cost of marketing at j. If the assembled product is actually consigned from i to j then the shadow value of the final product is equal to this sum. Thus

$$v_{1i} \leqslant \mu_{1i} + \varphi_{1ij} + [(1 - \tau_i)s_{1ij} + \tau_i - \tau_j]q_{1j} + (1 - \tau_i)\partial n_{Oj}/\partial x_{Oj} \qquad (7.34)$$

with equality if $x_{1ij} > 0$.

(h) The market sales decision

In each market the marginal revenue product cannot exceed the shadow value of the assembled product. When sales are positive the marginal revenue product is equal to the shadow value. Let $\varepsilon_i = -(\partial d_i/\partial p_i)p_i/d_i$ be the price elasticity of demand in the ith market; then

$$(1 - \tau_i)[1 - (1/\varepsilon_i)]p_i \leqslant v_{1i} \qquad (7.35)$$

with equality if $d_i > 0$.

The Kuhn–Tucker conditions confirm some intuitively obvious results.

(1) Whenever the unit cost of transport, net of tax relief, is positive there will be no cross-hauling of the product between any pair of locations. It is an immediate consequence of the routing conditions (7.28)–(7.30) that $m_{hij} > 0$ implies $m_{hji} = 0$ for any $j \neq i$.

(2) If for any origin i and any destination j there is a location l such that the unit net cost of transport *via* l is less than the unit net cost of direct shipment from i to j then nothing will be shipped directly from i to j. Using (7.28) and (7.30) shows that if

$$[1 - \tfrac{1}{2}(\tau_i + \tau_j)]a_{hij} > [1 - \tfrac{1}{2}(\tau_i - \tau_l)]a_{hil} + [1 - \tfrac{1}{2}(\tau_l - \tau_j)]a_{hlj}$$

then $m_{hij} = 0$.

(3) There is no disposal of output. Because, by assumption, there is no free production, the shadow cost of production is positive at any location where production occurs and hence the output constraint is always binding.

(4) In the absence of transfer-pricing there is no disposal of inputs either. Because production is costly and unit transport costs are non-negative, the value of supplies at any location is positive and so there is no disposal of inputs. However when transfer-pricing occurs the disposal of inputs is quite possible. When tax rates differ considerably between two countries and the fiscal authorities are flexible over transfer-pricing it may be profitable to ship a low-cost commodity at a high transfer-price from a high-tax country to a low-tax country even though the commodity has no use at its final destination.

The Kuhn–Tucker conditions can, in principle, be solved for the profit maximising monopolistic strategy. The solution determines the outputs of component production and assembly in each location x_{hi}, the prices of the final products, p_i, and the corresponding quantities sold, d_i, the pattern of international consignments, x_{hij}, the corresponding pattern of shipments, m_{hij}, the employments, n_{hi}, and the transfer prices q_{hi} as functions of the comparative disadvantages of labour in different locations, η_{hi}, the availability of non-tradeable inputs γ_{hi}, the input coefficients for components in the assembly process, b_h, the aggregate endowment of efficiency units in each location, N_i, the intensity of local demand, f_i, the unit costs of transport a_{hij}, the *ad valorem* tariff rates, s_{hij}, the profit taxation rates, τ_i, and the upper and lower bounds on the transfer prices, $Q_{hi}, Q'_{hi} (H = 1, \ldots, H+1; i = 1, \ldots, L)$.

The monopolist's strategy in turn determines the tariff and tax receipts at each location and, through the equity-ownership parameters g_i, the distribution of profit to each location as well. Income at each location then determines the local consumption of the competitive consumer good. The balance between local production and local consumption of this good determines the balance of trade.

7.5 A COMPUTABLE MODEL OF MULTINATIONAL LOCATION

This section presents a special case of the basic model, designed for practical computation. The model is well adapted to analysing the way that location adjusts to changes in technology and in market conditions.

On the supply side it is assumed that there are constant marginal returns to expanding production at a given location up to the capacity limit set by the labour endowment. On the demand side it is assumed that in the short run the product price in each market is fixed and the firm is committed to supplying all that is demanded at that price. In the long run the firm faces a demand at each location which diminishes linearly with respect to the product price.

Given these specifications, both the objective function and the feasible region faced by the monopolist are convex, and so the local maximum described by the Kuhn–Tucker conditions is a global maximum too. The short-run equilibrium of the firm can be determined from a linear programme, while the long-run equilibrium can be determined from a quadratic programme. Given the solutions of these programmes, the entire pattern of world trade can be deduced by arithmetic substitution into the equations for the competitive good industry.

The following example shows how the model can be applied to a short-run location problem. The accent is very much on simplicity. Four locations are distinguished: London, Brussels, Frankfurt and Madrid. Each location except Madrid is a potential source of demand for the monopoly product. The product is produced by assembling an engine and a frame. The transport costs for the engine and the frame are shown in Table 7.1. The assembled product is much bulkier than either of its components, and as a result, its unit transport cost is three times greater than for either of its components. The matrix of transport costs is assumed to be symmetric; only the elements to the right of the diagonal are shown in Table 7.1. To begin with tariffs are ignored and the rate of profit taxation is assumed to be the same at all locations.

Engine manufacture and assembly are feasible everywhere, but frame production is possible only in Madrid for example, because only

TABLE 7.1   *Transport costs for engines, frames and assembled products*

From/To	London	Brussels	Frankfurt	Madrid
London	—	2	4.5(4)	5
Brussels		—	2	4(3.5)
Frankfurt			—	1.5
Madrid				—

Madrid has the non-tradeable raw materials required or a geography suited to the disposal of pollutants. Labour costs (in efficiency units) differ significantly between locations. Table 7.2 shows that Frankfurt has a strong comparative advantage in engine manufacture and Madrid has a strong comparative advantage in assembly. The labour endowments in each location are shown in the final column of Table 7.2. The final demand for the finished product at each location is shown in Table 7.3.

In the short run the MNE's objective is to meet the final demands at minimum cost. It is not always necessary to invoke formal programming methods to solve a short-run location problem of this kind. The logical structure of the problem resolves the calculations into four fairly simple stages.

Because transport costs are linear and there is no capacity limit on the transport network the least-cost route between any two locations is independent of the quantity consigned between them. Thus the least-cost route for each consignment can be determined before the amounts to be consigned have been calculated.

Because production costs are linear, the costs of sourcing each location with an engine, a frame and an assembled product are

TABLE 7.2   *Labour costs*

| Location | Labour cost of | | | | Labour endowment |
	Engine	Frame	Assembly	Marketing	
London	16	—	10	2	3000
Brussels	15	—	8	2	3000
Frankfurt	10	—	8	2	4000
Madrid	20	6	3	2	1000

TABLE 7.3   *Final demands*

Location	Final demand
London	20
Brussels	30
Frankfurt	50
Madrid	0

independent of the quantities supplied – until, of course, the labour endowment at the source is exhausted. When calculating the cost of sourcing, it may be assumed that the least-cost route, determined in the first stage, is always employed. It is then quite straightforward to rank in terms of cost the alternative sources of engine and frames for each destination. (If tax rates differ between locations, however, the calculations are complicated by having to allow for the notional transfer of taxable profit between locations.)

To rank alternative sources of assembled products, it is assumed that each assembly plant is supplied with engines and frames from the lowest-cost sources (subject to capacity constraints). Adding the cost of the engine and the frame (inclusive of transport cost) to the labour cost of assembly makes it possible to rank in terms of cost the alternative sources of the assembled product for each market destination.

In the final stage a trial solution is considered in which each market is sourced from the lowest-cost location. If this allocation of production is feasible then it is also optimal. If some capacity limits are exceeded then the 'bottlenecks' must be relieved by switching some production to the next-lowest cost source. It is sensible to arrange for bottlenecks in assembly to be relieved before tackling bottlenecks in component production. If there are many bottlenecks then this heuristic approach is liable to break down and a formal procedure, for example, the simplex method (Baumol, 1977, Ch. 5) may need to be invoked. The simplex method differs from the heuristic approach in that it confines itself to investigating feasible solutions and it searches systematically across them. The heuristic approach can still be used, however, to provide an 'intelligent' trial solution from which the simplex procedure can commence.

Consider now the determination of the least cost routes. In Table 7.1 the figures without brackets indicate the cost of direct transport between the different locations. Inspection of the table reveals that in two instances it is cheaper to route consignments indirectly. Routing from London to Frankfurt via Brussels reduces the cost from 4.5 units to 4, whilst routing from Brussels to Madrid via Frankfurt reduces the cost from 4 units to 3.5. When these substitutions are made, the table may be reinterpreted as indicating the costs of consignment between the various locations, assuming that the consignment always follows the least-cost route. The least-cost routings are illustrated schematically by the solid lines in Figure 7.1.

Once the minimum costs of consignment have been derived, they can be combined with the data on labour costs in Table 7.2 to evaluate

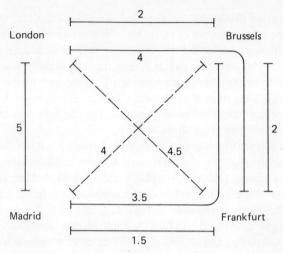

FIGURE 7.1   *Schematic representation of the solution of the least-cost routing*
problem

NOTE   Solid lines represent efficient routes

alternative assembly sourcing strategies. The relevant calculations are shown in Table 7.4. Subject to capacity constraints, it is efficient to concentrate all engine production in Frankfurt, irrespective of where assembly takes place.

Given the costs of the assembled product in the different locations, it is a straightforward matter to evaluate the costs of supplying each market from the various assembly points. The cost of supply is equal to the sum of the cost of the assembled product, the cost of transport to the market and the tariff payment (where applicable). The table shows that, subject to capacity constraints, it is efficient to service the London, Brussels and Madrid markets entirely from local assembly and to service the Frankfurt market entirely from Madrid. It follows that all the engines produced in Frankfurt will be exported to assembly plants at the other three locations.

Given the international distribution of final demands shown in Table 7.3, it is readily established that the pattern of specialisation described is compatible with the assumed labour endowment: the assumption of incomplete specialisation of production at each location (Section 7.3) is validated. The resulting matrix of trade flows is shown in Table 7.5. The implications of this matrix for employment at each location are shown in Table 7.6. It can be seen that in Frankfurt a high proportion

TABLE 7.4   *Determination of efficient assembly sourcing strategies*

	Location of assembly			
	London	Brussels	Frankfurt	Madrid
Delivered cost of engine from				
London	16	18	20	21
Brussels	17	15	17	18.5
Frankfurt	14*	12*	10*	11.5*
Madrid	24	23.5	21.5	20
Minimum	14	12	10	11.5
Delivered cost of frame from Madrid	11	9.5	7.5	6
Cost of local assembly	10	8	8	3
Minimum cost of assembled product	35	29.5	25.5	20.5
Delivered cost of assembled product in				
London	35*	35.5	37.5	35.5
Brussels	41	29.5*	31.5	31
Frankfurt	47	35.5	25.5	25*
Madrid	50	40	30	20.5*

NOTE   An asterisk identifies the cost-minimising source.

TABLE 7.5   *Matrix of trade flows for engines, frames and assembled products*

From/To		London	Brussels	Frankfurt	Madrid	Total
London	Engine	0	0	0	0	0
	Frame	0	0	0	0	0
	Assembly	20	0	0	0	20
Brussels	Engine	0	0	0	0	0
	Frame	0	0	0	0	0
	Assembly	0	30	0	0	30
Frankfurt	Engine	20	30	0	50	100
	Frame	0	0	0	0	0
	Assembly	0	0	0	0	0
Madrid	Engine	0	0	0	0	0
	Frame	20	30	0	50	100
	Assembly	0	0	50	0	50
Total	Engine	20	30	0	50	100
	Frame	20	30	0	50	100
	Assembly	20	30	50	0	100

TABLE 7.6   *The international allocation of labour*

Location	Engine manu- facturing	Frame manu- facturing	Assembly	Marketing	Transport	Competitive production	Total
London	0	0	200	40	70	2690	3000
Brussels	0	0	240	60	100	2600	3000
Frankfurt	1000	0	0	100	252.5	2647.5	4000
Madrid	0	600	150	0	222.5	1027.5	2000

of the labour force is involved in the production, transport and marketing of the monopoly product – in particular in the manufacture of engines, their outward transport to London, Brussels and Madrid, and the transport back of the assembled product from Madrid. Labour is also committed to the transport of frames from Madrid to Brussels, as these are routed through Frankfurt. Madrid is engaged extensively in frame manufacture and assembly, in the import of engines and the export of the frames and the assembled product. Labour in Brussels and London is engaged in assembly, the import of components and the marketing of the final product.

This example illustrates very clearly the three types of investment mentioned in Section 7.1. Import-substituting investment is exemplified by the location of assembly in London. London is the highest-cost location for assembly and is also remote from the manufacture of components in Frankfurt and Madrid. Assembly in London is efficient only because of the very high cost of transporting the assembled product instead of the components. The high cost of transporting the 'output' of assembly relative to its 'inputs' accords assembly a high degree of 'effective protection' (Balassa, 1971). London's 'effective protection' is sufficient to outweigh the labour cost savings that would be achieved by assembling elsewhere.

Export platform investment is exemplified by the specialisation of engine manufacture in Frankfurt. This specialisation accords with comparative advantage, and is exploited fully because of the relatively low transport costs for components and the fairly central position of Frankfurt within the transport network ('centrality' being defined with respect to the transport cost metric). Madrid is, to a lesser extent, an export platform for assembly. Like engine manufacture in Frankfurt assembly in Madrid is exclusively for export – though for different reasons: all engines are exported from Frankfurt because of vertical specialisation within the component production-assembly sequence whereas all assembled products are exported from Madrid simply because there is no local final demand for the product.

Raw materials investment is exemplified by the specialisation of frame manufacture in Madrid. Essentially this is an extreme form of comparative advantage in frame manufacture arising from exclusive access to an indispensable resource. Since the advantage is so strong, the fact that Madrid is on the 'periphery' of the transport network does not affect the incentive to locate frame manufacture in Madrid.

It is possible to measure the economies of vertical specialisation by comparing this situation with a situation in which, because of more primitive product design it is not feasible to separate the production of the engines and frames from the assembly of the product. If labour productivity in manufacturing were exactly the same as before but there were either no components, or the components were not tradeable, then all production would have to be carried on in Madrid, where essential inputs to frame-production are located. The product cost would be 29 units (see the bottom line of Table 7.2). This would give a delivered cost in London of 44 units (compared with 35 units with vertical specialisation), in Brussels of 41 units (compared with 29.5), in Frankfurt of 33.5 units (compared with 25), and in Madrid of 29 units compared with 20.5.

As noted above, import substitution is encouraged by high transport costs, and export platforms are encouraged by low transport costs. Since transport costs are normally higher for assembled products than for components, import-substituting investment is most likely at the assembly stage and export-platform investment in component manufacture. It is a consequence of this that improvements in product design which lower the transport cost of the assembled product relative to that of the component (for example, by trivialising a final stage of assembly in which much of the bulk is created) will reduce the significance of import-substitution. If, for example, the bulk of the assembled product could be reduced by one-third then, with a corresponding saving in transport costs, the model predicts that import-substituting assembly would entirely disappear. Both London and Brussels would cease to assemble the product and assembly would be concentrated completely on Madrid.

Tariffs tend to be levied more frequently upon final products than upon components. It is because a tariff on a final product does not directly inhibit the vertical specialisation of production that a fairly low tariff on a final product can generate a fairly high degree of 'effective protection' for assembly. Thus in the model the imposition by Frankfurt of a 5 per cent tariff on imports of the assembled product from Madrid will be sufficient to switch assembly from Madrid to Frankfurt. The impact of tariffs can, however, be mitigated by transfer-pricing. If the MNE can transfer the assembled product from Madrid to Frankfurt at a notional price of less than 10 units rather than at the true cost of 25 units then the tariff payments will be too small to influence location, and assembly will remain in Madrid.

Suppose now that each location has a linear demand curve for the monopolised consumer-product. As noted in Section 7.3, one of the parameters of demand at each location is the endowment of labour efficiency units. Consistency requires that the demand curve at each location does not, under any circumstances, commit wage-earners to spend more than their labour endowment on the monopolised product. The demand schedules reported in the first column of Table 7.7 all satisfy this constraint. It is assumed that demand in Frankfurt is relatively inelastic, in London reasonably elastic and Brussels very elastic. Demand in Madrid is reasonably elastic too, but the intensity of demand is so low that the market does not warrant any supply.

TABLE 7.7   *The long-run marketing plan for the monopolist*

Location	Demand	Price	Quantity
London	$d = 110 - 2p$	45	20
Brussels	$d = 296 - 8p$	33.25	30
Frankfurt	$d = 125 - p$	75	50
Madrid	$d = 15 - 2p$	20.5	0

In the long run the monopolist maximises profits by setting prices in each of the markets so that the marginal revenue in each market is equal to the marginal cost of supply. Under these conditions long-run profit-maximisation generates the short-run final demands specified earlier. In Frankfurt a price of 75 units is charged and the quantity sold is fifty; in London the price is 45 units and the quantity sold is twenty; in Brussels the price is 33.25 units and the quantity sold is thirty. In Madrid the product is priced at cost – 20.5 units – but nothing is sold. The location strategy and the matrix of trade flows is therefore exactly the same as before.

7.6 CONCLUSION

This chapter has developed a simple computable model of the behaviour of a vertically- and horizontally-integrated MNE operating a rationalised production system in which different activities are linked through international trade. It has been suggested that the model is well adapted to analysing the impact on trade of changes in technology associated with increased division of labour and of reductions in transport costs. It also extends the results of previous models concerning the impact of tariffs and tax differentials on the location of production.

The model is developed with applications at the firm and industry level very much in mind. It enables the modeller to analyse import-substituting investment, export-platform investment and raw-materials investment within a single framework and to derive predictions through simulation using standard computational techniques.

The model can be extended in a number of ways. The assumption that production at each location is incompletely specialised is crucial in generating simple results. In particular, it means that because capacity constraints are never binding, it is unnecessary – in the context of this model – for the firm to resort to multiple sourcing of components. Each assembly process receives any given component from a single source. Introducing binding capacity constraints into the model would increase the problems of solution quite considerably, but would facilitate a detailed analysis of multiple sourcing. Still greater realism could be achieved by making the capacity constraints stochastic, so that the firm could also engage in diversifying the risk of disruption of supplies through multiple-sourcing.

Another useful extension of the model would be to allow the firm a choice of production technique at each location. To allow a meaningful choice of technique another factor of production would have to be introduced; by increasing the generality of the model in this way, the substitution possibilities analysed by the HO model would appear as a special case. The model therefore has great potentiality, though it is difficult to assess at this stage how far it is useful to pursue the quest for generality alluded to above.

8 Entrepreneurship and the Dynamics of Foreign Direct Investment

MARK CASSON

8.1 INTRODUCTION

Analysis of entrepreneurship has been very much neglected by economists. This weakness of orthodox theory is apparent in fields as diverse as economic development, comparative economic systems, investment and business cycles, industrial structure, and the distribution of income (Baumol, 1968). This chapter shows that by relaxing some of the restrictive assumptions of orthodox theory it is possible to develop an economic theory of entrepreneurship which offers insights into international business behaviour.

Cantillon and Say were among the earliest economists to discuss the entrepreneur, but it was left to J. S. Mill to popularise the concept among English economists (though in this respect his influence did not last for long). The most extensive literature on entrepreneurship is Austrian; the early writers of this school sought to defend profit against socialists' assertion of the workers' 'right to the whole produce of labour'; later, interest broadened to a comparison of markets and planning as co-ordinators of economic activity (Hayek, 1937, 1949; Mises, 1949).

All writers agree that an entrepreneur owns and/or controls productive activities, but there has been disagreement, or a difference of emphasis, over his precise role. This is evident in the various English translations of the word: undertaker, adventurer, merchant. It is therefore appropriate to begin by distinguishing various categories of entrepreneur, and examining the relation between them.

172

8.2 THE OWNER-ENTREPRENEUR AND THE MANAGER-ENTREPRENEUR

Knight (1921) defines the entrepreneur as someone who hires inputs and owns exclusive rights in the final product. The entrepreneur's relation with the factor inputs is a purely contractual one. The factor owner receives a fixed payment and in return foregoes any 'natural' or 'traditional' right to the product obtained by the utilisation of his factor. In practice the contractual arrangements are usually made in two stages, with a legal fiction – the firm – being the nominal party to the contracts.

Because payments for inputs are normally made at a time when receipts from output are uncertain, the owner-entrepreneur is a risk-bearer.

According to Knight business risks cannot be shifted on to professional insurers because the probabilities of alternative outcomes cannot be estimated. Each business situation is unique; there are no classes of outcomes where each has the same *a priori* probability, nor is there repeated sampling to allow estimation of relative frequencies.

However, it is doubtful whether Knight's argument establishes that business risks are uninsurable *per se*. Rather, the uniqueness of business situations increases the information the insurer requires about the insured; it is argued later that the costs of obtaining this information are a major influence on the institutional structure of entrepreneurship.

In neoclassical economics a manager is responsible for deciding upon and implementing the production plan, that is, for choosing technique, setting the scale of output and ensuring that each input is available in the right quantity at the right time and place. In institutional economics he is also responsible for choosing institutional arrangements and thereby determining the boundaries of the firm. The essence of the manager's role is not ownership but negotiation and control.

The work of negotiation delegated to the manager concerns both contracts of employment (negotiated with factor owners) and contracts of sale (negotiated with purchasers of output). It is the form of the contracts negotiated with factor owners – in particular labour – which gives the manager his customary powers of control (Coase, 1937; Williamson, 1975). Because of the cost of covering each contingency in an employment contract, or of renegotiating it in the light of each unforeseen change of circumstances, employees normally agree to accept a certain degree of managerial discretion in the use of their labour; this allows managers to redeploy labour without further negotiation. The agreement of employees is obtained because the cost savings are sufficient to finance higher wages to compensate them for any additional risks involved in this form of contract.

Brokerage costs in labour markets mean that once an employer has found an employee it is normally of mutual benefit for the employment to continue until circumstances change. Hence most employment contracts are open-ended, continuing automatically until they are terminated by one of the parties. This gives the manager his customary power to fire employees.

8.3 THE RELATION BETWEEN OWNERSHIP AND MANAGEMENT

There is controversy over the extent of managerial discretion in business behaviour. In Knight's view the manager is fully accountable to the owner; management is simply one of the factors of production hired by the owner-entrepreneur. If accurate appraisal of managerial performance is costless and managers are interchangeable at will, then competition for managers will ensure that each manager's performance is fully reflected in his market valuation, that is, in the present value of his earnings. In such an ideal market the costs of avoidable managerial inefficiency are borne by the manager himself, in terms of foregone salary. Market incentives harmonise the interests of owner and manager; all the owner has to do to ensure efficient management is to pay the manager his market-determined salary (Alchian, 1969).

But in practice the appraisal of managerial performance is difficult, and interchanging managers incurs costs (for example due to a failure to recoup the training expenses of managers who leave). Under such circumstances the disciplines of the market cannot, unaided, provide adequate managerial incentives. The onus rests with the owner to provide his own internal incentives, by monitoring managers and rewarding the successful ones through promotion, payment by results, etc. (Chandler, 1962; Williamson, 1970).

The importance of internal incentives will normally depend on the ability of the manager and the size of the firm. Ambitious managers in small firms where the promotion ladder is short will recognise the necessity of performing well in order to be competitive when applying for higher paid posts in large firms; hence they are continually conscious of the discipline of the external market. On the other hand managers who do not wish to move, or who are sceptical of their outside promotion prospects, will be conscious mainly of internal incentives; this applies particularly to low- or middle-level management posts in large firms, where it is difficult for outsiders to appraise the quality of individual performance.

It appears therefore that there are certain 'ownership skills' concerned with efficient delegation of management, which are particularly important in large firms; these skills involve devising monitoring procedures and internal incentive schemes. However the prevalence of joint-stock organisation and the diffused ownership of voting shares in large corporations may make the cost of enforcing management accountability relatively high, while brokerage costs and the threat of government intervention may be a deterrent to outright take-over (Alchian, 1977, pp. 127–49). Thus even where ownership skills are available it may be difficult to exercise them. Although the objectives of owners determine the bounds within which managers operate, these bounds may leave considerable scope for managerial discretion. This analysis suggests that the actual extent of discretion will be greater, the greater are the frictions in the management and capital markets.

8.4 INNOVATION AND ARBITRAGE

It would be quite possible to stop the analysis at this point. We could say that we have distinguished two intangible factors of production – business risk-bearing and management. Because the market for management is imperfect there are certain 'ownership skills' which the bearer of business risk requires, namely knowledge of monitoring procedures and of internal incentive schemes. It is the possession of these skills, amongst other things, which distinguishes the bearer of business risk from the insurer against natural hazard. Profit is shared among the factors of production in relation to their 'marginal products'. If marginal returns diminish in appropriate fashion then there will be a finite optimum size of firm where there are constant returns to a marginal change of scale and profit is just exhausted by factor payments. The theory could be tested by examining the distribution of income between ownership and management, and assessing the extent to which portfolios are specialised in either bearing business risk or insuring against natural hazard.

But to stop here would be to repeat a cardinal error of neoclassical theory, namely to provide a static analysis of a fundamentally dynamic problem. The model described assumes a state of equilibrium in which, conditional on their state of knowledge, transactors' plans are fully reconciled by the prices prevailing in equity and management markets. But in practice equilibrium is continually being disturbed by changes in the market environment or in knowledge of that environment. Both product and factor markets are susceptible to unforeseen changes. A major role of the entrepreneur is in creating such change and/or in responding to it. The activities of entrepreneurs continually move markets away from one equilibrium and adjust them towards another. The movement away from equilibrium is associated mainly with innovation, the movement towards equilibrium with arbitrage. Innovation and arbitrage are, to some extent, merely different facets of the same phenomenon: spill-overs from innovation by one entrepreneur change the environment of other entrepreneurs and thereby create arbitrage opportunities for them.

Schumpeter (1934, 1939) contrasts innovation with invention. Invention represents a change in the state of the arts, innovation occurs only when resources are diverted to exploit the new state of the arts and a new, improved or cheaper product is produced. As a consequence of successful innovation, markets for substitute products contract and resources specialised in their production become obsolete; this is a process of 'creative destruction'.

However, the concept of innovation need not be restricted to technical advances. Improvements in marketing and management techniques are equally important, and are often closely linked to technological change, for example, the design of management information systems has been strongly influenced by computerisation. Some of the most influential innovations have been the creation of new types of institution (or the adaptation of existing institutions to new purposes) for example, the development of trading banks, unit trusts and conglomerate holding companies.

It should also be noted that much innovative activity is not of the pioneering kind pictured by Schumpeter, in which the new product or process bears little relation to what has gone before. Many innovations consist in the modification of earlier concepts and techniques, often arising from a need to adapt them to new environments; and many more consist simply in transferring an idea from one environment to another, with little or no adaptation. While the pioneer is undoubtedly the highest order of entrepreneur, the lower orders of adaptors and transferors have played a major role in the international diffusion of economic change. It is only the imitator – who replicates activities within the same environment – who may legitimately be denied the title of entrepreneur (in its dynamic sense).

Arbitrage consists of buying 'cheap' in one segment of a market and selling 'dear' in another (Kirzner, 1973). Arbitrage is the fundamental economic mechanism by which price uniformity is achieved. The arbitrager sets up transactions in an attempt to appropriate the discrepancy between the lowest selling price and the highest buying price. In doing so he raises the lowest selling price and reduces the highest buying price and so creates a tendency to price-uniformity. The gains to transactors from specialising arbitrage in the hands of middlemen arise from economies of scale in information-handling and from exploiting the middlemen's personal comparative advantage in such activities.

In a stationary economy the arbitrager's role would be a transitory one. Competing arbitragers would gradually eliminate one another's profits until equilibrium was achieved. But when patterns of demand and supply are continually changing some segments of the market expand while others contract. Thus there are continual profit-opportunities in buying up supplies in segments where supply is expanding relative to demand and selling them in segments where demand is expanding relative to supply.

Arbitrage can take a number of forms. Some of the most common are:

(1) inter-industry arbitrage, where capitalists liquidate their assets in low-profit industries and switch them to high-profit industries; this is the long run entry and exit mechanism which equalises rates of return in different sectors of the economy;
(2) spatial arbitrage, where goods (or consumers of services) are transported between different locations to take advantage of inter-regional price differentials;
(3) intertemporal arbitrage, where dealers equalise international interest rate differentials and forward exchange premia;
(4) interpersonal arbitrage, where dealers link buyers and sellers who would not otherwise transact because of mutual ignorance.

8.5 THE SYNTHESIS OF INFORMATION

Innovation and arbitrage are two special cases of entrepreneurial activity. The key function of the entrepreneur – the one that may be regarded as defining his role – is to take important decisions that are difficult to make. If the 'wrong' person took such a decision, error of judgement would lead to a very costly mistake. The entrepreneur may take decisions acting either as a principal – that is, as the owner of a firm – or as a delegate – that is, as a manager hired by the owners. Most important decisions involve searching out, identifying and exploiting profit-opportunities. Successful decision-making of this kind requires the entrepreneur to synthesise different kinds of information from very diverse sources.

The successful innovator needs to synthesise four main types of information: (i) the technology of transforming inputs into an output, (ii) the supply price of the inputs, (iii) the demand price of the output, and (iv) the law and institutions governing transactions in the input and output markets. The successful arbitrager needs to combine information about (i) the technology of moving goods within or between markets, (ii) price differentials between markets or sub-markets, and (iii) the law and institutions governing transactions in these markets. In each case none of the items of information is by itself sufficient to indicate a profit-opportunity; only when technical, marketing and institutional aspects are combined does the information acquire commercial value (Leibenstein, 1968; Penrose, 1959; Richardson, 1960).

Information acquired by an entrepreneur is not necessarily of absolute certainty, nor is it even necessarily correct. All that entrepreneurial activity demands is that the synthesiser has sufficient confidence in the information that the expectation of profit outweighs the subjective risk involved. Entrepreneurs who act on correct information will tend to be successful, while those whose information is incorrect are liable to fail. The relationship is by no means exact however; for example, projects based on false information may turn out successfully for reasons which were wholly unforeseen.

8.6 THE MONOPOLY OF INFORMATION

An essential feature of a profit-opportunity is that the entrepreneur has a monopoly of its exploitation. This is not to deny that there are everywhere competitive constraints which determine the size of the profit that can be appropriated. But if two or more entrepreneurs independently exploit identical commercial information then they will bid up buying prices and bid down selling prices until all profit has been eliminated.

A monopoly in the exploitation of commercial information can be achieved either by legal patent or by maintaining secrecy about a discovery. In orthodox neoclassical theory the patent is the only source of monopoly that is recognised, for it is an assumption of the theory that all individuals are equally well-informed. But in practice lags in the diffusion of information create inequalities in access to information which may form the basis of temporary monopoly.

The distinction between patent and secrecy is crucial for the way the information is exploited. If commercial information is patented then it is possible in principle for the discoverer to license the information to those who have a comparative advantage in its exploitation. But attempts to license a secret will encounter the problem of buyer uncertainty, and this provides a strong incentive for a discoverer of commercial information to exploit it himself (see Chapter 3).

Another aspect of the same problem is that it is difficult to share the risk involved in the exploitation of a commercial secret. Without patent protection the discoverer cannot afford to supply potential equity investors with full information because they may pre-empt the profit-opportunity (having, as they do, superior access to risk capital). But without access to the information the investors are likely to face much greater subjective risks than does the discoverer. This 'information barrier' may be surmounted by a combination of two strategies. First, the discoverer may put some of his own capital at risk. Even if this is only a small proportion of the total capital required, it may be sufficient to convince investors of his integrity, particularly if his exposure represents a large proportion of his personal wealth. But this will not suffice to convince investors of his qualities of judgement. This second problem can be resolved if both parties agree to delegate the crucial decision on the exploitation of the information to a hired manager with proven reputation. The risk capital is put up on the condition that the final decision whether or not to sink it in exploitation rests with the manager rather than with the discoverer himself. Thus the exploitation of information takes place within a corporate organi-sation, where the discoverer is part minority shareholder and part employee; as employee he is accountable to a manager appointed by the major shareholders.

The effects of patentability on the organisation of entrepreneurship are summarised schematically in Figure 8.1.

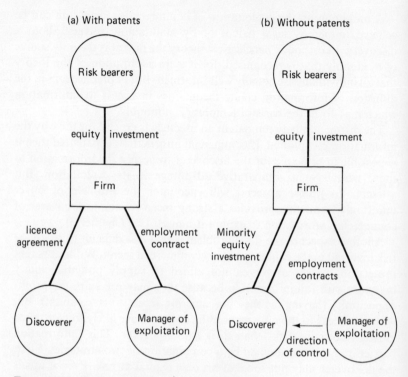

FIGURE 8.1   *The organisation of entrepreneurship*

8.7 THE STRATEGY OF ENTREPRENEURSHIP

It is sometimes suggested that entrepreneurial success is purely a matter of chance. The entrepreneur pursues diversity as an end in itself; each project is an experiment, and statistical laws determine that on average a certain proportion will be successful (Alchian, 1950). Indirect confirmation of this view comes from the high proportion of new businesses which fail, the robustness of simple stochastic processes in explaining income distribution and so on. But this evidence is also consistent with a more sophisticated view, namely that entrepreneurship is the outcome of rational choice, the parameters of which can be identified, and that it is the values of these parameters which are distributed at random among the population. Differences in parameter values between individuals reflect different preferences, abilities, endowments of wealth, etc. Differences in the average values of parameters between societies reflect differences in attitudes, laws and institutions, and general social and economic structure.

This section considers the principles underlying the strategy of a rational entrepreneur and develops a number of predictions concerning his behaviour. The analysis also has implications for the personal qualities needed by a successful entrepreneur.

The first stage of entrepreneurship is gaining access to information. Table 8.1 lists a number of ways of gathering information, classified according to whether the information is obtained first-hand, or from an

TABLE 8.1 *Some of the more important ways in which an entrepreneur gains information*

Method	Examples
By direct observation	
Attend markets	Visit trade fairs, exhibitions, auctions, markets, shops
Monitor public behaviour	Study the outdoor behaviour of people travelling, working or at leisure
Take employment	Study employer's technology and operating methods; identify his major customers and suppliers
Scientific experiment	Conduct experiments in physical and biological sciences; develop prototype products and improve them by trial and error
By communication from another person	
Study published information (news and advertisements)	Read notices, newspapers and books, and monitor broadcasts
Direct enquiry	Write or phone requesting information; conduct market research by questionnaire
Social contact	Exchange information through conversation with social contacts
Eavesdropping	Overhear conversations; read confidential documents by stealth
Announce offer to trade and monitor response	Advertise in order to elicit a response from potential transactors
Formal instruction	Attend conferences, short courses, etc.

intermediate source. An examination of this table indicates that in many cases information is not acquired as the result of full-time specialised search, but instead emerges as a joint product generated in the course of some other activity. Very often the choice of this activity will have been determined by its production and consumption characteristics and not by any specific information requirements. In such cases the type of information generated may be wholly unforeseen, so the entrepreneur must be good at recognising its significance and reacting quickly to it; this quality has been termed 'alertness' (Kirzner, 1973).

In other cases the choice of the activity may be dictated by the need for specific information. A particularly interesting case is where the activity is needed to provide a legitimate reason for entering a particular environment. The activity provides a 'cover', without which the searcher would not be admitted because of the desire of those who share the environment to maintain confidentiality. The pursuit of such a search strategy may involve a good deal of subterfuge.

It has already been noted that the synthesis of commercial information involves drawing on a diversity of sources. Where the information covers a variety of subject areas the entrepreneur will need a wide background knowledge to understand all of it; and where the information originates in different countries he may require a good grasp of local cultures and languages to interpret it. Given the diversity of sources it is tempting to imagine the entrepreneur connected to his sources by a network of telecommunications, but perusal of Table 8.1 suggests that many ways of acquiring information are based on face-to-face contact. First-hand observation requires the observer to be close to the subject of the information. Effective communication often depends on face-to-face contact too, so that the reliability of information can be checked by cross-examination, and any concealment detected. The importance of face-to-face contact, coupled with the diversity of information sources, points to the need for the entrepreneur to be both geographically and socially mobile, that is, he must be good at travelling and at getting along with people from diverse backgrounds.

The picture which emerges is of an entrepreneur who spends relatively little time 'running his business' and much of it developing contacts with potential customers and suppliers, competitors' employees, public administrators, pressure groups, etc. Although his activities may seem somewhat aimless, they are in fact designed to achieve maximum face-to-face contact with information sources in a diversity of environments.

Once the relevant information sources have been tapped, the next stage is to process the information from them to diagnose any profit-opportunities. The information-processing system consists of the entrepreneur together with whatever secretarial assistance, office equipment, computer services, etc. he considers it economic to provide. Ultimately the efficiency of the system depends on the entrepreneur's ability to organise and delegate routine information handling and his imagination or flair in analysing the summary information made available to him.

When a profit-opportunity has been diagnosed the entrepreneur must maximise the profit he can appropriate from it. The principal constraints on his behaviour are the actions and reactions of other entrepreneurs. Since there is continual competitive search for information, any delay in exploiting the opportunity increases the risk that it will be discovered by someone else (either independently, or through a 'leak'). On the other hand if the opportunity is exploited hurriedly then costs may rise. Furthermore the very act of exploitation may attract the notice of others and so speed up the diffusion of the information; so that if the information is exploited before there has been time for its wider implications to be worked out, the initiative in adapting the idea, or transferring it to new environments, may pass to others.

The ease with which a profit-opportunity can be fully pre-empted depends on a number of factors. Some opportunities can be exploited by a once-for-all stock adjustment, for example, buying up agricultural land and exploiting mineral resources underneath it. Other opportunities can only be exploited by initiating a flow, for example, introducing a new product. The difference would not be important were it practicable to set up long-term forward contracts for flows of inputs and outputs. The long-term contracts would tie factor owners and purchasers of the product to the innovating firm, and so establish an effective barrier to the entry of imitators. But in practice it is difficult to organise such contracts; for example, long-term contracts for one of the most important factor inputs – labour – cannot normally be enforced. This not only restricts employers in securing supplies of labour; it means that workers cannot easily capitalise their earning power and so cannot afford the outlays that long-term consumption contracts would require. Capitalisation of input and output streams can only be achieved when inputs and outputs are services generated by durable assets in which there are transferable property rights. In this case the innovating firm can pre-empt imitators by buying up supplies of the relevant durable assets (provided that the assets are in fixed or inelastic supply).

In some cases the habitual nature of economic behaviour may be exploited as a substitute for long-term contracts. If we suppose that individuals do not choose directly their consumption and production plans, but rather choose a pattern of habitual response to consumption and production stimuli, then the innovating firm may be able to pre-empt a profit-opportunity by encouraging people to change their habits. For example, an introductory offer on a new product, by subsidising consumers who experiment, may help to break old habits, while a coupon offer on repeat buys may reinforce the new habit.

Another policy for deterring imitators is to prevent the dissemination of information to anyone who is not a legitimate supplier or customer. For example, potential transactors may be screened before price negotiations are begun, to ensure that they are not acting as 'fronts' for competitors seeking price information, employees may be given only partial access to company information so that no individual is sufficiently well-informed to 'go independent' in competition with the firm, disclosure of profits and performance data may be kept to the minimum consistent with legal obligations, and so on. This is the obverse of the point made earlier, that seekers of commercial information must contend with discrimination unless they have a legitimate cover for their search activity.

The picture which emerges is that entrepreneurial activity is a competitive search for information, involving a race to be first to discover it and a struggle to defend it against potential imitators. The successful entrepreneur requires not only creative talents, such as imagination, skill in routine information-processing, wide background knowledge and an ability to communicate face-to-face, but also considerable tactical awareness, to be used in gaining information by subterfuge, exploiting habitual behaviour and countering espionage by transactors and employees.

8.8 TEAM ENTREPRENEURSHIP

The qualities required of a successful entrepreneur are exceptional. It is only rarely that someone will possess all (or even most) of them; those who do will command very high incomes. But it may be possible to organise a team of less-talented people who together can perform as well as a single more-talented individual.

The main advantage of team organisation is that each member is required only to exercise a limited range of skills (although he must have sufficiently broad knowledge to communicate effectively with other specialists in the team). Another advantage is that when outside contacts are geographically dispersed, team members, suitably located, can maintain face-to-face contact with outsiders (and with each other) at a relatively modest cost in travel time. By contrast the individual entrepreneur meeting the same number of contacts would spend almost all his time travelling. Alternatively he would have to substitute telecommunication for more reliable face-to-face contact.

An obvious disadvantage of team organisation is that imperfect communication between members may lead to delay or distortion in the processing of information. The extent of the problem will depend on how good an understanding can be built up between team members and this in turn depends on the stability of membership. Another problem is that incentives may suffer when it is difficult to attribute responsibility for success or failure to particular individuals; and even if praise or blame could be accurately apportioned, the importance of stability might make it very costly to replace an inefficient member.

On balance it seems that the more diverse are the skills required in entrepreneurship and the more dispersed are the information sources, the greater are the advantages of team organisation. A diversity of skills means not only that the demands on an individual entrepreneur are much greater, but also that the role of each team member is more easily distinguished and so personal accountability is more readily enforced. Geographical dispersion of information sources means that each team member will spend less time travelling than would the individual entrepreneur and so more time will be available for the creative work of analysing the information that has been acquired.

A team of entrepreneurs can be organised in various ways, the main difference being in the degree of centralisation involved. A highly centralised organisation involves a set of 'listening posts' or 'sensors' which are placed in strategic environments; they pass on their information to headquarters, where it is collated and analysed; instructions for the exploitation of profit-opportunities are then passed back to the peripheral units. A decentralised organisation involves largely autonomous entrepreneurs with common access to central services, data banks, etc. Where appropriate, entrepreneurs liaise directly with each other in developing profit-opportunities, instead of waiting for the initiative to come from headquarters.

The advantage of centralisation is that it allows very sophisticated profit-opportunities to be discovered, for example, arbitrage involving chains of transactions across different markets or the adaptation of a complex technology to an apparently alien environment. The advantage of the decentralised system is that it provides team members with the flexibility to respond rapidly to local profit-opportunities before independent entrepreneurs can pre-empt them.

The two structures can be integrated by giving each entrepreneur a certain area of autonomy, while requiring him to accept certain obligations to headquarters. The precise amount of autonomy given will depend on the nature of the market environment in which it is planned to operate. In most cases an integrated system of this kind should provide a viable alternative to the individual entrepreneur.

8.9 THE DYNAMICS OF FOREIGN DIRECT INVESTMENT

The remainder of this paper shows how the analysis of entrepreneurship can be applied to international business behaviour. Because the ramifications of the theory are so wide, it is necessary to confine the discussion to a single topic. We have chosen to show how analysis of the information flows associated with entrepreneurial activity can improve understanding of the links between the various stages in the growth of a multinational firm. We now consider in turn the dynamics of 'horizontal' and 'backward' foreign direct investment (FDI).

Horizontal integration

The typical horizontal foreign direct investor is a firm producing a differentiated product and protected by limited barriers to entry. Consider the firm in the early stages of its growth before foreign markets have been tapped. We begin by asking: how does the entrepreneur acquire information about potential overseas markets?

One important channel of information flow is migration, which brings people from one environment to live in another. If the entrepreneur himself is an immigrant then he will have first-hand knowledge of at least one overseas market. Alternatively he may have family relations who have emigrated. Although information from such sources is secondhand it will be more up-to-date than that available to an immigrant who has left home some time ago.

Another means of gaining information is by travel. This may be undertaken with the specific object of investigating overseas markets;

alternatively the information may be a by-product of social visits or holidays abroad.

Numerous permutations of the information networks can be generated, but the general principle is simple enough: migration and travel are potentially important channels of market information for introducing producers to overseas markets.

Having obtained some indication of local demand the entrepreneur may decide to export, perhaps using emigrant contacts to assist him in overseas distribution. As a result he obtains reliable information on the actual level of demand at quoted export prices. However if a local middleman is being used as sales agent then only a small proportion of the relevant information will normally be passed back to the exporting firm. This information could be purchased by buying out the middleman and establishing a sales subsidiary.

A sales subsidiary gives the exporting firm access to the local business world: social contacts can be developed, and information 'exchanged' through conversations with other traders; in particular some idea of local factor prices can be obtained. This facilitates an evaluation of sourcing strategy, as a result of which a decision may be made to replace exports with FDI (Johanson and Vahlne, 1977).

Once a production subsidiary has been established the firm will acquire a detailed knowledge of factor prices and other (environmental) influences on production cost. These can be compared with factor prices and environmental influences at home and at any other overseas production plants that the firm has established. This comparison may suggest ways of concentrating particular aspects of production at specific locations to take advantage of the international division of labour according to comparative costs. This movement will be strengthened if the activities which make up the production process exhibit economies of scale. The implementation of this strategy may involve the firm in redesigning the production process to allow the product to be assembled from a number of standardised components produced in different locations.

When a firm has completed the rationalisation of international production, has the evolution of its international operations come to an end? The answer must surely be no, provided that entrepreneurial talent still remains. The information on host-economies collected by foreign subsidiaries will not be confined to the firm's operations. All sorts of intelligence will come their way, particularly where the subsidiaries are large enough to be involved in consultations with government. Governments by nature are averse to *laissez faire* doctrines, and regularly intervene in the economy in response to various indicators. The ability to foresee the reactions of governments is a potentially large source of profit, particularly if it is possible to synthesise information on the policies of different governments in order to forecast movements in any sort of 'international differential' – for example, tax rates, interest rates, rates of inflation, rates of growth. The modern multinational firm is in a good position to undertake world-wide arbitrage operations in response to forecast movements in differentials of this kind.

The preceding discussion ties in well with what is known about the decision to invest abroad. The emphasis on migration as an information channel explains why, for example, British firms have often expanded into Commonwealth markets before they have tapped those in Europe or the US. The fact that the frequency of travel diminishes with the distance of the journey may be one reason why foreign investments are more often between neighbouring countries than they are between countries much further apart, despite the fact that the potential saving in transport costs of exported goods is much greater in the latter case. The importance of trade as an information channel may explain why many firms prefer to export for a time even though, in retrospect, it would seem to have been more profitable to invest immediately: exporting reduces the subjective risks of FDI by providing better information on host-country demand. Finally there is evidence that some large mature multinationals have already evolved into organisations oriented towards generalised arbitrage in productive assets within the world economy. The large US and European conglomerates, and to some extent the Japanese trading corporations, may fall into this category.

Backward integration

The typical form of backward FDI is the 'raw materials venture'. Of course, not all foreign-owned raw materials ventures represent backward integration; the extraction of raw materials typically requires more risk capital than is available from local resources, and so there is frequent recourse to foreign capital. Backward integration occurs only where the risk capital is supplied entirely by a foreign firm which uses the materials in its production.

The problem is to explain why the investment is made by the producing firm. In static analysis economies of vertical integration are often given as the reason, but dynamic analysis suggests an alternative explanation. The dynamic explanation is that the producing firm has superior information about the demand for the raw material which it combines with knowledge of supplies derived from its purchasing experience.

Since the demand for the material is a derived demand, changes in demand are likely to be signalled by earlier changes in demand for the final product. Suppose for example that there is an expansion of demand for the final product, perhaps associated with an improvement in product quality or marketing techniques. If the raw material is in inelastic supply then its price can be expected to rise. The firm which is first to recognise this can gain by buying forward to meet its own future needs. But if future markets are imperfect the best way of capitalising this gain is to buy the materials in the ground by purchasing rights over the appropriate land. Profit can be increased if the firm buys up rights over all intramarginal land, with a view to selling the surplus to other users at the higher prices.

This strategy may be particularly useful to a firm which has introduced a new consumer product based on the raw material and is seeking to defend itself by establishing barriers to entry. Immunity from competition may be difficult to achieve by strategy in the consumer market. But if the firm can buy up inputs which are in inelastic supply then it can at least profit from the purchasing requirements of its imitators. If the input is in totally inelastic supply then by cornering the market the firm can in principle eliminate the threat of imitation altogether. However if the surplus to the firm's needs is sold on the open market, it may be difficult in practice to prevent imitators getting access to it through intermediaries or by invoking fair trade laws.

This provides an incentive for the firm to expand its own activities to use up the surplus material. It may simply take over existing purchasers of the material, or it may invest in developing new products which utilise it. The first strategy is *de facto* a way of policing the use of the material to prevent imitators gaining access. The second strategy may lead to more product innovations. It is interesting to note that the firm's prior assurance of a barrier to entry acts as a stimulus for it to invest in R & D related to the monopolised material; conversely the fact that a barrier to entry exists is a deterrent to other firms to examine entrepreneurial possibilities in the same area. The net effect is to cause a strong bias in the firm towards activities which use the monopolised material.

A model of this kind may help to explain, for example, the backward integration of consumer-oriented firms in the food industry, and their subsequent diversification into other activities involving the exploitation of agricultural products. A similar, but less striking pattern, may be apparent in some of the metal-processing industries.

8.10   SUMMARY AND CONCLUSION

This chapter has developed, in outline, a general theory of entrepreneurial behaviour, which has been applied to analyse the dynamics of FDI.

The theory defines an entrepreneur as someone who specialises in taking decisions that call for a special quality of judgement. These decisions involve the entrepreneur in synthesising information from diverse sources and exploiting it through transactions in factor and product markets. In international operations, information sources are geographically widely dispersed. The increasing specialisation of knowledge, together with the dispersion of sources, means that in international firms the entrepreneurial function calls for team organisation. The main problem in team organisation is providing incentives for the individual team members. The importance of team stability in developing good internal communications makes it difficult to rely entirely on the discipline of the external management market. On the other hand, the role of this market must not be underestimated: a salaried team member will initiate profit-maximising entrepreneurial activity provided he believes this will ultimately lead to promotion, or to recruitment to highly paid jobs in other firms.

The entrepreneur is engaged in purposeful pursuit of information. However, much of the information can only be obtained as a by-product of other activities. The information-generating capacities of different activities, coupled with the networks through which the information passes to entrepreneurs, determine the dynamics of innovation and arbitrage.

Competition involves a race between entrepreneurs to discover and pre-empt profit-opportunities. The most fundamental barrier to the entry of imitators is secrecy, but this normally provides only temporary immunity. Because patents also provide very limited protection, the successful entrepreneur needs considerable skill in devising barriers to entry; these can range from marketing techniques which exploit habitual purchasing behaviour, to buying up necessary inputs which are in inelastic supply. Without barriers to entry of some kind, competition between entrepreneurs would become so intense that all reward from entrepreneurial activity would be eliminated and entrepreneurial activity would effectively cease.

The application of the theory to FDI suggests an explanation of the dynamics of both horizonal and backward integration. The theory complements, but does not supplant, the insights afforded by the static theories of FDI which emphasise the importance of market imperfections.

9 Testing Theories of the Multinational Enterprise: A Review of the Evidence

PETER J. BUCKLEY

9.1 INTRODUCTION

As Chapter 1 showed, a rich variety of theoretical perspectives on the multinational enterprise now exist. However, there have been few systematic attempts to test the predictions of this body of theory. This has been partly because of the difficulties in framing the right kind of data to test the theories. It is also true that the theories have not been cast in such a way as to project testable hypotheses which can be subjected to empirical scrutiny. The maturity of the theory now makes testing the next task on the research agenda.

This chapter addresses a number of empirical issues: the growth of the multinational enterprise (Section 9.2), the industrial composition of multinationals (9.3), the effects of nationality of ownership (9.4), the destination of foreign direct investment (9.5), the diversification pattern of multinationals (9.6), and their market-servicing and sourcing policies (9.7). The concluding section (9.8) examines the difficulties inherent in testing the type of theory which has been put forward to date and attempts to suggest the direction of future research.

Difficulties in confronting theories with relevant evidence are common scientific problems. A theory – a complete system of interrelated thought – generates a number of hypotheses: single statements which attempt to explain or predict a single phenomenon. Consequently, general theoretical statements must have restrictions imposed upon them in order to generate testable hypotheses. A theory such as that outlined, which relies heavily on the very general (at worst, tautological) concept of internalisation, requires a precisely defined set of restrictions to generate testable hypotheses. Consequently we move from a general theory to a number of restricted special theories, which, given precisely defined conditions, generate testable hypotheses. Thus the general theoretical statement that imperfect markets will be internalised until the benefits of internalisation are equalled by the costs, must be restricted by carefully defining costs and benefits in relation to a set of extant markets at points of time and across limited economic space. Modelling of the costs and benefits can now take place. Considerable progress has been made in modelling arrangements (Casson, 1984) and in assessing the markets upon which transaction costs bear heavily. A specification of the nature of property rights is a further adjunct to the general approach which needs to be carefully specified. We can then predict which markets will be internalised and go on to list the consequences in terms of observed patterns of allocation.

In developing hypotheses with a dynamic content, we should be able to specify the timing of strategic outcomes. Consequently, in order to predict the timing of a foreign direct investment the incidence of costs and their time profile must be specified (Chapter 5). The heroic assumptions introduced give specificity to these costs and a limit-pricing strategy in a market growing according to a logistic pattern determines the demand conditions. The firm's decisions are then determined by the interplay of these factors over time. Similar specifications can yield predictions on other strategic decisions, for instance ownership policies and the choice between greenfield entry into a foreign market versus an acquisition entry.

A number of specific hypotheses are generated by the material presented in earlier chapters. In Chapter 2, it was suggested that the incidence of transaction costs gives operational content to the concept of internalisation but it also shows that in one particular type of market, where it is essential to monitor for product quality, the imperative to internalise is very strong. Thus we can test the hypothesis that quality control as a type of monitoring activity causes an incentive for backward integration at the level of the firm. Consequently, the prediction is that firms engaged in consumer marketing, where quality control is essential, will integrate backward to co-ordinate and control high quality inputs. This empirical observation can then be confronted by relevant data at firm and industry level to predict the scope of such firms and their direction of expansion. This approach also generates hypotheses concerning the nature of branding and product differentiation and suggests a category of multinational firms specialising in market-making whose growth and pattern can again be confronted with empirical evidence.

The idiosyncracies in the market for information and the important subset of markets in technology also give predictions on the incidence of multinational enterprises in these fields. Chapter 3 assessed attempts to achieve the transfer of industrial technology to a less-developed country whilst simultaneously relaxing the control of multinational enterprises over its utilisation. The existence of buyer uncertainty, which complicates arms-length transactions in information, bears heavily on the institutional arrangements which can be designed to effect transfer. Limitations of the rights transferred in space and time and a reduction in the scope of these rights make externalisation of the transfer more feasible and more manageable. The design of contingent contracts and the creation of new institutions and property rights represent attempts to make transfer more flexible and more amenable to modifications in objectives as the change of ownership is effected. Consequently we can suggest areas where internalised transactions can be replaced by partially externalised ones and contrasting areas where this is difficult. The pattern of transfer across the spectrum of industries can thus be predicted. The nature and type of information can be related to the institutional form of transfer most likely to exist; non-patentable and non-codifiable information is more likely to be internalised than is information which can be patented or codified.

Chapter 4 compared and contrasted multinational single firm monopolies with international cartels. it is conceivable that cartels will re-emerge as an important institutional form under the combined pressures of increased protectionism, collusion in the supply of raw materials, a slowing down of technological progress in a number of industries and political reorientations. If this hypothesis is correct, identification of the types of industry likely to be (or remain) cartelised is important. The analysis suggests that industries with inelastic product demand, few sellers and atomistic buyers, particularly where minimum efficient scale of plant is large relative to the market, will be cartelised. Varied products, dynamic technology and management and vulnerability to entry are all inimical to the operation and formation of cartels, as is the pursuit of vigorous anti-trust policies by governments. The decline of cartels following their heyday in the inter-war period and the dominance of the integrated multinational firm following World War Two is attributable to the more open world economy, progress in technology and the development of international management skills such that international multiplant operating costs fell relative to international collusion costs based on domestic plants. The analysis in this chapter raises important issues for the future development of the world economy.

Chapter 6 integrates the theory of international capital markets with the theory of the international firm and the theory of international trade. It focuses attention on the availability of different financial instruments – equity and debenture debt in different countries – and suggests that specialisation in risk-bearing is an important influence on location decisions. Such an approach provides predictions of nationality of ownership effects and the origins of funding of multinational firms.

The theory of location of multinational firms is extended by the model developed in Chapter 7. A profit-maximising location strategy is computed which gives solutions for the efficient location of the various stages of production, assembly and distribution. The prices of final products and internal transfer prices are also determined. External constraints such as tax and tariff rates are included in the determination of optimal location strategy. Such a model can be fitted to the location policy of a given multinational firm with a view to predicting the impact of changes in conditions of trade, production and government intervention on the firm's plans. Simulation techniques can be used to identify those factors which have the greatest impact on location.

The analysis of entrepreneurial behaviour gives a further dynamic to the theory – the distribution of entrepreneurial competence between firms and nations is a further explanatory variable in the growth and spatial distribution of multinational firms (Chapter 8). The importance of the monitoring and feedback of information by foreign subsidiaries enables superior forecasting of future profit opportunities to which the individual multinational firm can respond rapidly. The building maintenance of such information channels is an important stimulus to further internationalisation. The necessity to build and control an entrepreneurial team explains the personnel policies adopted in 'locking in' key employees.

Thus the theory outlined yields testable predictions at the levels of industry, nationality of ownership, individual firm and intra-firm policy. The scope of these hypotheses varies, as does their generality. It is now possible to confront some of these predictions with data.

9.2 THE GROWTH OF THE MULTINATIONAL ENTERPRISE

Many predictions have been made concerning the growth of multinational enterprises. Most rely on straight-line projection or on naive scenarios. In 1968, Polk predicted that by the end of this century, the 200 or 300 largest multinationals would account for one half of the world's output (Polk, 1968).

Recent figures, however, suggest that the rapid growth of foreign direct investment relative to world output and world trade in the 1960s did not occur in the 1970s. The total growth of GNP for market economies was 8.4 per cent between 1960 and 1970 and 15.2 per cent between 1970 and 1980; world trade grew at rates of 10.4 per cent and 20.5 per cent in these two decades, whilst the rate of growth of foreign direct investment only grew in current prices from 10.2 per cent to 15.6 per cent (UNCTC, 1983). Thus foreign direct investment has kept in step with world output and fallen behind the growth of world trade. The multinational enterprise and its investment cannot be said to be replacing world trade (although as we shall see, it can be said to exercise control over world trade) nor to be rapidly increasing its share of world output.

Examinations of the growth of the multinational enterprise, measured in terms of rate of growth of worldwide sales, have found significant non-linearities in its relationship with firm size. Using a specification

$$g = f(s, s^2) \tag{9.1}$$

$$\text{or } g = f(\varphi, \varphi^2) \text{ where } \varphi = \log s \tag{9.2}$$

where g is rate of growth of the firm's sales and s is firm size at the beginning of the period, growth has been found to be negatively related to size but positively related to size squared. This u-shaped relationship suggests that in the periods tested (from the late 1950s to the late 1970s) growth may show as firms approach a critical size, but after this point, for the very largest firms, there may be stimuli to further growth (Rowthorn and Hymer, 1970; Buckley, Dunning and Pearce, 1978).

The relationship between firm size and profitability, specified on the same basis, is not strong or as stable as that between size and growth. Difficulties of specifying profitability accurately and differences in accounting traditions nationally make it difficult to arrive at firm conclusions of the independent influence of size on profitability (Buckley, Dunning and Pearce, 1978; Stopford and Dunning, 1983). However, at the firm level, internalisation of know-how and R & D establishes the connection between multinationality, growth and profitability (Buckley and Casson, 1976). This suggests that an approach disaggregated to the level of individual firms and groups of firms by industry and nationality is likely to prove more fruitful for the testing of hypotheses.

A considerable amount of attention has been given to smaller multinational enterprises (Buckley, Berkova and Newbould, 1983) and to firms undertaking direct foreign investment for the first time (Newbould, Buckley and Thurwell, 1978; Aharoni, 1966). Aharoni found that first-time investors require a major stimulus (or 'initiating force') in order to begin internationalising, whilst Newbould *et al.* (1978) found that the management process is a critical determinant of a successful initial move abroad and that careful planning could reduce the risk which can be a major obstacle to first-time investors.

9.3 THE INDUSTRIAL COMPOSITION OF MNEs

Foreign direct investment and multinational firms are concentrated by industrial sector. The theory of the multinational enterprise based on the internalisation of markets vertically, in research-intensive industries and in skill-intensive activities (Chapters 2 and 8; Buckley and Casson, 1976) suggests that the types of industries shown in Table 9.1 will be dominated by multinational firms.

In a study of the foreign penetration of UK industry in 1968, the following characteristics were positively associated with foreign penetration at industry level:

(1) High wage rate
(2) High salary level
(3) Ratio of staff to operatives
(4) Ratio of royalty payments to net output
(5) Industry concentration
(6) Advertising expenditure as a percentage of net output

The first five were significant in a rank correlation analysis at the 1 per cent level, the last one at the 5 per cent level (Buckley and Casson, 1976). Such a nexus of characteristics is consistent with an industry group dependent on the internalisation of specialised knowledge, embodied largely in skilled individuals and technology intensive machinery, and protecting its position by erecting barriers to entry based on product-differentiation and quality competition.

Further significant differences between domestic and foreign firms emerge in the management of industrial relations and labour utilisation in a study of foreign investors in the UK (Buckley and Enderwick,

TABLE 9.1   *Industries predicted to be dominated by multinational firms*

Industry	Examples
PRIMARY	
Perishable agricultural products requiring careful monitoring of product quality	Bananas Tobacco
Raw materials whose deposits are geographically concentrated	Oil Copper
MANUFACTURING	
High-technology, research-intensive industries with intermediate flows of specialised knowledge and skills	Computers Pharmaceuticals
Capital-intensive industries requiring the services of sophisticated plant and machinery	Earth-moving equipment Heavy electrical machinery
SERVICES	
Skill-, knowledge- and communication-intensive services	Banking Distribution

1984). The industrial relations practices of foreign multinationals in the UK differ in type and degree from local firms. Foreign firms take some workplace relations out of joint negotiations and indulge in single-employer bargaining. Foreign firms rely much more heavily on formalised agreements and plant- or company-based agreements. A more effective use of labour is a major source of the foreign multinational's productivity advantage and this arises from a simplified union representation and increased worker flexibility. However this increased utilisation of labour is achieved at a price. This price is usually higher wage rates but also more conflict over labour utilisation issues and a higher incidence of unconstitutional disputes result. The policies of foreign firms in dealing with these difficulties attempt to increase the cost to employees of taking industrial action.

There is a wages differential in British industry between foreign and domestic firms, even after account has been taken of plant size. Indeed, the largest differentials occur in the small and the very large plant sizes (Buckley and Enderwick, 1984). This positive differential arises because of productivity levels, plant bargaining and policies designed to buy out restrictions on labour utilisation and to discourage unionism. In testing an exit-voice model of strike activity in UK industry (Enderwick and

Buckley, 1984) strike activity was found to depend on both structural and cost factors. Multinationals attempt to discourage strike action by a high wage policy but transnational production enables national unions to exploit their leverage in disrupting integrated activities.

Studies of the growth, profitability and policy decisions of multinational firms have consistently shown important industry differences. Representing industry differences by dummy variables and assuming that industry effects (and, later, nationality effects) are additive, Equation (9.1) becomes

$$g = a + bs + cs^2 + \sum_{i=1}^{n} d_i I_i + \sum_{j=1}^{m} f_j N_j + e \qquad (9.3)$$

where b, c are regression coefficients, a is the intercept I_i takes a value 1 for industry i and 0 otherwise, N_j takes a value 1 for nationality j and 0 otherwise, d_i and f_j are differences from arbitrarily chosen d_{n+1} and f_{m+1} respectively, and e is the error term.

Industry effects are then tested by omitting all industry terms from Equation (9.3) and testing the ratio of incremental variance explained by inclusion of these terms in the full equation to the remaining incremental variance in the full equation by means of an F-test. In general industry differences in growth and profitability and policy are significant. To develop this hypothesis, industry differences have been replaced by groupings based on research intensity, with limited success, possibly because research and development is measured at industry, not firm level and so this measure misses intra-industry differences in R & D intensity (Buckley and Pearce, 1981).

9.4 THE EFFECTS OF NATIONALITY OF OWNERSHIP

Multinationals are highly concentrated by country of ownership. The three largest source countries have controlled more than 68 per cent of world foreign investment from the beginning of the century, although the identity of the three countries has changed. (Table 9.2 shows the concentration rates to be 92.8 per cent in 1900, 90.1 per cent in 1914, 87.5 per cent in 1930, 89.1 per cent in 1960, 76.7 per cent in 1967, 72.3 per cent in 1971 and 68.0 per cent in 1977.)

However, recent changes in world economic power have seen the rapid rise in Japanese, Dutch and Swiss foreign investment, the re-emergence of Germany after its second expropriation this century and the beginnings of foreign direct investment from nations which had

TABLE 9.2   *Non-Communist* countries' stock of foreign investment held abroad,*
by percentage distribution, 1900–77

Country	Percentage						
	1900	1914	1930	1960	1967	1971	1977
US	2	6.3	35.3	59.1	55.0	52.0	48.1
UK	50.8	50.5	43.8	24.5	16.2	14.5	13.7
France	21.8	22.3	8.4	4.1	5.5	5.8	4.8
Germany	20.2	17.3	2.6	1.1	2.8	4.4	6.2
Switzerland	neg.	neg.	neg.	neg.	3.9	4.1	4.7
Canada	neg.	0.5	3.1	5.5	3.4	3.6	3.1
Japan	neg.	neg.	neg.	neg.	1.3	2.7	4.5
Netherlands	4.6	3.1	5.5	3.1	2.1	2.2	3.5
Sweden	neg.	0.3	1.3	0.9	1.4	2.1	1.6
Others	neg.	neg.	neg.	1.0	8.2	8.5	9.8
Total amount (billions of US dollars)	23.8	38.6	41.6	53.8	102.8	159.2	311.5

NOTES   * The exclusion of communist countries makes little difference to the figures. It has been estimated that the *stock* of foreign direct investment by Comecon countries stood at only 0.72 billion dollars at the end of 1978, although the figure is higher for fixed assets (4.48 billion dollars). See, for example, C. H. McMillan, 'Growth of External Investments by the Comecon countries', *The World Economy*, September 1979.

The percentages for the years 1900–60 are calculated from figures for total foreign investments, i.e. including portfolio investments overseas.

The percentages for 1967–77 are calculated from figures for direct investments only.

All figures are derived from *actual*, not licensed, amounts, except for Japan in 1967 and 1971.

The 1960 figures for France and the Netherlands are estimates, as is the 1977 amount for Switzerland.

SOURCE   For years 1900–60, Woodruff, W. *The Impact of Western Man*, St. Martins Press, 1967. For 1967–71, United Nations, '*The MNC in World Development*', 1972. Figures for 1977 calculated from data in the *Balance of Payments Yearbook* (IMF, 1979).

previously only been host-countries, including a small number of significant third world foreign investors.

It is conceivable that the concept of nationality of ownership is in need of more careful redefinition. Chapter 4 showed that when financial markets are globally integrated, a firm may produce in one set of countries but be funded by debenture holders in another set of countries (Casson, 1984). Its management culture may derive from yet another set. The implicit assumption in the literature is that these sets (except production) can be identified with one, or unusually, two countries of ownership and casual empiricism suggests that we have not yet reached the truly international corporation as envisaged by Kindleberger (1969, p. 182). Most of the largest multinationals can still be identified unequivocally with one or two nations of ownership. This may not continue to be the case if markets permit separation of the above functions.

Econometric studies of nationality of ownership effects in foreign direct investment show them to be highly significant, frequently more significant than industrial differences in explaining growth, profitability and policy decisions. A plausible hypothesis here is that multinationality is greater for firms based in traditionally open economies which form part of a wider social and ethnic grouping than for firms based in traditionally closed economies which are socially and politically isolated (Buckley and Casson, 1976). Post-imperial countries, UK, Netherlands, Belgium and France exhibit a high propensity to invest abroad, partly as a result of the reduction in psychic distance from common post-governance structures.

Further, it can be hypothesised that certain national cultures are more viable than others as bases for managing internal markets. Such culturally-inspired managerial styles may reduce the costs of organising internal markets and provide an impetus to multinationality. Foreign direct investment enables the internal transfer of efficient managerial culture unavailable to host-country firms (Buckley, 1983). The identification of 'hierarchy' as the alternative to 'market' as modes of organisation (Williamson, 1975) may have obscured the role of national cultures in evolving internationally viable competitive systems within firms. Evidence is presented in Table 9.3.

The Impact of Multinationality

The independent impact of multinationality on growth and performance has been a source of controversy. Adding a term in M (degree of multinationality: sales of foreign affiliates excluding goods imported from the parent for resale divided by total worldwide group sales) to equation (9.3) and testing to significance via an F-test has given mixed results in the explanation of profitability and growth (Buckley *et al.*, 1978 and 1983). Part of the reason for this difficulty lies in the problems

TABLE 9.3   *Selected countries: the average propensity to invest abroad*[a]

Country	Average propensity to invest overseas			Rank in	
	1965	1971	1977	1965	1971
United Kingdom	8.6	12.1	18.2[b]	1	1
Netherlands	7.8	11.9	14.5	2	2
Sweden	4.7	5.0	7.9[b]	4	3
USA	7.3	4.5	6.7	3	4
W. Germany	2.3	4.9	5.1	7	5
Norway	0.3	2.6	4.7[c]	15	6
Belgium	2.3	6.2	4.2	7	7
Canada	2.3	2.8	4.0	7	8
France	3.5	2.6	3.7[b]	5	9
Japan	0.9	1.5	3.6[b]	12	10
Venezuela	0.0	n.a.	3.3	18–21	11
Italy	3.0	4.1	3.2	6	12
Finland	0.4	4.4	2.9	14	13
Australia	1.1	3.3	2.3[b]	11	14
Brazil	0.0	0.02	2.3[b]	18–21	14
Austria	1.8	2.2	2.0[b]	10	16
Columbia	0.0	0.5	1.7[c]	18–21	17
Spain	0.3	0.6	1.3	15	18
S. Africa	0.7	2.6	1.0[c]	13	19
Philippines	0.2	0.7	0.9	17	20
S. Korea	0.0	1.2	0.7	18–21	21

[a] The average propensity to invest abroad $= \dfrac{\text{Flow of FDI}}{\text{GNP in same year}} \times 1000$

[b] 1976 figure

[c] 1975 figure

All figures are calculated from actual – not licensed – capital movements.

SOURCE   Calculated using figures derived from the IMF publication, *International Financial Statistics* and *The Balance of Payments Yearbook* (various issues).

of accurately measuring the degree of multinationality but the direction of causation is also unclear. Multinationality may be suggested to increase profitability as firms seek the highest possible returns from their worldwide foreign investments. However, profitability may be depressed if foreign direct investment is undertaken to diversify the firm's income, that is, for a given return to reduce variability. Consequently, further testing of the impact of this variable is dependent on clear assumptions on the strategy of the firm. Shapiro (1983) suggests that advantages attributed to multinationality are in fact specifically related to particular nationalities (in the case of Canada, to US ownership) rather than being general. Tests which can discriminate between these effects more carefully are necessary in the design of a crucial experiment.

9.5 THE DESTINATION OF FDI

Location effects enter the theory of the multinational firm in two main ways. First, as 'location endowments' (Dunning, 1981) of host-countries, stimulating (in the traditional Ricardian fashion) trade-flows and giving rise to factor-flows. Second, location factors provide the motives for the different types of foreign indirect investment. The key motives are:

(1) market-induced direct investment
(2) raw-material-induced direct investment, and
(3) labour-induced investment, a subset of which is 'offshore production'.

Table 9.4 shows that the major recipients of foreign direct investment are advanced countries. The share of foreign direct investment which goes to third-world countries remains very low: 21.8 per cent of the world total in 1980.

When we examine further the less-developed countries which do receive inward investment, they represent quite a distinct subset of all developing countries. Either they have large protected markets (for example, Brazil, Argentina, India) or they have significant raw-material resources (for example, oil, copper) which are geographically concentrated or they are 'newly industrialising', that is, they attract inward investment to a cheaper labour country with a well-developed infrastructure and to an enclave industrial environment (for example, Singapore, South Korea).

9.6 THE DIVERSIFICATION PATTERN OF MULTINATIONALS

The theory of the multinational firm has been brought to bear on the issues of diversification and strategy with respect to two major decisions. First, the issues of take-over of foreign firms can be presented

TABLE 9.4 Inflows of foreign direct investment by country and region, 1970–80
(Millions of dollars)

Country and region	1970	1971	1972	1973	1974	1975	1976	1977	1978	1979	1980
Developed market economies											
Australia	898.0	1 148.4	1 042.3	138.3	1 334.9	433.5	1 054.1	1 150.0	1 658.9	1 678.3	2 124.1
Austria	95.0	79.2	77.1	107.3	172.0	99.6	107.4	124.9	157.8	192.5	239.5
Belgium	318.0	446.3	386.5	718.9	1 137.7	958.0	871.7	1 273.8	1 429.8	1 134.4	1 547.5
Canada	866.0	929.8	625.4	825.0	862.3	709.1	−191.7	1 030.9	1 184.4	1 608.5	622.1
Denmark	104.0	125.4	163.9	212.2	…	267.1	−190.5	75.9	88.9	103.4	…
Finland	18.0	25.1	36.9	13.1	34.9	68.0	58.9	47.9	33.8	27.1	28.6
France	622.0	525.6	687.3	1 126.6	1 853.3	1 555.3	1 062.2	2 021.0	2 919.7	2 537.5	3 249.9
Germany, Federal Republic of	595.0	1 131.4	1 932.6	2 026.6	2 140.7	692.1	1 073.7	840.6	1 540.0	1 111.1	1 119.3
Greece	50.0	42.1	55.4	62.0	67.3	24.3	10.4	24.5	17.5	19.4	74.2
Iceland	5.0	20.1	3.3	−1.2	13.2	42.5	4.6	4.7	7.5	2.6	23.4
Ireland	32.0	25.1	31.5	52.5	51.7	159.1	173.2	135.4	375.6	337.2	…
Italy	606.0	518.5	1 803.4	619.9	600.1	631.4	95.8	1 138.3	509.6	360.5	−744.5
Japan	94.0	209.6	162.9	−35.8	204.4	230.7	115.5	23.4	12.5	232.6	273.3
Netherlands	537.0	585.7	603.7	858.3	952.5	977.4	349.8	359.6	671.1	1 200.3	1 241.7

New Zealand	23.0	55.2	83.6	–32.2	166.0	193.0	179.0	168.1	12.5	33.6	37.7
Norway	64.0	94.3	120.5	208.6	346.4	214.9	372.9	765.9	485.8	399.2	58.6
Portugal	335.0	...	72.7	95.4	105.8	115.3	52.0	49.0	56.3	47.8	114.5
South Africa	222.0	259.8	117.3	27.4	692.7	184.6	18.5	–121.4	–127.7	–484.5	...
Spain	108.0	201.6	268.2	389.8	358.4	307.2	221.7	520.7	919.0	1 397.9	1 492.9
Sweden	850.0	83.2	67.3	72.7	75.8	80.1	4.6	80.6	71.4	112.4	251.2
United Kingdom	1 464.0	1 078.2	1 017.3	1 783.4	1 997.6	1 364.7	1 453.5	2 310.5	2 501.5	3 881.2	4 885.9
United States		366.1	955.4	2 801.5	4 762.5	2 634.7	4 341.0	3 712.7	7 900.1	11 860.6	10 854.8
Sub-total	7 906.0	7 950.6	10 314.2	12 070.3	17 930.2	11 942.4	11 238.1	15 737.0	22 425.8	27 793.5	27 494.8
Developing countries											
Latin America	815.0	1 555.6	1 019.5	2 389.0	1 894.2	3 428.8	1 749.1	3 082.3	4 059.0	5 396.7	5 249.1
Africa	369.0	852.5	570.0	603.2	689.1	302.3	431.8	678.3	565.9	2 028.4	2 187.9
West Asia	142.0	–133.4	192.2	–468.5	–3 557.4	2 288.7	–1 086.4	1 056.6	855.1	–980.6	–3 097.6
South and East Asia	486.0	561.7	780.6	1 425.8	1 445.6	1 709.6	1 690.2	1 437.2	1 888.0	2 286.8	3 230.4
Europe	22.0	27.1	22.8	28.6	39.7	35.2	46.2	59.5	78.9	87.9	84.6
Sub-total	1 834.0	2 863.5	2 585.1	3 978.1	508.7	7 764.5	2 830.9	6 313.9	7 446.9	8 819.2	7 654.3
Total – listed countries	9 740.0	10 814.1	12 899.3	16 048.5	18 438.9	19 706.9	14 069.0	22 051.0	29 872.7	36 612.7	35 149.1

A minus sign (–) reflects a reduction in the stock of foreign direct investment in the country.
SOURCE International Monetary Fund, *Balance of Payments Yearbook* (Washington, DC), various issues.
Reproduced from UNCTC (1983).

as a test of the theory; second, the form of diversification adopted by individual firms can be explained and to some extent predicted by the application of the theory.

Take-overs

The framework used by Baumann (1975) can be used to analyse the factors leading to the take-over of domestic firms by foreign entrants. The demand price of foreign firm A for domestic firm B can be represented as the difference between the expected profits of the combined firm C and the existing firm A as in equation (9.4):

$$D_A = \sum_{t=0}^{\infty} \frac{[(\Pi_C^A)_t - (\Pi_A^A)_t]}{(1+R_A)^t} \tag{9.4}$$

where Π_C^A is expected profits of the combined firm according to A's managers Π_A^A is expected profits of A alone, and R_A is the discount rate of A's managers. The supply price of firm B is the present value of its expected future profits as in equation 9.5:

$$S_B = \sum_{t=I}^{\infty} \frac{(\Pi_B^B)_t}{(1+R_B)^t} \tag{9.5}$$

where $\Pi_B SO^B$ are the expected profits according to B's managers and R_B is the discount rate of B's managers. Consequently a take-over is feasible when $D_A > S_B$. The factors which may bring about this situation are instructive.

First, the profits of the combined firm may exceed the profits of the two firms separately, that is $(\Pi_C^A)_t - (\Pi_A^A)_t > (\Pi_B^B)_t$. This may arise because the combined firm gains monopoly power over prices or because of economies of scale or synergy between the previously independent firms. Second, $R_A < R_B$ will cause a divergence in valuations. This may occur either because of different attitudes to risk between the two management groups or, following Aliber (1970) and (1971), because the financial market's valuations of earnings in two currencies diverge because of investor myopia, enabling a strong-currency firm to take over one in a weak-currency area. Finally, management views may differ such that A's expectations of profitability may be greater than B's.

Diversification

Industrial and geographical diversification can be regarded as alternatives for firms with excess managerial capacity and particular types of technical know-how (Wolf, 1977). Testing of such hypotheses has been limited but Pearce (1983), using data from the world's largest firms discovered weak relationships in a cross-section study relating industrial diversification negatively to industrial diversification and finding industrial diversification to be negatively related to foreign production and positively to exporting from the parent. This suggests that industrial diversification is followed by 'R & D'-intensive firms producing new products (that is, at the early stage of a product cycle) which tend to be low-volume producers servicing foreign markets by exporting. Firms which are geographically (internationally) diversified may be characterised as adaptors (and adopters) who match existing products to new markets, carry out high volume production and service markets through foreign direct investment and local production. Such firms may be 'free riders' on others' development or may license technology inwards; their strength lies in the marketing function in which they may well be innovators.

Empirical data-testing of some of these tentative hypotheses has been advanced in Buckley (1981) which examined recent British and continental European take-overs in the USA, 1976–9. Tables 9.5 and 9.6 show that the overwhelming number (65.2 per cent) of such take-overs were of the horizontal take-over type, with only two firms following this pattern in an unrelated technology field. Vertical diversification and concentric diversification represented 29.0 per cent of take-overs and conglomerate diversification only 5.8 per cent of the total. In a study of US foreign direct investment Kopits (1979) found that conglomerate diversification (at the two digit SIC level) accounted for 22.3 per cent of US direct investment in 1968 as against 14.1 per cent in 1962. Kopits finds 'no evidence that direct investment abroad (in horizontal and forward vertical forms) is inversely related to product diversification at home' (Kopits, 1979, p. 12). The conflict between the Kopits and Pearce results suggest that more clearly specified hypotheses need to be derived in this area.

9.7 MARKET-SERVICING AND SOURCING POLICIES

The choice between exporting, the foreign licensing of technology and

TABLE 9.5   *Classification of 144 recent UK take-overs of US firms: 1976–9*

New missions	New products	
Customers/Products	Related technology	Unrelated technology
Same type	77	1
Firm its own customer	22	1
Similar type	9	5
New type	7	8

Not known: 14

Type of take-over: UK firms		Number of firms
Horizontal diversification		78
Vertical diversification		23
Concentric diversification		21
of which	(a) Marketing- and technology-related	9
	(b) Marketing-related	5
	(c) Technology-related	7
Conglomerate diversification		8
		130
	Not known	14
	Total	144

SOURCES   Classification from H. Igor Ansoff *Corporate Strategy* (Harmondsworth: Penguin, 1968)
Basic data from author's researches
Reproduced from Buckley (1981).

foreign direct investment has been subject to intense analysis. The theory of the multinational enterprise suggests that the relative weight of benefits and costs of internalising a market will discriminate between market solutions (licensing) and internal organisational solutions (foreign direct investment). Efficiency considerations will determine the optimum location between the home country (exporting), the end use country (licensing or foreign direct investment) or third countries (offshore production or out-sourcing).

Recent research suggests a positive association between internal exports (exports to foreign affiliates) and foreign production, although extra group exports may be negatively related to foreign production (Buckley and Pearce, 1983). However such effects may be swamped by

TABLE 9.6 *Classification of 97 recent European take-overs of US firms (excluding UK) (1976–9)*

New missions	*New products*	
Customers/Products	*Related technology*	*Unrelated technology*
Same type	56	1
Firm its own customer	9	0
Similar type	4	1
New type	2	4

Not known: 20

Type of take-over		*Number of firms*	
Horizontal diversification		57	
Vertical diversification		9	
Concentric diversification		7	
of which	(a) Marketing- and technology-related		4
	(b) Marketing-related		1
	(c) Technology-related		2
Conglomerate diversification		4	
		77	
	Not known	20	
	Total	97	

SOURCES As Table 9.5

changes in relative international competitiveness. The market-servicing decision (exports versus foreign production) can be analysed in terms of influences arising from the size of firm, the industry of operation and the nationality of ownership. The balancing of plant level economies of scale and firm level economies, the latter encouraging foreign operation, modifies the optimal strategy.

9.8 CONCLUSION

This partial review of empirical work in testing theories of multinational firms has revealed a number of deficiencies, both in the theory and in its application. This concluding section examines difficulties in fusing neoclassical with institutional economics and testing the outcome, in drawing on the managerial literature and in difficulties in the field of the economics of business strategy.

Institutional and Neoclassical Economics

The theory of the multinational enterprise has moved into an area where the neoclassical theory of the firm is integrated with the tools of institutional economics. The concepts of transactions costs (and governance costs as in Teece, 1983) has become central in explaining the pattern of behaviour observed in international trade and investment. Efforts are now being made to recast these concepts in a framework conducive to dynamic analysis (Casson, 1981; Buckley, 1983).

Significant problems remain, however. First, markets and hierarchies frameworks are amenable to explaining all states of the world and to induce a bias towards the *status quo* (Buckley, 1983; Dugger, 1983). Second, a clearer view of transactions cost and its measurement needs to be taken in order to give minimisation of such costs a clear meaning. Third, the concept of efficiency drawn from neoclassical analysis is in need of clarification when other types of costs are included. Issues of distribution of benefits also become entangled with efficiency criteria. Fourth, the issue of whether hierarchy is necessarily an alternative to market as a means of allocation needs explicit treatment. The internalisation literature suggests that replacement of external by internal market may improve allocative efficiency by the substitution of a more perfect market based on shadow prices. Hierarchy may not be the only internal mode of organisation.

The internalisation literature is not without problems. The necessity to move from general to special applications of the concept of internalisation requires limiting assumptions which need careful justification, otherwise it too can explain (and justify) all states of the world.

Integrating the Managerial Literature

The problems of drawing on the literature intended mainly for management have existed for some time. The interpretation of work aimed at improving managerial performance, refining strategy and motivating decision-makers remains imperfect. Moreover, theorists are unsure how to interpret data derived from business history, particularly single-firm histories (how many observations do such works give to the researcher?). Business policy and industrial economics treat the same subject matter in very distinct ways and a certain amount of antipathy and intolerance clouds the possibility of fusion.

A possible solution exists in a convincing economics of business strategy. So far, attempts in this area have bemoaned the weakness of neoclassical theory of the firm but have failed to replace it (Moss, 1981; Kay, 1979). The twin problems of imperfect information and interdependence between decision-makers have not been fully incorporated into models of management decision-making except in partial and largely descriptive fashion. Two of the better attempts at these respective issues are Aharoni (1966) and Knickerbocker (1973). Neither is claimed to be a general explanation of foreign investment behaviour, however.

Finally, the business strategy problem is complicated by the difficulties of fixing exogeneity. Market imperfections in the internalisation rubric are given. In the managerial literature they can be created by product differentiation, collusive practices and branding. A more careful specification of exogeneity and a more cohesive theory of barriers to entry are necessary foundations for progress.

Asking the Right Questions

Empirical data on multinational enterprises at both aggregate (UNCTC, 1983) and individual firm level (Dunning and Pearce, 1981; Stopford, Dunning and Haberich, 1980; Stopford and Dunning, 1983) is more plentiful than ever. Testing of hypotheses can now be carried out more extensively and at a more sophisticated level. The duty of theory is now to be more precise in order to enable rejection of false hypotheses. More careful distinctions now need to be made on such basic concepts as 'internalising a market' (Casson, 1984). Only when this is achieved can progress-testing and a new generation of theorising then result.

Bibliography

Agmon, T. and C. P. Kindleberger (1977) *Multinationals from Small Countries* (Cambridge, Mass.: MIT Press).

Aharoni, Y. (1966) *The Foreign Investment Decision Process* (Boston Mass.: Graduate School of Business Administration, Harvard University).

Aharoni, Y. (1971) 'On the Definition of a Multinational Corporation', *Quarterly Review of Economics and Business*, vol. 11, pp. 27–37.

Alam, G. and J. Langrish (1981) 'Non Multinational Firms and Transfer of Technology to Less-developed Countries', *World Development,* vol. 9, pp. 383–7.

Alchian, A. A. (1950) 'Uncertainty, Evolution and Economic Theory', *Journal of Political Economy*, vol. 58, pp. 211–21.

Alchian, A. A. (1959) 'Costs and outputs' in M. Abramavitz *et al.* (eds) *The Allocation of Economic Resources* (Stanford: Stanford University Press) pp. 23–40.

Alchian, A. A. (1969) 'Corporate Management and Property Rights' in H. Manne (ed.) *Economic Policy and the Regulation of Corporate Securities* (Washington: American Enterprise Institute).

Alchian, A. A. (1977) *Economic Forces at Work* (Indianapolis: Liberty Press).

Alchian, A. A. and H. Demsetz (1972) 'Production, Information and Economic Organisation', *American Economic Review*, vol. 62, pp. 777–95.

Aliber, R. Z. (1970) 'A Theory of Direct Foreign Investment' in *The International Firm* (ed. C. P. Kindleberger) (Cambridge, Mass.: MIT Press) pp. 17–34.

Aliber, R. Z. (1971) 'The Multinational Enterprise in a Multiple Currency World' in J. H. Dunning (ed.) *The Multinational Enterprise* (London: George Allen & Unwin).

Archibald, G. C. (ed.) (1971) *The Theory of the Firm* (Harmondsworth: Penguin).

Arrow, K. J. (1962) 'Economic Welfare and the Allocation of Resources for Invention' in *The Rate and Direction of Inventive Activity* (Princeton: National Bureau of Economic Research, Princeton University Press).

Arrow, K. J. (1970) *Essays in the Theory of Risk-Bearing* (Amsterdam: North-Holland).

Arrow, K. J. (1975) 'Vertical Integration and Communication', *Bell Journal of Economics*, 5, pp. 173–83.

Asch, P. and J. J. Seneca (1975) 'Characteristics of Collusive Firms', *Journal of Industrial Economics*, vol. 23, pp. 223–37.

Bacharach, M. (1976) *Economics and the Theory of Games* (London: Macmillan).

Bain, J. S. (1948) 'Output Quotas in Imperfect Cartels', *Quarterly Journal of Economics*, vol. 62, pp. 617–22.

Bain, J. S. (1956) *Barriers to New Competition* (Cambridge, Mass.: Harvard University Press).

Balassa, B. *et al.* (1971) *The Structure of Protection in Developing Countries* (Baltimore: Johns Hopkins University Press).

Balasubramanyam, V. N. (1973) *International Transfer of Technology to India* (New York: Praeger).

Balasubramanyam, V. N. (1980) *Multinational Enterprises and the Third World*, Thames Essay No. 26 (London: Trade Policy Research Centre).

Baldwin, R. (1970) 'International Trade in Inputs and Outputs', *American Economic Review*, vol. 60, pp. 430–4.

Baldwin, R. (1979) 'Determinants of Trade and Foreign Investment: Further Evidence', *Review of Economics and Statistics*, vol. 61, pp. 40–8.

Baranson, J. (1967) *Manufacturing Problems in India* (Syracuse: Syracuse University Press).

Baranson, J. (1978) *Technology and the Multinationals* (Lexington, Mass.: D. C. Heath).

Baranson, J. (1981) *North-South Technology Transfer* (Mt. Airy, Maryland: Lomond Publications).

Baumann, H. G. (1975) 'Merger Theory, Property Rights and the Pattern of US Direct Investment in Canada', *Weltwirtschaftliches Archiv.*, vol. 111, pp. 676–98.

Baumol, W. J. (1968) 'Entrepreneurship in Economic Theory', *American Economic Review (Papers and Proceedings)*, vol. 58, pp. 64–71.

Baumol, W. J. (1967) *Business Behavior, Value and Growth* (New York: Harcourt, Brace, Jovanovich).

Behrman, J. N. and W. A. Fischer (1980) *Overseas R & D Activities of Transnational Companies* (Cambridge, Mass.: Delgeschlager).

Behrman, J. N. and H. W. Wallender (1976) *Transfers of Technology within Multinational Enterprises* (Cambridge, Mass.: Ballinger).

Bertrand, J. (1883) Review of 'Theorie Mathematique de la Richesse Sociale', *Journal des Savants*, vol. 68, pp. 499–508.

Bivens, K. K. and E. B. Lovell (1976) *Joint Ventures with Foreign Partners* (New York: National Industrial Conference Board).

Brooke, M. Z. and J. Holly (1981) 'International Management Contracts' in L. Otterbeck (ed.) *The Management of Headquarters–Subsidiary Relationships in Multinational Corporations* (Farnborough: Gower Press).

Brown, W. R. (1976) 'Islands of Conscious Power: MNCs in the Theory of the Firm', *MSU Business Topics*, vol. 24, pp. 37–45.

Buckley, P. J. (1981) 'The Entry Strategy of Recent European Direct Investors in the USA', *Journal of Comparative Corporate Law and Securities Regulation*, vol. 3, pp. 169–91.

Buckley, P. J. (1983) 'New Theories of International Business: Some Unresolved Issues' in Mark Casson (ed.) *The Growth of International Business* (London: George Allen & Unwin).

Buckley, P. J., Z. Berkova and G. D. Newbould (1983) *Direct Investment in the UK by Smaller European Firms* (London: Macmillan).

Buckley, P. J. and M. Casson (1976) *The Future of the Multinational Enterprise* (London: Macmillan and New York: Holmes-Meier).

Buckley, P. J. and M. Casson (1978) 'A Theory of International Operations' in J. Leontiades and M. Ghertman (eds) *European Research in International Business* (Amsterdam: North-Holland).

Buckley, P. J. and H. Davies (1980) 'Foreign Licensing in Overseas Operations: Theory and Evidence from the UK' in R. G. Hawkins and A. J. Prasad (eds) *Technology Transfer and Economic Development* (Greenwich, Conn.: JAI Press).

Buckley, P. J., J. H. Dunning and R. D. Pearce (1978) 'The Influence of Firm Size, Industry, Nationality and Degree of Multinationality in the Growth and Profitability of the World's Largest Firms', *Weltwirtschaftliches Archiv.* vol. 114, pp. 243–57.

Buckley, P. J., J. H. Dunning and R. D. Pearce (1984) 'An Analysis of the Growth and Profitability of the World's Largest Firms 1972 to 1977', *Kyklos*, vol. 37, pp. 3–26.

Buckley, P. J. and P. Enderwick (1983) 'Comparative Pay Levels in Domestically-owned and Foreign-owned Plants in UK Manufacturing – evidence from the 1980 Workplace Industrial Relations Survey', *British Journal of Industrial Relations*, vol. 21, pp. 395–400.

Buckley, P. J. and P. Enderwick (1984) *The Industrial Relations Practices of Foreign-owned Firms in British Manufacturing Industry* (London: Macmillan).

Buckley, P. J. and A. M. Mathew (1980) 'Dimensions of the Market Entry Behaviour of Recent UK First Time Direct Investors in Australia', *Management International Review*, vol. 20, pp. 35–51.

Buckley, P. J. and R. D. Pearce (1979) 'Overseas Production and Exporting by the World's Largest Enterprises – A Study in Sourcing Policy', *Journal of International Business Studies*, vol. 10, pp. 9–20.

Buckley, P. J. and R. D. Pearce (1981) 'Market Servicing by Multinational Manufacturing Firms: Exporting versus Foreign Production', *Managerial and Decision Economics*, vol. 2, pp. 229–46.

Buckley, P. J. and R. D. Pearce (1984) 'Exports in the Strategy of Multinational Enterprises', *Journal of Business Research*, forthcoming.

Buckley, P. J. and B. R. Roberts (1982) *European Direct Investment in the USA before World War I* (London: Macmillan: New York: St Martin's Press).

Byé, M. (1958) 'Self-financed Multiterritorial Units and Their Time Horizon', *International Economic Papers No. 8* (London: Macmillan).

Calvet, A. L. (1981) 'A Synthesis of Foreign Direct Investment Theories and Theories of the Multinational Firm', *Journal of International Business Studies*, vol. 12, pp. 43–60.

Calvet, A. L. and M. Naim (1981) 'The Multinational Firm in Less Developed Countries: A Markets and Hierarchies Approach', Barcelona, Spain: *Paper presented at AIB/EIBA Conference.*

Carstairs, R. T. and L. S. Welch (1981) *A Study of Outward Foreign Licensing of Technology by Australian Companies* (Licensing Executives Society of Australia).

Casson, M. C. (1979) *Alternatives to the Multinational Enterprise* (London: Macmillan).

Casson, M. C. (1981) 'Foreword' to A. M. Rugman, *Inside the Multinationals* (London: Croom Helm).

Casson, M. C. (1982) *The Entrepreneur: An Economic Theory* (Oxford: Martin Robertson).

Casson, M. C. (1984) *General Theories of the MNE; A Critical Examination* (University of Reading Discussion Papers in International Investment and Business Studies).

Caves, R. E. (1971) 'International Corporations: The Industrial Economics of Foreign Investment', *Economica* (New Series) vol. 38, pp. 1–27.

Caves, R. E. (1974) 'Multinational Firms, Competition and Productivity in Host-country Markets', *Economica*, vol. 41, pp. 176–93.

Caves, R. E. (1982) *Multinational Enterprise and Economic Analysis* (Cambridge: Cambridge University Press).

Caves, R. E. and M. E. Porter (1977) 'From Entry Barriers to Mobility Barriers', *Quarterly Journal of Economics*, vol. 9, pp. 241–61.

Chamberlin, E. H. (1933) *The Theory of Monopolistic Competition: A Reorientation of the Theory of Value* (Cambridge, Mass.: Harvard University Press).

Chandler, A. D., Jr (1962) *Strategy and Structure* (Cambridge, Mass.: MIT Press).

Chandler, A. D., Jr (1977) *The Visible Hand: The Managerial Revolution in American Business* (Cambridge, Mass.: Belknap Press of Harvard University Press).

Coase, R. H. (1937) 'The Nature of the Firm', *Economica* (New Series), vol. 4, pp. 386–405.

Contractor, F. J. (1981a) *International Technology Licensing: Compensation, Costs and Negotiation* (Lexington, Mass.: D. C. Heath).

Contractor, F. J. (1981b) 'The Role of Licensing in International Strategy', *Columbia Journal of World Business*, vol. 16, pp. 73–83.

Contractor, F. J. and F. Sagafi-Nejad (1981) 'International Technology Transfer: Major Issues and Policy Responses', *Journal of International Business Studies*, vol. 12, pp. 113–36.

Corden, W. M. (1977) 'The Theory of International Trade' in J. H. Dunning (ed.) *Economic Theory and the Multinational Enterprise* (London: George Allen & Unwin).

Cournot, A. (1838) *Researches into the Mathematical Principles of the Theory of Wealth* (London: Hafner, 1960).

Cubbin, J. (1983). 'Apparent Collusion and Conjectural Variations in Differentiated Oligopoly', *International Journal of Industrial Organisation*, vol. 1, pp. 155–63.

Cyert, R. and R. G. Marsh (1963) *A Behavioural Theory of the Firm* (Englewood Cliffs: Prentice Hall).

Davies, H. (1977) 'Technology Transfer through Commercial Transactions', *Journal of Industrial Economics*, vol. 26, pp. 161–75.

Dollinger, P. (1970) *The German Hansa* (translated by D. S. Ault and S. H. Steinberg) (London: Macmillan).

Dugger, W. M. (1983) 'The Transaction Cost Analysis of Oliver E. Williamson: A New Synthesis?', *Journal of Economic Issues*, vol. 17, pp. 95–114.

Dunning, J. H. (1958) *American Investment in British Manufacturing Industry* (London: George Allen & Unwin).

Dunning, J. H. (1971) 'Comment on the Chapter by Professor Aliber' in J. H. Dunning (ed.) *The Multinational Enterprise* (London: George Allen & Unwin).

Dunning, J. H. (1972) *The Location of International Firms in an Enlarged EEC: An Exploratory Paper* (Manchester: Manchester Statistical Society).

Dunning, J. H. (1973) 'The Determinants of International Production', *Oxford Economic Papers*, vol. 25, pp. 289–335.

Dunning, J. H. (1977) 'Trade, Location of Economic Activity and the Multinational Enterprise: A Search for an Eclectic Approach' in B. Ohlin *et al.* (eds) *The International Allocation of Economic Activity* (London: Macmillan).

Dunning, J. H. (1979) 'Explaining Changing Patterns of International Production: In Defence of the Eclectic Theory', *Oxford Bulletin of Economics and Statistics*, 161 41, pp. 269–95.

Dunning, J. H. (1980) 'Towards an Eclectic Theory of International Production', *Journal of International Business Studies*, vol. 11, pp. 9–31.

Dunning, J. H. (1981) *International Production and the Multinational Enterprise* (London: George Allen & Unwin).

Dunning, J. H. (1982) 'Non Equity Forms of Foreign Economic Involvement and the Theory of International Production', *University of Reading Discussion Papers in International Investment and Business Studies*, No. 59.

Dunning, J. H. (1983) 'Changes in the Structure of International Production: the Last 100 Years' in M. C. Casson (ed.) *The Growth of International Business* (London: George Allen & Unwin).

Dunning, J. H. and P. J. Buckley (1977) 'International Production and Alternative Models of Trade', *Manchester School*, vol. 65, pp. 392–403.

Dunning, J. H. and M. McQueen (1981) *Transnational Corporations in International Tourism* (New York: UN Commission on Transnational Corporations).

Dunning, J. H. and M. McQueen (1982) 'The Eclectic Theory of the Multinational Enterprise and the International Hotel Industry', in A. M. Rugman (ed.) *New Theories of the Multinational Enterprise* (Beckenham, Kent: Croom Helm) pp. 79–106.

Dunning, J. H. and R. D. Pearce (1981) *The World's Largest Industrial Enterprises* (Farnborough: Gower Press).

Ellison, R. (1977) 'Management Contracts' in M. Z. Brooke and H. L. Remmers, *The International Firm* (London: Pitman).

Emmanuel, A. (1982) *Appropriate or Underdeveloped Technology?* (Chichester and New York: Wiley/IRM).

Enderwick, P. and P. J. Buckley (1982) 'Strike Activity and Foreign Ownership: An Analysis of British Manufacturing', *British Journal of Industrial Relations*, vol. 28, pp. 308–21.

Enderwick, P. and P. J. Buckley (1983) 'The Determinants of Strike Activity in Foreign-owned Plants: Inter-industry Evidence from British Manufacturing Industry 1971–3', *Managerial and Decision Economics*, vol. 4, pp. 83–8.

Fama, E. F. (1976) *Foundations of Finance* (New York: Free Press).

Fellner, W. (1949) *Competition Among the Few: Oligopoly and Similar Market Structures* (New York: Alfred A. Knopf).

Finger, J. M. (1975) 'Tariff Provision for Offshore Assembly and the Exports of Developing Countries', *Economic Journal*, vol. 85, pp. 365–71.

Finger, J. M. (1976) 'Trade and Domestic Effects of Offshore Assembly Provision in the US Tariff', *American Economic Review*, vol. 66, pp. 598–611.

Finger, J. M. (1977) 'Offshore Assembly Provisions in the West German and Netherland Tariffs: Trade and Domestic Effects', *Weltwirtschaftliches Archiv.*, vol. 113, pp. 237–49.

Finnegan, M. B. (1976) *Current Trends in Domestic and International Licensing* (New York: Practising Law Institute).

Flowers, E. B. (1976) 'Oligopolistic Reaction in European and Canadian Direct Investment in the United States', *Journal of International Business Studies*, vol. 7, pp. 43–55.

Fog, B. (1956) 'How are Cartel Prices Determined?', *Journal of Industrial Economics*, vol. 5, pp. 16–23.

Franko, L. G. (1976) *The European Multinationals* (London: Harper & Row).

Friedman, B. W. (1983) *Oligopoly Theory* (Cambridge: Cambridge University Press).

Friedman, W. F. and Kalmanoff, G. (eds) (1981) *Joint International Business Ventures* (New York: Columbia University Press).

Friend, I. and E. Losq (1979) 'Advantages and Limitations of International Portfolio Diversification' in M. Sarnat and G. P. Szego (eds) *International Finance and Trade*, vol. 2, pp. 3–15 (Cambridge, Mass.: Ballinger).

Gabriel, P. R. (1967) *The International Transfer of Corporate Skills: Management Contracts in Less Developed Countries* (Cambridge, Mass.: Harvard University Press).

Gabriel, P. R. (1972) 'Multinationals in the Third World: Is Conflict Inevitable?', *Harvard Business Review*, vol. 50, pp. 93–102.

Galbraith, J. K. (1967) *The New Industrial State* (London: Hamish Hamilton).

Galbraith, J. K. (1974) *Economics and Public Purpose* (London: André Deutsch).

Geroski, P. A. (1979) 'Review of Direct Foreign Investment by Kiyoshi Kojima', *Economic Journal*, vol. 89, pp. 162–4.

Giddy, Ian H. (1978) 'The Demise of the Product Cycle Model in International Business Theory', *Columbia Journal of World Business*, vol. 13, pp. 90–7

Giddy, I. and A. M. Rugman (1979) 'A Model of Foreign Direct Investment, Trade and Licensing', Graduate School of Business, Columbia University, New York, *Mimeo*.

Giddy, I. H. and S. Young (1982) 'Conventional Theory and Unconventional Multinationals: Do New Forms of Multinational Enterprise require New Theories?' in A. M. Rugman (ed.) *New Theories of the Multinational Enterprise* (Beckenham, Kent: Croom Helm) pp. 55–78.

Gonedes, N. (1976) 'Capital Market Equilibrium for a Class of Heterogeneous Expectations in a Two-parameter World', *Journal of Finance*, vol. 31, pp. 1–15.

Gravelle, H. and R. Rees (1981) *Microeconomics* (Harlow, Essex: Longman).

Gray, M. P. (1972) *The Economics of Business Investment Abroad* (London: Macmillan).

Grossman, S. (1976) 'On the Efficiency of Competitive Stock Markets Where Traders Have Diverse Information', *Journal of Finance*, vol. 31, pp. 573–85.

Grubel, H. G. (1968) 'Internationally Diversified Portfolios: Welfare Gains and Capital Flows', *American Economic Review*, vol. 58, pp. 1299–314.

Grubel, H. G. (1977) 'A Theory of Multinational Banking', *Banca Nazionale del Lavoro Quarterly Review*, no. 123, pp. 349–64.

Grubel, H. G. and P. J. Lloyd (1975) *Intra-Industry Trade: The Theory and Measurement of International Trade in Differentiated Products* (London: Macmillan).

Gutman, P. and F. Arkwright (1976) 'Co-operation Industrielle Tripartite', *Politique Etrangère*, vol. 41, pp. 615–41.

Hall, G. R. and R. E. Johnson (1970) 'Transfers of United States Aerospace Technology to Japan' in R. Vernon (ed.) *The Technology Factor in International Trade* (New York: National Bureau of Economic Research, Columbia University Press).

Hayek, F. A. (1937) 'Economics and Knowledge', *Economica*, New Series, vol. 4, pp. 33–54.

Hayek, F. A. (1949) 'The Meaning of Competition' in F. A. Hayek, *Individualism and Economic Order* (London: Routledge & Kegan Paul).

Helleiner, G. K. (1975) 'The Role of Multinational Corporations in the Less Developed Countries' Trade in Technology' in K. Kojima and M. Wionczek (eds) *Technology Transfer in Pacific Economic Development* (Tokyo: Japan Economic Record Centre).

Hennart, J. F. (1982) *A Theory of Multinational Enterprise* (Ann Arbor: University of Michigan Press).

Hexner, E. (1945) *International Cartels* (Durham, North Carolina: University of North Carolina Press).

Hirsh, S. (1967) *The Location of Industry and International Competitiveness* (Oxford: Oxford University Press).

Hirsh, S. (1976) 'An International Trade and Investment Theory of the Firm', *Oxford Economic Papers*, vol. 28, pp. 258–70.

Hirshman, A. O. (1972) 'How to Divest in Latin America and Why' in A. Kapoor and P. A. Grub, *The Multinational Enterprise in Transition* (Princeton, New Jersey: Darwin Press).

Hood, N. and S. Young (1979) *The Economics of Multinational Enterprise* (London: George Allen & Unwin).

Horst, T. O. (1971) 'The Theory of the Multinational Firm: Optimal Behaviour under Different Tariff and Tax Rates', *Journal of Political Economy*, vol. 79, pp. 1059–72.

Horst, T. O. (1972a) 'Firm and Industry Determinants of the Decision to Invest Abroad: An Empirical Study', *Review of Economics and Statistics*, vol. 54, pp. 258–66.

Horst, T. O. (1972b) 'The Industrial Composition of US Exports and Subsidiary Sales to the Canadian Market', *American Economic Review*, vol. 57, pp. 37–45.

Hufbauer, G. C. (1966) *Synthetic Materials and the Theory of International Trade* (London: Duckworth).

Hufbauer, G. C. (1970) 'The Impact of National Characteristics and Technology on the Commodity Composition of Trade in Manufactured Goods' in R. Vernon (ed.) *The Technology Factor in International Trade* (New York: Columbia University Press for National Bureau of Economic Research) pp. 145–213.

Hymer, S. H. (1970) 'The Efficiency (Contradictions) of the Multinational

Corporation', *Papers and Proceedings of the American Economic Association*, May.

Hymer, S. H. (1971) 'The Multinational Corporation and the Law of Uneven Development' in J. N. Bhagwati (ed.) *Economics and World Order* (New York: World Law Fund).

Hymer, S. H. (1976) *The International Operations of National Firms* (Lexington, Mass.: Lexington Books).

Hymer, S. H. and R. Rowthorn (1970) 'Multinational Corporations and International Oligopoly: The Non-American Challenge' in C. P. Kindleberger (ed.) *The International Corporation* (Cambridge, Mass.: MIT Press) pp. 57–91.

India Investment Centre (1981) *Foreign Investment in India – Opportunities and Incentives* (New Delhi: India Investment Centre).

Intriligator, M. D. (1971) *Mathematical Optimisation in Economic Theory* (Englewood Cliffs, New Jersey: Prentice-Hall).

Izraeli, D. (1972) *Franchising and the Total Distribution System* (London: Longman).

Jaques, E. (1951) *The Changing Culture of a Factory* (London: Heinemann).

Johanson, J. and J. E. Vahlne (1977) 'The Internationalisation Process of the Firm – a Model of Knowledge Development and Increasing Market Commitments', *Journal of International Business Studies*, vol. 8, pp. 23–32.

Johnson, H. G. (1968) *Comparative Cost and Commercial Policy Theory for a Developing World Economy* (Wicksell Lectures 1968) (Stockholm: Almquist & Wiksell).

Johnson, H. G. (1970) 'The Efficiency and Welfare Implications of the International Corporation' in C. P. Kindleberger (ed.) *The International Corporation* (Cambridge, Mass.: MIT Press).

Johnson, H. G. (1975) *Technology and Economic Interdependence* (London: Macmillan).

Kaldor, N. (1937) 'The Equilibrium of the Firm', *Economica*, vol. 4, pp. 386–405.

Kay, N. (1979) *The Innovating Firm* (London: Macmillan).

Kemp, M. C. (1962) 'The Benefits and Costs of Private Investment from Abroad: Comment', *Economic Record*, vol. 38, pp. 108–10.

Kidron, M. (1965) *Foreign Investments in India* (Oxford: Oxford University Press).

Kindleberger, C. P. (1969) *American Business Abroad* (New Haven: Yale University Press).

Kirzner, I. M. (1973) *Competition and Entrepreneurship* (Chicago: University of Chicago Press).

Knickerbocker, F. T. (1973) *Oligopolistic Reaction and Multinational Enterprise* (Cambridge, Mass.: Harvard University Press).

Knight, F. H. (1921) *Risk, Uncertainty and Profit* (Chicago: University of Chicago Press (1971).

Kojima, K. (1973) 'A Macroeconomic Approach to Foreign Direct Investment', *Hitotsubashi Journal of Economics*, vol. 14, pp. 1–21.

Kojima, K. (1975) 'International Trade and Foreign Investment: Substitutes or Complements', *Hitotsubashi Journal of Economics*, vol. 16, pp. 1–12.

Kojima, K. (1978) *Direct Foreign Investment: A Japanese Model of Multinational Business Operations* (London: Croom Helm).

Kojima, K. (1982) 'Macroeconomic Versus International Business Approach to Direct Foreign Investment', *Hitotsubashi Journal of Economics*, vol. 23, pp. 1–19.

Kopits, G. (1979) 'Multinational Conglomerate Diversification', *Economia Internazionale*, vol. XXXII, pp. 3–15.

Krimpas, G. E. (1975) *Labour Input and the Theory of the Labour Market* (London: Duckworth).

Kumar, K. and M. G. McLeod (1981) *Multinationals from Developing Countries* (Lexington, Mass.: Lexington Books).

Lall, S. (1973). 'Transfer Pricing by Multinational Manufacturing Firms', *Oxford Bulletin of Economics and Statistics*, vol. 35, pp. 173–95.

Lall, S. (1978a) 'The Pattern of Intra-firm Exports by US Multinationals', *Oxford Bulletin of Economics and Statistics*, vol. 40, pp. 209–22.

Lall, S. (1978b) 'Transnationals, Domestic Enterprises, and Industrial Structure in Host LDCs: A Survey', *Oxford Economic Papers*, vol. 30, pp. 217–48.

Lall, S. (1980) 'Offshore Assembly in Developing Countries', *National Westminster Bank Quarterly Review*, August, pp. 14–23.

Lall, S. (1981) 'Technology and Developing Countries: A Review and an Agenda for Research' in S. Lall (ed.), *Developing Countries in the International Economy* (London: Macmillan).

Lall, S. and P. Streeten (1977) *Foreign Investment, Transnationals and Developing Countries* (London: Macmillan).

Lamers, E. A. A. M. (1976) *Joint Ventures between Yugoslav and Foreign Enterprises* (Tilburg: Tilburg University Press).

Lancaster, K. (1979) *Variety, Equity and Efficiency* (Oxford: Basil Blackwell).

Lecraw, D. (1977) 'Direct Investment by Firms from Less Developed Countries', *Oxford Economic Papers*, vol. 29, pp. 442–57.

Leibenstein, J. (1968) 'Entrepreneurship and Development', *American Economic Review (Papers and Proceedings)*, vol. 58, pp. 72–83.

Leibenstein, H. (1976) *Beyond Economic Man* (Cambridge, Mass.: Harvard University Press).

Lenin, V. I. (1970) *Imperialism: The Highest Stage of Capitalism* (Moscow: Progress Publishers).

Lessard, D. (ed.) (1979) *International Financial Management: Theory and Application* (Boston: Warren, Gorham and Lamont).

Levcik, F. and J. Stanokvsky (1979) *Industrial Co-operation between East and West* (New York: M. E. Sharpe, White Plains and London: Macmillan).

Levy, H. (1911) *Monopoly and Competition: A Study in English Industrial Organisation* (London: Macmillan).

Levy, H. and M. Sarnat (1978) *Capital Investment and Financial Decisions* (Englewood Cliffs: Prentice-Hall).

Liefmann, R. (1932) *Cartels, Concerns and Trusts* (Introduction by D. H. Macgregor), (London: Methuen).

Loasby, B. J. (1976) *Choice, Complexity and Ignorance* (Cambridge: Cambridge University Press).

Long, F. (1981) *Restrictive Business Practices, Transnational Corporations and Development, A Survey* (The Hague: Martinus Nijhoff).

Lundgren, N. (1977) 'Comment on Professor Dunning's paper' in G. Ohlin *et al.* (eds) *The International Allocation of Economic Activity* (London: Macmillan).

Luoskarinen, R. (1980) *Internationalization of the Firm* (Helsinki: Helsinki School of Economics).

MacDougall, G. D. A. (1960) 'The Benefits and Costs of Private Investment from Abroad: a Theoretical Approach', *Economic Record*, vol. 36, pp. 13–35.

Macgregor, D. H. (1906) *Industrial Combination* (London: George Bell & Sons).

Macrosty, H. W. (1907) *The Trust Movement in British Industry: A Study of Business Organisation* (London: Longmans, Green).

Magee, S. P. (1977a) 'Multinational Corporations, Industry Technology Cycle and Development', *Journal of World Trade Law*, vol. 11, pp. 297–321.

Magee, S. P. (1977b) 'Information and the Multinational Corporation: An Appropriability Theory of Direct Foreign Investment' in J. N. Bhagwati (ed.) *The New International Economic Order* (Cambridge, Mass.: MIT Press).

Malmgrem, H. B. (1961) 'Information, Expectations and the Theory of the Firm', *Quarterly Journal of Economics*, vol. 75, pp. 399–421.

Mansfield, E., A. Romeo and S. Wagner (1979) 'Foreign Trade and US Research and Development', *Review of Economics and Statistics*, vol. 61, pp. 49–57.

Marris, R. (1964) *The Economic Theory of Managerial Capitalism* (London: Macmillan).

Mason, E. S. (1946) *Controlling World Trade: Cartels and Commodity Agreements* (New York: McGraw Hill).

Mason, R. H. (1981) 'Comment on Professor Dunning's Paper' in T. Sagafi-Nejad, R. W. Moxon and H. V. Perlmutter (eds) *Controlling International Technology Transfer* (New York and Oxford: Pergamon Press).

Mason, R. H., R. R. Miller and D. R. Weigel (1975) *The Economics of International Business* (New York: Wiley).

McManus, J. C. (1972) 'The Theory of the International Firm' in G. Paquet (ed.) *The Multinational Firm and the Nation State* (Toronto: Collier Macmillan).

McMillan, C. H. (1981) 'Trends in East–West Industrial Co-operation', *Journal of International Business Studies*, vol. 12, pp. 53–68.

Mises, L. von (1949) *Human Action: A Treatise on Economics* (London: William Hodge).

Modelski, G. (ed.) (1979) *Transnational Corporations and World Order: Readings in International Political Economy* (San Francisco: W. H. Freeman).

Moss, S. (1981) *An Economic Theory of Business Strategy* (Oxford: Martin Robertson).

Moxon, R. W. (1974) 'Offshore Production in the Less Developed Countries', *The Bulletin*, July (New York: Institute of Finance, New York University) pp. 698–9.

Murray, R. (1972) 'Underdevelopment, International Firms and the International Division of Labour' in *Towards a New World Economy* (Rotterdam: Rotterdam University Press).

Newbould, G. D., P. J. Buckley and J. Thurwell (1978) *Going International: The Experience of Smaller Companies Overseas* (London: Associated Business Press).

Norman, G. (1979) *Economies of Scale, Transport Costs and Location* (The Hague: Martinus Nijhoff).

O'Brien, D. P. and D. Swann (1968) *Information Agreements, Competition and Efficiency* (London: Macmillan).

Oman, C. (1980) 'Research Project on Changing International Investment Strategies: The New Forms of Investment in Developing Countries – a "State of the Art"' (Paris: OECD Development Centre, Working Document no. 7).

Osborne, D. K. (1976) 'Cartel Problems', *American Economic Review*, vol. 86, pp. 835–44.

Ozawa, T. (1979a) *Multinationalism, Japanese Style: The Political Economy of Outward Dependency* (Princeton, New Jersey: Princeton University Press).

Ozawa, T. (1979b) 'International Investment and Industrial Structure: New Theoretical Implications from the Japanese Experience', *Oxford Economic Papers*, vol. 31, pp. 72–92.

Paliwoda, S. J. (1981) *Joint East–West Marketing and Production Ventures* (Farnborough: Gower Press).

Parker, J. E. S. (1978) *The Economics of Innovation: The National and Multinational Enterprise in Technological Change* (2nd edn) (London: Longman).

Parry, T. G. (1975) 'Trade and Non-trade Performance of US Manufacturing Industry: Revealed Comparative Advantage', *Manchester School*, vol. 43, pp. 158–72.

Pearce, R. D. (1983) 'Industrial Diversification amongst the World's Leading Multinational Enterprises' in M. Casson (ed.) *The Growth of International Business* (London: George Allen & Unwin).

Penrose, E. T. (1956) 'Foreign Investment and the Growth of the Firm', *Economic Journal*, vol. 66, pp. 230–5.

Penrose, E. T. (1959) *The Theory of the Growth of the Firm* (Oxford: Basil Blackwell).

Perlmutter, H. V. and T. Sagafi-Nejad (1981) *Controlling International Technology Transfer: Issues, Perspectives and Policy Implications* (New York and Oxford: Pergamon Press).

Pierce, F. (1907) *The Tariff and the Trusts* (New York: Macmillan).

Plummer, A. (1934) *International Combines in Modern Industry* (London: Pitman).

Polk, J. (1968) 'The New World Economy', *Columbia Journal of World Business*, vol. 3, pp. 7–16.

Posner, M. V. (1961) 'International Trade and Technical Change', *Oxford Economic Papers*, vol. 13, pp. 323–31.

Prachowny, M. F. J. (1972) 'Direct Investments and the Balance of Payments of the United States' in F. Machlup, W. S. Salant and L. Tarshis (eds) *International Mobility and Movement of Capital* (New York: Columbia University Press).

Prasad, S. J. (1981) 'Technology Transfer to Developing Countries through Multinational Corporations' in R. G. Hawkins and A. J. Prasad (eds) *Technology Transfer and Economic Development* (Greenwich, Conn.: JAI Press).

Ragazzi, G. (1979) 'Theories of the Determinants of Direct Foreign Investments', *IMF Staff Papers*, vol. 20, pp. 471–98.

Read, R. A. N. (1983) 'The Growth and Structure of Multinationals in the

Banana Export Trade', in M. Casson (ed.), *The Growth of International Business* (London: Allen & Unwin) pp. 180–213.

Reader, W. (1970, 1975) *Imperial Chemical Industries: A History*, 2 volumes (London: Oxford University Press).

Richardson, G. B. (1960) *Information and Investment* (Oxford: Oxford University Press).

Robertson, D. H. (1948) *Control of Industry* (Cambridge: Cambridge University Press).

Robinson, E. A. G. (1931) *The Structure of Competitive Industry* (London: Nisbet).

Robinson, E. A. G. (1934) 'The Problem of Management and the Size of Firms', *Economic Journal*, vol. 44, pp. 242–57.

Robinson, E. A. G. (1941) *Monopoly* (London: Nisbet).

Robock, S. H., K. Simmonds, and J. Zwick (1977) *International Business and Multinational Enterprises*, revised ed. (Homewood, Illinois: Irwin).

Rowthorn, R. and S. Hymer (1970) *International Big Business* (Cambridge: Cambridge University Press).

Rugman, A. M. (1975) 'Motives for Foreign Investment: The Market Imperfections and Risk Diversification Hypothesis', *Journal of World Trade Law*, vol. 9, pp. 567–73.

Rugman, A. M. (1976) 'Risk Reduction by International Diversification', *Journal of International Business Studies*, vol. 7, pp. 75–80.

Rugman, A. M. (1977a) 'Risk, Direct Investment and International Diversification', *Weltwirtschaftliches Archiv.*, vol. 113, pp. 487–500.

Rugman, A. M. (1977b) 'International Diversification by Financial and Direct Investment', *Journal of Economics and Business*, vol. 30.

Rugman, A. M. (1978) 'Review of the International Operations of National Firms: a Study of Direct Foreign Investment by Stephen Hymer', *Journal of International Business Studies*, vol. 9, pp. 103–4.

Rugman, A. M. (1979) *International Diversification and the Multinational Enterprise* (Farnborough: Lexington).

Rugman, A. M. (1981) *Inside the Multinationals* (London: Croom Helm).

Rugman, A. M. (ed.) (1982) *New Theories of the Multinational Enterprise* (London: Croom Helm).

Salem, M. and M. A. Sansom (1979) *Les Contrats 'Clés en Main' et les Contracts 'Produits en Main'* (Paris: Libraires Techniques).

Samuelson, P. A. (1937) 'Some Aspects of the Pure Theory of Capital', *Quarterly Journal of Economics*, vol. 51, pp. 469–96.

Scherer, F. M. *et al.* (1975) *The Economics of Multi-Plant Operation – An International Comparisons Study* (Cambridge, Mass.: Harvard University Press).

Schumpeter, J. A. (1934) *The Theory of Economic Development* (Cambridge, Mass.: Harvard University Press).

Schumpeter, J. A. (1939) *Business Cycles* (New York: McGraw-Hill).

Scriven, J. G. (1980) 'Joint Ventures in Poland: A Socialist Approach to Foreign Investment Legislation', *Journal of World Trade Law*, vol. 15, pp. 424–38.

Seers, D. (ed.) (1981) *Dependency Theory: A Critical Reassessment* (London: Francis Pinter).

Shapiro, D. M. (1983) 'The Comparative Profitability of Canadian and

Foreign-owned Firms', *Managerial and Decision Economics*, vol. 4, pp. 97–106.

Sherman, R. (1972) *Oligopoly: An Empirical Approach* (Lexington, Mass.: D. C. Heath).

Shubik, M. (1959) *Strategy and Market Structure: Competition, Oligopoly and the Theory of Games* (New York: John Wiley & Sons).

Singer, H. (1980) *New Forms of International Co-operation for Technical Assistance* (London: George Allen & Unwin).

Smith, C. H. (1981) *Japanese Technology Transfer to Brazil* (Ann Arbor, Michigan: UMI Research Press).

Solnik, B. (1974) 'An Equilibrium Model of the International Capital Market', *Journal of Economic Theory*, vol. 8, pp. 500–14.

Southard, F. A. (1931) *American Industry in Europe* (Boston: Houghton Mifflin).

Stackelberg, H. von (1952) *The Theory of the Market Economy* (translated by A. T. Peacock) (London: William Hodge).

Stevens, G. V. G. (1972) 'Capital Mobility and the International Firm' in F. Machlup *et al.* (eds), *International Mobility and Movement of Capital* (New York: Columbia University Press).

Stevens, G. V. G. (1974) 'The Determinants of Investment' in J. H. Dunning (ed.) *Economic Analysis and the Multinational Enterprise* (London: George Allen & Unwin).

Stigler, G. J. (1964) 'A Theory of Oligopoly', *Journal of Political Economy*, vol. 72, pp. 44–61.

Stocking, G. W. and M. W. Watkins (1946) *Cartels in Action: Case Studies in International Business Diplomacy* (New York: Twentieth Century Fund).

Stocking, G. W. and M. W. Watkins (1948) *Cartels or Competition? The Economics of International Controls by Business and Government* (New York: Twentieth Century Fund).

Stone, L. (1956) *An Elizabethan: Sir Horatio Palavicino* (Oxford: Clarendon Press).

Stopford, J. M., J. H. Dunning and K. O. Haberich (1980) *The World Directory of Multinational Enterprises* (London: Macmillan).

Stopford, J. M. and J. H. Dunning (1983) *Multinationals: Company Performance and Global Trends* (London: Macmillan).

Stopford, J. M. and K. O. Haberich (1976) 'Ownership and Control of Foreign Operations', *Journal of General Management*, vol. 3, pp. 3–20.

Sukijasović, M. (1970) 'Foreign Investment in Yugoslavia' in I. A. Litvak and C. J. Maule (eds), *Foreign Investment: The Experience of Host Countries* (New York and London: Praeger).

Sutherland, L. S. (1936) 'Sir George Colebrooke's World Corner in Alum, 1771–73', *Economic History*, vol. 3, pp. 237–58.

Swedenborg, B. (1979) *Multinational Operations of Swedish Firms* (Stockholm: Almquist & Wiksell).

Tabe, A. (1975) 'The Diffusion of Technology in Manufacturing: The Development of Skills' in K. Kojima and M. S. Wionczek (eds) *Technology Transfer in Pacific Economic Development* (Tokyo: Japan Economic Record Centre).

Teece, D. J. (1976) *The Multinational Corporation and the Resource Cost of International Technology Transfer* (Cambridge, Mass.: Ballinger).

Teece, D. J. (1977) 'Technology Transfer by Multinational Firms: The Resource Cost of Transferring Technological Know-how', *Economic Journal*, vol. 87, pp. 242–61.

Teece, D. J. (1983) 'Technological and Organisational Factors in the Theory of the Multinational Enterprise' in M. Casson (ed.) *The Growth of International Business* (London: George Allen & Unwin).

Teichova, A. (1974) *An Economic Background to Munich: International Business and Czechoslovakia 1918–1938* (Cambridge: Cambridge University Press).

Telesio, P. (1979) *Technology, Licensing and Multinational Enterprises* (New York: Praeger Special Studies).

Thompson, D. (1982) 'The UNCTAD Code on Transfer of Technology', *Journal of World Trade Law*, vol. 16, pp. 311–37.

Tomlinson, J. W. C. (1970) *The Joint Venture Process in International Business: India and Pakistan* (Cambridge, Mass.: MIT Press).

United Nations Commission on Transnational Corporations (1978) *Transnational Corporations in World Development: A Re-examination* (New York: UNCTC).

United Nations Centre on Transnational Corporations (1979) *Measures Strengthening the Negotiation Capacity of Governments in their Relations with Transnational Corporations: Technology Transfer through Transnational Corporations. A Technical Paper* (by M. S. Wionczek) (New York: UNCTC).

United Nations Commission on Transnational Corporations (1983) *Transnational Corporations in World Development: Third Survey* (New York: UNCTC).

United Nations Economic and Social Council Economic Commission for Europe on the Development of Trade (1978) *Promotion of Trade Through Industrial Co-operation: Case Studies in Industrial Co-operation: Results of a Survey of Five Western Enterprises* (New York: UNESC Trade R373/Add 3).

Utton, M. A. (1979) *Diversification and Competition* (Cambridge: Cambridge University Press).

Vaitsos, C. V. (1974) *Intercountry Income Distribution and Transnational Enterprises* (Oxford: Oxford University Press).

Vaughn, C. L. (1979) *Franchising* (2nd Edn) (Lexington, Mass.: D. C. Heath).

Vernon, R. (1966) 'International Investment and International Trade in the Product Cycle', *Quarterly Journal of Economics*, vol. 80, pp. 190–207.

Vernon, R. (1971) *Sovereignty at Bay* (Harmondsworth: Penguin).

Vernon, R. (1974) 'The Location of Economic Activity' in J. H. Dunning (ed.) *Economic Analysis and the Multinational Enterprise* (London: George Allen & Unwin).

Vernon, R. (1977) *Storm over the Multinationals: The Real Issues* (London: Macmillan).

Vernon, R. (1979) 'The Product Cycle Hypothesis in a New International Environment', *Oxford Bulletin of Economics and Statistics*, vol. 41, pp. 255–67.

Viner, J. (1931) 'Cost Curves and Supply Curves', *Zeitschrift fur Nationalökonomie*, vol. 3, pp. 23–46. Reprinted in *Readings in Price Theory* (American Economic Association) (1953), pp. 198–232 (London: George Allen & Unwin).

Watanabe, S. (1971). 'Subcontracting, Industrialisation and Employment Creation', *International Labour Review*, vol. 104, pp. 51–76.

Watanabe, S. (1972) 'International Subcontracting: Employment and Skill Promotion', *International Labour Review*, vol. 106, pp. 425–49.

Weigand, R. E. (1980) 'Barters and Buy-Backs: Let Western Firms Beware!', *Business Mergers*, June, pp. 54–61.

Wells, L. T. (1972) *The Product Life Cycle and International Trade* (Cambridge, Mass.: Harvard University Press).

Weralski, M. (1980) 'The New Policies and Legislation concerning Joint Ventures in Poland', *European Taxation*, vol. 20, pp. 99–105.

Whittlesey, C. R. (1946) *National Interests and International Cartels* (New York: Macmillan).

Wildsmith, J. R. (1973) *Managerial Theories of the Firm* (London: Martin Robertson).

Wilkins, M. (1970) *The Emergence of Multinational Enterprise: American Business Abroad from the Colonial Era to 1914* (Cambridge, Mass.: Harvard University Press).

Wilkins, M. (1974) *The Maturing of Multinational Enterprise: American Business Abroad from 1914 to 1970* (Cambridge, Mass.: Harvard University Press).

Wilkins, M. (1977) 'Modern European Economic History and the Multinationals', *Journal of European Economic History*, vol. 6, pp. 575–95.

Williamson, O. E. (1970) *Corporate Control and Business Behaviour* (Englewood Cliffs, New Jersey: Prentice-Hall).

Williamson, O. E. (1975) *Markets and Hierarchies: Analysis and Anti-trust Implications* (New York: Free Press).

Williamson, O. E. (1981) 'The Modern Corporation: Origins, Evolution, Attributes', *Journal of Economic Literature*, vol. 19, pp. 1537–68.

Wolf, B. M. (1975) 'Size and Profitability among US Manufacturing Firms: Multinational vs. Primarily Domestic Firms', *Journal of Economics and Business*, vol. 28, pp. 15–22.

Wolf, B. M. (1977) 'Industrial Diversification and Internationalisation: Some Empirical Evidence', *Journal of Industrial Economics*, vol. 26, pp. 177–91.

Wright, P. *et al.* (1982) 'The Developing World to 1990: Trends and Implications for Multinational Business', *Long Range Planning*, vol. 15, pp. 116–25.

Wright, R. W. (1981) 'Evolving International Business Arrangements' in K. C. Dhawan, H. Etemad and R. W. Wright (eds), *International Business: A Canadian Perspective* (Don Mills, Ontario: Addison-Wesley).

Zaleski, E. and H. Wienert (1980) *Technology Transfer between East and West* (Paris: OECD).

Index

In this index MNE = multinational enterprise

227